THE ART OF THE NASTY

Nigel Wingrove and **Marc Morris**

THE ART OF THE NASTY

© SALVATION FILMS LTD. BCM BOX 9235 LONDON WC1N 3XX

The copyright in the original video cover designs is retained
by the individual video companies, artists, photographers
and designers. Most of these video distributors no longer
exist - forced out of business by the 1984 Video Recordings Act
and the high cost of censorship. However, every attempt has
been made to obtain copyright clearance on all images contained
herein. We would like to thank all those distributors whose artwork
included in this review, particularly Go Video, Astra, and Vipco.
Any copyright holder omitted please contact Salvation Films Ltd
so that the situation may be rectified in future editions.

The moral rights of the authors have been asserted

Published by SALVATION FILMS LTD

First Edition, November 1998

Printed by Mablo Colour Ltd
101-109 Fairfield Road
London E3 2QA

ACKNOWLEDGEMENTS

The Authors would like to express their thanks as follows:-

Nigel Wingrove:

I would particularly like to thank John Martin for his assistance and for his book 'The Seduction of the Gullible', which has proved to be an invaluable source of reference. I would also like to thank my lawyers, Tim Woolley and Roger Holmes at Edmonds Bowen, Kate Spicer, Chris, Emily and Louise for their help in the office, and the ICA team for their support. And as always, Eileen and Walley (aka Tompkins Longtail) for being lovely.

Marc Morris:

I'd like to give a big thank you to Francis Brewster for his invaluable research and assistance. Keep up the work on those databases! Thanks also go to Nathan Bradbury, Martin Brooks, Nigel Burrell, Chris Charlston, Paul Everett, Harvey Fenton, David Flint, Julian Grainger, Adrian Luther-Smith, David McGillivray, and last but not least, Eva for her patience and encouragement.

THE NASTIES A PERSONAL VIEW

An anagram of *American Psycho* author Brett Easton Ellis's name is 'To Sell, Be Nastier'. The same ethos, for good or bad, was probably in the minds of the early players of the evolving video industry. To understand the phenomenon of the 'nasty', one has to realise just how much of a threat to society this upstart technology, and the films that it initially carried, were regarded as posing. The early eighties establishment, in the form of Government, politicians, mainstream film distributors, the media (in particular the tabloid press), together with various pressure groups from Mary Whitehouse's *Viewers and Listeners' Association*, through to some sections of the feminist movement and various social study groups, were to combine forces in a kind of unholy alliance against a single enemy – video.

Video had arrived quietly enough in the late seventies, in the dying days of punk and what would turn out to be the last Labour government for 18 years. Unemployment was rising fast, the unions were, seemingly, on a death wish, any company employing more than two people appeared to be on strike, mentally disturbed social workers with bizarre hair styles, wearing hideously non-threatening fabrics were increasingly strident in their demands to create a caring society, and dungareed sirens with attitude and a venomously draconian attitude to pornography had begun to march through the red light districts of Britain's main cities carrying candles and smashing the windows of sex shops. On top of all this an odd looking woman with a squeaky voice, who quoted from Saint Francis of Assisi and talked international economics in terms of grocery prices, had just arrived in Downing Street.

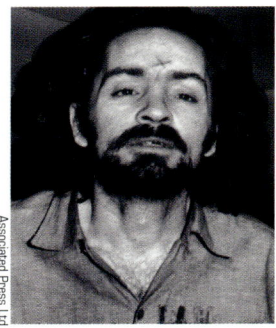

The seventies had basically pushed everything from music to politics to the limit, and people wanted a change. It's easy to forget now in the closing days of the caring nineties, where there are more ''sms' than letters of the alphabet, and it is de rigueur to hug your co-workers after instruction from your company's Human Resources Management person, that the seventies was primarily ANTI anything that moved. But the seventies was created out of the sixties. There is a general belief that seems to grow in strength with each passing year, that the sixties were about 'peace and love', people forget that the sixties had ended in serious violence. Students had clashed with the forces of government throughout the West, Woodstock had metamorphosised into Altamont, and in California some hippies had met a man called Manson and swapped their flowers for knives, and the anti-establishment forces that found the ways of democracy just a tad slow had discovered a more direct way of getting their views across – terrorism.

This desire to shock and challenge mainstream society was, by the advent of video, ingrained within virtually all aspects of English culture, whether deliberate as with punk, or as a by-product like football hooliganism. Everything aimed to shock yet nothing shocked. It was almost as if any creative product or thought that didn't provoke a response was, by its very lack of provocation, somehow lessened in its value. This attitude had grown seemingly organically out of the sixties sub-culture into mainstream consciousness as an almost incipient desire to shock and confront.

For over ten years then, prior to the arrival of video, the marketing of a large percentage of creative or cultural product used some form of provocation to get its message across. Throughout the decade, in all areas of the Arts, 'straight' society had its sensitivities and values trammelled. Cinema premiered **The Exorcist**, **A Clockwork Orange**, **The Devils**, **Straw Dogs**, **The Texas Chainsaw Massacre**, **Last Tango in Paris**, **Blow Out**, **The Night Porter**, **Emmanuelle**, **Taxi Driver**, **In the Realm of the Senses**, **The Life of Brian**, **Caligula** and **Salo** amongst many, as well as about half of the key Nasties.

In theatre the decade opened with *Oh Calcutta!*, which had a totally nude cast, and closed with Roman soldiers gang raping British peasants in *Romans in Britain*. Music saw David Bowie announce his bisexuality, Alice Cooper cavorting with snakes and 'dead babies', and *Black Sabbath's* Ozzy Osborne biting the heads off chickens. *The Sex Pistols*, adorned with Swastikas and an inverted Christ, spat in the face of everything and, for a while, everyone seemed either caked in make-up, pumped full of drugs and generally fucked, or out for a fight, or sex or whatever. What no one wanted was to seem to be straight, to be part of the 9 to 5 work cycle with 2.4 kids, a mortgage and a wardrobe consisting of Crimpline and drip-dry nightmares in a range of pleasing shades.

THE NASTIES A PERSONAL VIEW

THE NASTIES A PERSONAL VIEW

Publishers were just as keen as the rest of the media world to be seen as hip and trendy, and the seventies saw an explosion in new magazine titles that pushed back the boundaries of taste, sex and morality. The anti-establishment began launching titles that were from the 'underground' and consequently *weally, weally* hip. Their readers eagerly awaited news of the coming revolution as they endlessly discussed Maoist theories and gazed gooey-eyed at the pictures of Che Guevara that adorned the walls of their Ladbroke Grove bedsits.

Mainstream women's magazines championed the sexual freedoms and ideas formulated in the sixties. Titles like *Cosmopolitan*, which launched with a male nude centrefold in 1972, and *Spare Rib*, which described itself as a 'women's liberation magazine', and was the antithesis of *Cosmo*, both challenged the accepted norms. *Penthouse's* Bob Guccione launched a pseudo fashion and sex title aimed at women called *Viva,* which WH Smiths refused to stock because of its explicit nudity. There was no such trouble for the sex mags which exploded during the seventies, becoming more and more explicit and pushing the boundaries towards full hardcore.

It was the underground publications though, from *Oz* in the early seventies to punk's *Sniffing Glue* with its ubiquitous opinions on young life that really set the seal on the decade's "fuck you big time" stance. *Oz* in particular, with its visual mêlée of sex, drugs and 'fucking-in-the-streets' politics felt the full ire of the establishment (as the nasties would ten years later) as the police raided their offices, impounded "*Oz* 28, the School Kids issue", charged the publishers and editors with obscenity and, after the longest obscenity trial in history, sentenced them to fifteen months in prison (quashed on appeal). *Sniffing Glue*, whilst not in *Oz's* league, represented a youth movement that quite literally, to the nation's press, seemed to threaten the whole fabric of society as we know it. Hell hath no fury like a tabloid newspaper with a willing victim, and punk sat up and begged for it. 1976 and 1977 saw the tabloids unleash one savage attack after another on the key figures in punk. The police and public responded by duly doing their duty: the police by raiding punk venues and by general harassment, and the public by beating up any seventeen year old with spiky hair and a dog collar. Things were beginning to get vicious.

All this ANTI-NESS was eventually to have an effect on mainstream society as a whole. The power of being ANTI was that as a state of mind it was pervasive and invidious, it left reasoned argument aside in favour of argument for argument's sake, and if that didn't work then there was always the boot. In a sense, the packaging of film on video was a sort of visual kick — the culmination of a decade's worth of shock, *must* shock, and shock hard. It was unfortunate for the video nasty that it shocked too hard, too much, in the wrong place, at the wrong time.

The victory in 1979 of the Conservatives, led by Margaret Thatcher, had been brought about as much by the outgoing Labour Government's failures as it had by any great faith in the incoming Tories. Labour had agreed an incomes policy with the unions, wages were to be controlled by consent, a *social contract* in fact, inflation would be brought under control, and basically everything in the garden would be rosy. And of course pigs would fly. The deal collapsed in the *winter of discontent*, a series of bitter disputes that left corpses unburied and mountains of rubbish in the streets. Clashes between strikers, their supporters — the dreaded 'agitators' so feared by Fleet street — the police, and those who wished to work (the loathsome 'scabs') were, in the main, degenerating into heavy duty scraps. The country was now getting nervous. The establishment feared it was going to the dogs bigtime. But the nation was about to get a saviour, a modern Bodicea, though this one pushed a shopping trolley rather than riding a chariot.

Margaret Thatcher arrived in Downing Street confident, and with a vision to make Britain Grrreeeattt again. This vision was inspired by Churchill, by the monetarist and free market theories of Milton Friedman, by an indefinable interpretation of England's past glories, and by a desire to get rid of the nanny state and to bring 'freedom' to the individual. This new

society would be wrapped up in Thatcher's own concept of 'Victorian values', a personal hybrid of the petty bourgeoisie, net-curtain twitching and castrated libertarianism that had, presumably, developed during her years in her parents' greengrocers shop in Grantham.

This vision had a mass of real and imagined enemies, some tangible like the Unions, the left, the welfare state, the civil service, local councils, homosexuals and lesbians, students and so on, and on the other side the intangibles like the 'sixties', the 'permissive' society, 'declining morals' and, a Tory favourite, 'the erosion of the family'. Thatcher had been elected into a country that was, in the eyes of many, on the verge of social collapse - a fear that was compounded by serious riots in the St Pauls area of Bristol on 2 April 1980, rapidly rising unemployment and an economy whose industrial base was stymied by a combination of bad management and Trade Unions whose working practices were totally antiquated. All of which meant that the United Kingdom entered the 1980's with the entrepreneurial potential of a luddite cloned from a retrogressive Telaban, inhabited by a population of amoral, work-shy, hypocritical, sexual deviants with a penchant for begging.

The Tories set about reshaping the nations psyche and simultaneously took on the Unions and the economy. The results were predictable and extreme. Within two years Britain's inner cities, from Brixton to Toxteth, were burning, unemployment had rocketed to over three million, crime was out of control and businesses screamed out loud as interest rates and the recession culled great sways of industry. On top of all this there was the battle for the country's moral soul.

Thatcher's rise had been supported by a loose collective of radical rightwing theorists, from politicians and think tanks like the *Adam Smith Institute* and the *Centre for Policy Studies*, to leading industrialists and media tycoons like Rupert Murdoch, who, through his chosen mouthpiece *The Sun*, would be an invaluable champion of Thatcher and Thatcherite values. Although there were obvious targets for change, or enemies to be taken out like the Unions, the public sector and inflation, there was also another, less tangible target for change - *family values*, or rather their restoration.

It was, and probably still is, a widely held view amongst many radical right thinkers that a free market, and the society that feeds off it, can only be truly tolerable if its people follow a moral code, a moral code that had once been inextricably linked to the State by Christianity and the Church. This mixture of natural or moral law and conventional civil law was, by the time of the election of Margaret Thatcher, beginning to totally fragment as religion played less and less of a role in people's lives, both in schools and in society generally, particularly a society that had become secular and collectivist. Instead of Christian principles, precepts and values were driven by causes, by pressure groups, by lobbyists, and, most importantly by the people's newly revitalised and greatest former of opinions and arbiters of taste, the tabloid newspaper.

The tabloid came into its own in the early eighties, the Falklands War allowing headline writers a chance to flex their jingoistic muscles to great effect. Through papers like *The Sun* and *The Mail*, the tabloid championed, and to a great degree interpreted, Thatcherite values, vociferously supporting 'her' causes and equally vociferously attacking 'her' enemies. But these values were, in a way, still being formulated, progressing like an intellectual virus throughout the eighties, evolving eventually into a mass of contradictions, hypocrisy and family values gobbledygook, a substantial amount of which would soon crystallise into an outpouring of vicious invective tabloid claptrap directed at video.

In effect, these tabloids, according to political journalist Martin Jacques, were 'the mirror, the interlocutor, the enabler of this new society...the source of information and opinion, symbols and humour...the template of society, defining success and failure in everything from sport to politics, from entertainment to ideas'. Biographers of *The Sun*, though they could have been writing about any of the tabloids, stated savagely, 'The absorption of its readers in sexual intercourse, television celebrities and sport reflects a country in which millions of people are leading stunted and demoralised lives, which they

have lost the will to escape or improve. Their newspapers gratify their desire to belittle all great men and women, all high endeavours, great causes and original ideas, and to judge...'.

The modern tabloid is, in effect, an addict to sensation, to sales and to forming mass opinion. This is not unique - papers have always been driven by the need for sales, and using sensationalism to achieve them, but what is different now is the society that they operate in, and the power that they have to influence that society. What was to make the video nasty furore so frightening was that it was one of the first contemporary press frenzies, and that it was driven by the overriding demand that 'something must be done'- a cry that has eagerly been taken up again and again over the last fifteen years by opportunist politicians keen for their fifteen minutes in the spotlight. They rapidly put their names to an often ill conceived and rushed piece of legislation, that may be endorsed by parliament, but is, in fact, made up of the ephemeral words and ideas of countless newspaper editorials. In effect they would make sure that *something was done*.

The Video Nasty brouhaha was slow to start – a comment here, a raised eyebrow there, an article here, a bigger story there, a concerned parent, then a worried councillor, then an article that used the word 'nasty' and then the *...video nasty ate my son's brain and raped my wife and murdered my neighbour with an axe and ate their bodies before being tortured to death by crazed vigilanties who were shot to death by drugged up neo nazi police officers who raped my wife...* type of stories appeared every day. *Something must be done!*

The first clammerings of trouble came early in 1982 when a letter of complaint was published in the February issue of *Television and Video Retailer* objecting to an advertisement that had been printed in an earlier issue for the video release of a film called **SS Experiment Camp** *(Distributor: Go Video).* This infamous Italian, Nazi, sex, death and sleaze epic from 1976 was advertised by a crude drawing of a semi-naked, crucified and inverted woman, whilst in the background loomed a grim faced Nazi, behind him the barbed wire fence of a Concentration camp.

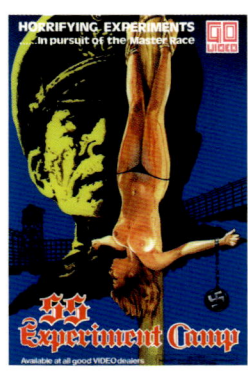

Offensive and gratuitous, this was to become a key nasty and its packaging would make it one of a core of titles that would be at the eye of the coming storm. Its distributors, *Go Video,* responded to the criticism in a glib and fatuous way by stating, correctly, that in the original Italian artwork the woman was completely naked. They had had the woman adorned with a pair of badly drawn black knickers stating pompously 'to this extent we imposed our own moral censorship'. *Go Video* further stated that it was no use their toning down their packaging if none of the other distributors did. The trade magazine sympathised saying that 'as the industry gets fatter and the publicity material spreads wider and wider, there must be a case for public moral acceptability'. It concluded that the industry was unlikely to come up with a voluntary code of practice. *Go Video* were to go on to produce some of the most extreme video covers including **Cannibal Holocaust** and **The Demons**, concentrating always on sex and violence, although the public were at least spared the sight of blood crazed cannibals wearing neatly drawn-on lace panties.

It was another four months before the national press picked up on things when, on May 7th, *The Daily Star* reported that 'the video boom is giving youngsters a chance to see some of the most horrific and violent films ever made'. *The Star* also quoted James Ferman (Director of the BBFC) as being 'furious', at the situation, and that 'they are watching shocking scenes that we would never allow in a cinema, even under an 'X' certificate' – *quelle horreur!*

What was to be one of the driving issues behind the impending nasty hysteria, was control. Video was outside state control, it was unregulated, uncensored and untouchable, and the first body to be really pissed off was James Ferman and his collection of censorious zealots at the then called *British Board of Film Censors (BBFC).* The word 'censor' would, ironically enough, be dropped in 1984 when it was replaced by the euphemistic and less contentious sounding 'classification'. The two main bodies that could control film, that is the censors and the police, could not touch video. According to the Obscenity Act, video did not exist.

The same was true of the *BBFC's* remit which only covered films due for a theatrical release. Basically for now, any film or programme could be released on video, and the new breed of gung-ho distributor was to do just that.

Films like the **Story of O**, **The Exorcist**, **The Driller Killer**, **Violation of the Bitch**, **Faces of Death**, **Snuff**, **Debbie Does Dallas**, **SS Girls**, **Straw Dogs**, **Mark of the Devil** and thousands of others were released to fill the shelves of Britain's other new growth area, the video rental shop. Video was now a commercial success, a phenomenon. From 1979 to 1982, in just over two years, video had grown from a fledgling business to a massive, totally unregulated industry. The UK at this stage had more video players per household than any other country in the world.

This rapid success, at a time of recession and three million unemployed, meant big profits for the distributors, the rental outlets and the producers, and none of them wanted regulation. In fact, in a simplistic way, the impending media storm would be seen by many within the industry as a case of 'any publicity is good publicity'. That, and as an opportunity for more sales of course.

By May 1982 the story of the easy availability of uncensored horror videos had spread to the broadsheets. *The Sunday Times* reported that videos were "available to anyone of any age", that they exploited "extremes of violence", that "the 'nasties' are far removed from from the suspense of the traditional horror film", and that they "dwell on murder, multiple rape, sado-masochism, mutilation of women, cannibalism and Nazi atrocities". *The Sunday Times* also highlighted what was, and to some still is, one of the great dangers of video, that it offered "the chance for renters to use slow-motion and freeze-frame facilities to revel in the gory bits as often as they like".

The Sunday Times then went on to quote from two video distributors whose comments were both naïve and cretinous, and were, unfortunately, to be typical of the raison d'être espoused by the early defenders of the 'nasty'. The head of Astra Video commented 'there's no censorship law on video at all, what can they do about it?', and in a piece of utter bollocks, a spokesman for distributor *Vipco* claimed that "we are feeding a demand, not creating it. People want to see this sort of stuff, and we are giving them what they want. I agree that that there's a lot of violence and that is probably bad, but who are we to decide? There really ought to be a line drawn somewhere, but there isn't". It was quite obvious that many of the early champions of video were to have as much trouble constructing a valid argument against censorship as they were with public relations, which was a pity as things were about to get nasty for the 'nasty'.

Since the advent of video the competition between distributors to get *their* titles onto the rental shelves was intense, hence the spate of lurid trade advertisements. Even more competitive though was the battle for the potential renter, and this is really where the nasty was born, for it was the packaging and presentation of films on video that created it. Looking at the thousands of video covers that were produced prior to regulation one aspect that comes across is sensation. Whatever the subject of the film, distributors implied sex or violence, or both. In fact, the video sleeves were no different from the lurid pulp covers of the 1930's and 40's, which promised oodles of sex and violence where there was usually none. Often a dull title, or a totally innocuous family film, would be presented in a way that might imply that it contained something dodgy, or at least a bit iffy. Whilst some of the 'nasties' were indeed 'nasty', most were not, and it is very likely that had a bit more restraint be shown by the distributors in their cover art then a lot of the ensuing legislation may never have happened.

The video industry had, from the beginning, set out to shock and sell, and they were to be successful on both counts. People did not need to see films like **The Driller Killer** (Distributor: Vipco) or **Poor White Trash** (Distributor: Intervision) to be shocked, and the covers certainly ensured they sold. The sight of a bloodied man screaming out while a drill bit is screwed into his head or the close up shot of a woman's throat being torn to pieces by barbed wire on the video covers

THE NASTIES A PERSONAL VIEW

was enough for most people. But most people who were shocked by the packaging did not watch the video. What the over-the-top packaging and trade adverts were doing was bringing the exploitation horror film to the attention of an establishment already reeling from the previous decade's excesses. The newly emerging Thatcherite consciousness needed a battle, an enemy for all their disparate supporters to unite against, and the truculent and sensation driven 'video nasty' was to provide an ideal villain.

The video nasty furore encapsulated within it all the major bugbears of Thatcherite values. The nasty represented a veritable cornucopia of sleaze. From the cover of each fetid video cassette leered a seemingly endless array of dribbling psychos whose crazed features were sweetness and light to the jaded editors of Fleet Street, always keen to nail their colours to the mast of Family Values and stamp out the threat of the indecent.

From May 1982 onwards the press, and pressure groups like Mary Whitehouse's *Viewers and Listeners' Association*, would begin the process of applying persistent and constant pressure on the Government to bring in legislation to control video. It is worth noting that the Conservatives were originally opposed to any statutory laws being used to control video, preferring to leave the *BBFC* and the *British Videogram Association (BVA)* who had set up a joint working party, to look into the whole question of video, and to sort out the 'problem' of certification by developing a voluntary solution. But it was Mary Whitehouse's growing hysteria that was now to propel the issue, and keep it in the press. From now on any sense of reasoned argument or calm debate was out the window, for, in the words of Mary Whitehouse, the distributors of video were 'merchants of menace' threatening the safety of the nation's children.

By June 1982 perceived video nasties were being seized by the police, who were keen to see if the films' content justified their being sent to the *Director of Public Prosecutions (DPP)* for prosecution under the *Obscene Publications Act (OPA)*. The first title to merit this honour was the salaciously packaged **SS Experiment Camp**, followed in rapid succession by **The Driller Killer** and **I Spit on Your Grave**, two titles well known for their restrained packaging. In the meantime the *BVA/BBFC* working party were quoted in the press as being "deeply disturbed by some of the material they have seen" and that they would not "be able to give a grade to the sort of material that would not pass a normal cinema certificate, which would exclude most of the nasties".

There was to be a succession of titles hauled up before the DPP over the coming months. With more and more films being cited by the press as potential 'nasties' it was all the police could do to seize them fast enough to keep up. Then on the 15 July the *Daily Mail* reported that Tory MP Graham Bright was planning to introduce a private members bill to control and censor video. At this stage though, despite the growing press uproar there was still no indication that the Government were particularly keen on new legislation.

The Government's initial lack of interest in video is not particularly surprising as 1982 was a pretty hectic year for the Tories. It had started with unemployment topping three million for the first time. In April, Britain declared war on Argentina after a bunch of shifty latin 'scrap dealers' set up camp on a pile of rocks nobody had heard of somewhere in the middle of the South Atlantic. On top of all this the *IRA* had bombed London, killing ten soldiers. For light relief the *Greater London Council (GLC)*, led by the newt loving Ken Livingstone, and the launch of *Channel 4* were offering the tabloids huge opportunities for spontaneous outbursts of moral indignation and a bit of fun: the *GLC* by funding lesbian defence classes and homosexual dance lessons thus giving rise to the phrase 'loony left'; and *Channel 4*, according to the then Home Secretary Willie Whitelaw, by transmitting an unrelenting diet of filth and programmes that were anti Conservative. And oh dear, oh dear, oh dear, there was also to be a general election within twelve months.

Despite the Union Jack waving that greeted the returning Falklands Task Force and Thatcher's lamentable entreaties to the population to rejoice, all was not sweetness and light in the green and pleasant land. Since the Conservative's victory in 1979, crime had exploded. The left blamed, or in some cases justified its rise by citing a corresponding rise in unemployment. The right blamed anything but unemployment, citing everything from single mothers to the welfare state. Whatever the reason, 1981's riots and a really rapid rise in burglary, mugging, vandalism and crime generally had put the Government in a position where it needed to be seen to do something.

The Government's *Short, Sharp, Shocks* (a system designed to tackle criminal behaviour amongst juvenile offenders) and the *YOP* (youth opportunity programmes) schemes had induced derision and failed. It was obvious that something a little more creative in the law and order department was going to be needed if the Government was going to be taken seriously. And what better than to blame something that was already perceived in the public mind as corrupting, a possible cause of crime and a danger to society, and where a campaign was already being widely waged in the press to end its existence. "'Video nasty', that'll do nicely sir".

On 17th March 1983, despite six months of police seizures, *DPP* involvement, constant press coverage, and direct pleas from politicians of all political parties that legislation be introduced to control the availability of video, the Home Secretary William Whitelaw stated that "there is a very real point of principle that it would be wrong to involve the government so directly in matters of censorship...If legislation is needed in this field we must clearly ensure that it is in the form best designed to achieve its objective without undesirable and unintended side-effects. As you know, the BVA are introducing their own scheme for voluntary classification and I think we both agreed that, if at all possible, it is preferable to rely on effective measures of self-regulation".

One month later the Conservative election manifesto stated that "We will also respond to the increasing public concern over obscenity and offenses against public decency, which often have links with serious crime. We propose to introduce legislation to deal with the most serious of these problems, such as the spread of violent and obscene video cassettes".

The reason for this rapid volte-face was simple political expediency: the party of law and order was being seen as the party of disorder. In 1971 there were 1,665,700 notifiable offenses recorded by the police in England and Wales per 100,000 of the population. By 1981, the figure had rocketed to 2,963,760*.

By calling the 1983 election nearly a year and half before she had to, Thatcher was cynically exploiting every drop of blood the 255 servicemen who died in the Falklands conflict had shed. The *Falklands Factor* had a sell by date, and time was running out. But victory in the Atlantic was no guarantee of victory at home and the Conservatives would have to fight the election against a backdrop of mass unemployment, cruise missiles and the rise of *CND (Campaign for Nuclear Disarmament)*, cuts in all the social services and mass social unrest, with one main phrase in their defence - There Is No Alternative, or TINA for short.

In a way they were right, because despite the Conservatives, and Thatcher in particular, being genuinely hated by a sizable section of the electorate, the official opposition were totally useless. A group of eminent Labour party MP's had decided that the Labour Party was a political turkey and had left to form the *SDP (Social Democratic Party)*, The militant tendency and assorted left wing nutters, whose fashion sense was on a par with wet seaweed, were passing the sort of policy resolutions that would have made Stalin nervous, and would guarantee making Labour unelectable for years. In control of this ragbag party was an affable intellectual *CND* supporter in a duffel coat.

*Source: Criminal Statistics, England and Wales Annual Command Papers; B.R. Mitchell.

THE NASTIES A PERSONAL VIEW

But though there was very little in the immediate sense the Conservatives could do about the economy and unemployment, except wait for it to get better, there was still crime, and they could at least be *seen* to be doing something about that. Within three weeks of the Conservatives resounding re-election on 10th June 1983, three things were to happen on the same day, all of which were obviously a bizarre coincidence.

Firstly, in the House of Commons in response to a Parliamentary question on video legislation Margaret Thatcher commented "I recognise the great concern caused by this matter. That is why we referred to it in our party manifesto during the Election campaign. It is not enough to have voluntary legislation. We must bring in a law to regulate the matter. My Right Honourable and learned friend the Home Secretary is now considering precisely what form the law should take". That Home Secretary was Sir Leon Brittan, perceived by many as a far tougher proposition than Whitelaw. Secondly, for maximum impact, The *Daily Mail* relaunched its *'Ban the Sadist Videos'* campaign, and thirdly, for good measure, the *DPP* announced a list of some 52 'official' nasties.

By a further amazing coincidence the next day the *Daily Mail* was able to crow that, "within hours of The *Daily Mail* campaign moving into top gear…Graham Bright, Conservative MP for Luton South announces his intention of introducing a private members Bill on the control of 'video nasties' ".

In order to bring in this private members Bill, Bright had had to resign his post as a *minor* Parliamentary private secretary (only back-benchers can bring a private members Bill, but I suspect he was too stupid to warrant a major post anyway), a truly noble act, on which Sir Leon Brittan commented "I was determined to get something through as soon as possible so we formulated a policy and Graham Bright has kindly taken it up". Which, translated basically means 'we needed someone expendable to get this dross through and Bright did the honours'. It's worth bearing in mind that Bright's political career since has, apart from a brief attempt to ban rave parties in the early nineties, had all the excitement and longevity of a determined sprout.

Now that the Government were committed to legislation, the media, Mary Whitehouse and other pressure groups, were able to enlist the support of sympathetic MP's to ensure that the Bill would be truly draconian. What was to follow was twelve months of ranting, and imbecilic claptrap from a lot of people who should have known better.

High in the padded cell stakes was the *Daily Mail*, whose editorial of 30 June 1983 reads like a cross between the hysterical outpourings of an evangelist with an attack of the vapours and an article by the Nazi Jew baiter Julius Streicher in his party newspaper *Der Stürmer*. Except in the *Daily Mail's* case, Jews had been replaced by the video nasty, other than that, the argument was on about the same level.

The headline screamed "Rape of our children's minds" which was restrained compared to the diatribe of complete crap and hatred that spat out from the editorial itself. For example, "so how many more women will be savaged and defiled by youths weaned on a diet of rape videos", and "turn back this tide of degenerate filth", and "women being defecated on by thugs". It continued in this vein before entering serious loony land with "…An electric drill slowly grinding away a man's brain. Nazi death camp sadism, complete with the screams of the Jewish girl victims, played for kicks. And rape, rape, rape… Britain fought the last World War against Hitler to defeat a creed so perverted that it spawned such horrors in awful truth. Are we insane? Are we bent on rotting our own society from within? Are we determined to spur to a gallop the forces of decadence that threaten to drag us down?" The *Mail* was also clear that it had its finger on the nation's pulse as it quipped that "years ago, children went off with their Saturday sixpence to see Roy Rogers and Trigger. Now for 50p, they gather in sniggering groups to view **SS Experiment Camp**".

Whilst the *Daily Mail's* editorial team were working themselves up into a rabid frenzy, two other future bastions of family values and defenders of public morals, Conservative MP's Jerry Haynes and David Mellor (both of whom were to be caught up in sex

scandals a few years later) would launch bitter attacks against the 'immoral' middle classes and critics of Bright's Bill (some had dared criticise the proposed legislation, but to do so was to invoke some pretty nasty abuse). From Hayes, "I bitterly regret that those middle-class people who sit on beanbags wearing Gucci accessories in their Hampstead flats which are bedecked with Laura Ashley decorations and talk about world affairs should allow their children to see the type of video films with which we are dealing".

Mellor was altogether more sanguine in his support for the proposed legislation, and clever in its defence, by directly linking the video nasty to some of the most disgusting and upsetting areas of modern life thus leaving its opponents wide open to attack from all fronts. "No one has the right to be upset at a brutal sex crime or a sadistic attack on a child or mindless thuggery on a pensioner if he is not prepared to drive sadistic videos out of our high streets". What Mellor was very effectively doing was re-enforcing the Government's line that video violence caused crime. Crime was rising but by banning video nasties they would begin the process of fighting back, of reducing crime and making Britain a safe and decent place again, where family values ruled.

The Government's line and its way of attacking those that criticised the *Bright Bill* was to imply that they were apologists for sadists, pederasts, murderers, thugs and all the worst elements of the criminal world, and it proved very effective. *The Daily Mail*, already crusading tirelessly for Bright's legislation with all the vigour of a monomanian pit bull, commented that there were 'sinister forces' at work trying to wreck Bright's Bill and, on the public's predilection for video, that "The public has shown its preference, but in this case the public is wrong".

There were, however, a few brave souls willing to suffer the venomous invective of the tabloids and assorted MP's in order to criticise Bright's proposed dirge. Amongst the most notable were Nigel Andrews of the *Financial Times*, MP's Austin Mitchell (Labour) and Richard Shepherd (Conservative), Labour peer Lord Houghton of Sowerby and John Mortimer QC, who had previously defended *Oz* magazine during its obscenity trial. Mortimer wrote in the *Sunday Times* that "It might be thought that a Conservative government with an avowed belief in family responsibility would think that what we see and read in our own homes, and what we allow our own children to watch, is better decided by individual parents than by persons designated by the Secretary of State. It might be hoped that any government would resist the temptation to undermine our constitutional liberties for the sake of a populist, unthought out and unnecessary act of Parliament".

However, despite a reasoned, articulate and, unfortunately rather rare opposition, the *Video Recordings Act* gained its Royal Assent on 12 July 1984. Amongst the hideous sanctimonious claptrap that our guardians had just made law were:-

1. That it was an offense to supply, or offer to supply an uncertified videogram (tape or disc).
2. That it was an offense to possess an uncertified videogram for supply.
3. That it was an offense to supply, or offer to supply a videogram to a person below the age specified in the certificate.
4. That it was an offense to supply, an 18R (restricted) videogram on premises other than a licensed sex shop.
5. Supplying, or offer to supply, a videogram in such a way that the labelling requirements are infringed, ie in an un-marked transit box or where the symbols and statements are of the wrong colour or have become defaced and obscured, was an offence.
6. Supplying, or offering to supply, a falsely-labelled videogram was an offence.

Penalties:

The first two offenses can result in a fine of up to £20,000 on conviction. The others carry a maximum of £2,000 fines. There is no provision for prison sentences. The Act empowers the police to search, seize and arrest. Videograms for which people are convicted under the Act are subject to forfeiture.

Exemptions from the act: Material designed to be informative, educational or instructive; videos concerned with sport, religion or music; video games; and videos produced for use in schools.

Exemption is lost if material deals to any significant extent with:

1 Human sexual activity or acts of force or restraint associated with such activity.
2 Mutilation or torture or other acts of gross violence towards humans or animals.
3 Human genital organs, human urinary or excretory functions, or if the product is designed to a significant extent to stimulate or encourage acts listed in the above two categories.

Exempt supplies include:

1 If the supply is neither for reward nor in the course of business (as a gift).
2 Where an original supplier supplies a videogram to another supplier, as long as it is not intended to reach the public.
3 Exports
4 Supplying videos made to record events like weddings for those who took part in them, providing they don't depict or are designed to stimulate sex or violence.
5 Supplies to bona-fide cinemas and broadcasters, and the censoring authority are exempt, along with medical training films.

Norman Abbott of the *BVA* comments that the Bill "will make Britain the only European country to have state censorship of video".

The 'nasty' had not though, been laid to rest for good. In a way, the tabloids had done too good a job of demonising it, of making it a definable creature with the sole aim of creating and perpetuating evil. In fact, the nasty has become part of modern English folklore, like satanic abuse in Cleveland, giant beasts on the loose on Bodmin moor, sex-crazed Scout masters, or hot and horny hooligans with one collective fist in society's face and the other up their own patriotic arses – *oooh eer*.

Ever since the tabloids foaming at the mouth stance on nasties, the video has been perceived as something totally unholy, a force for evil. So when events that could not be defined by normal rational, or understandable human behaviour like the awful Bulger murders, the Hungerford shootings or the slaughter in Dunblane, then society looks for contemporary demons to blame.

The video nasty is now, as far as the United Kingdom is concerned, part of our collective psyche. Rational thought, scientific evidence, motivation, proof or normal rules of debate no longer apply. Evil is tangible, evil is everywhere, evil has a name, *video nasty*. To question this argument is heresy, and heretics are evil.

It is now nearly fifteen years since the nasties furore and the introduction of laws that have made Britain one of the most heavily censored democracies on earth, and still the popular cry is for yet more censorship. Crime in the UK is now officially higher for all crimes other than murder than it is in the United States, though the gap is narrowing for that too.*

The United States is, like the United Kingdom, a democracy, though its representatives do not arrogantly state as ours do at every opportunity that their country is the mother of all democracies. As if somehow Britain's were a greater democracy for being the first. In fact, as a nation we seem to subconsciously desire less democracy, to welcome state interference, to yearn for a National nanny and the control of the individual. Britain is the only country in the Western world to censor strong sexual material intended for an adult audience, and (alongside the freedom loving governments of China and Singapore) to have called for censorship of the Internet. And why? Because it is an easy target. It is another example of the *something must be done* way of tackling crime or protecting the family.

By blaming the intangibles for our society's woes, society seeks intangible solutions. Each act of government censorship becomes, in the public mind, a blow against crime, drug dealers, antisocial behaviour or whatever, and for that night at least the public sleep easy in their beds.

* according to a study carried out by the US Department of Justice, reported in October 1998.

There are some pretty horrible films around, some of which do contain scenes of exploitative rape, torture, violence, and probably every other vile act that the human imagination can come up with, but should they be banned? In other countries, if the film's content does not break criminal law and is made by consensual adults, performed by consensual actors and other adults want to watch it, then so be it. These are, after all, commercially made films to be sold to, and viewed by, consumers in a free market. That is not to say that some adults may not be affected by what they see on screen. It is probable that some individuals may have a negative reaction, and some rare individuals may be influenced enough to commit copycat crimes. It has happened, and will no doubt happen again.

The same can be said of some adults who drink alcohol, or attend football matches, some react very violently, or at the very least antisocially, yet no-one has called for the prohibition of alcohol or the banning of football. Too many people would be affected. It would not be populist, so the populist newspapers and politicians would not seek legislation, though every day people will suffer violence and assault directly linked to drink. But the state should not seek to legislate for the lowest common denominator. In the case of film, for censorship to be really effective, it would have to include cutting violent or sexual material from mainstream movies and this would not be a viable or popular option.

If Britain is to live up to its boastful claim that it is the mother of all democracy then it must stop looking for easy solutions to its difficult problems. It is not films that kill people, or for that matter drink, it is people. To absolve offenders of responsibility by citing film, or drink as cause and effect is shameful, simplistic and ruefully irresponsible. Individuals must be made to take responsibility for their actions. If a person drinks and drives he (or she) knows what he is doing in the same way that someone who saw **A Clockwork Orange** in the seventies, and then dressed up as a Droog and went looking for tramps to beat up did. In both cases it is the individual's decision to act as they do, and the individual who must face the consequences.

Democracy and freedom is not just about sitting around a table while sensible, well balanced people discuss contradictory views in measured, or even slightly heated tones - that is a facet, and a good facet at that. But democracy is also about being able to tolerate extremes of views, from the most bestial racist to the most intolerant fundamentalist; from pornography to gratuitous violence on film. As long as they stay within the law people have a right to voice those views, in the street, on video, or on the Internet. Society has laws which cover criminal activity and any film or distributor, or artist, writer, or political group that breaks those laws can be dealt with in the courts. Other than that the State should have no role whatsoever in the creative freedoms or political opinions of its citizens.

If Britain is to have a truly democratic future, then as a society we have to learn to accept that banning what offends us is not the answer. Censoring films, books, plays or music, or even, God forbid, tabloid newspapers, are easy options that offer no lasting solutions. If they did, Britain would today probably have one of the lowest crimes rates in the western world. The *Daily Mail* forgot, when it evoked the memory of World War Two in its diatribe against video and its fight to preserve our freedom, that part of that freedom was their right to publish what many might regard as drivel, as it is theirs to criticise others for watching what they in turn might regard as drivel. Because ultimately democracy is not about the nice it is fundamentally about the nasty.

Nigel Wingrove
Soho, London
October 1998

1 THE OFFICIAL NASTIES

The 39 films deemed obscene by the Director of Public Prosecutions

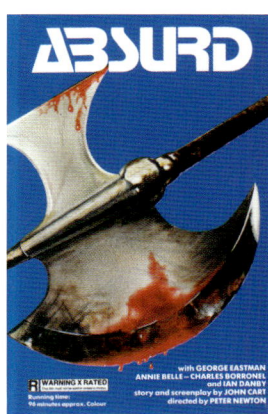

Absurd
Original Title: **Rosso sangue**
Country: **Italy**
Director: **Aristide Massaccesi** (as Peter Newton)
Year: **1981** Time: **90m 06s**
Video Label: **Medusa**

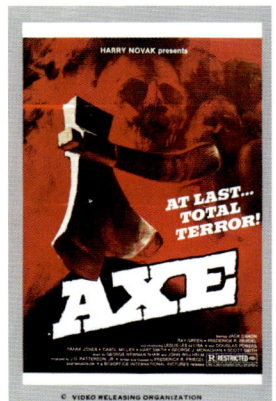

Axe
Original Title: **Lisa**
Country: **USA**
Director: **Frederick R. Friedell**
Year: **1977** Time: **64m 49s**
Video Label: **Video Network**

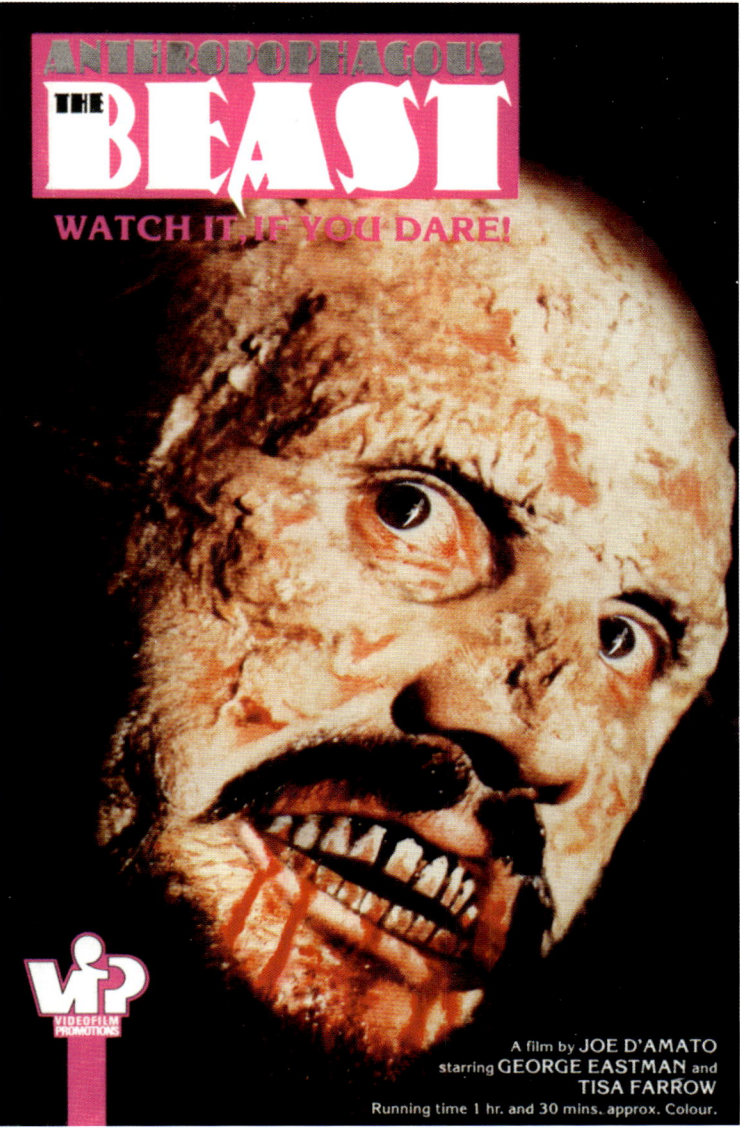

Anthropophagous the Beast
Original Title: **Antropophagus**
Country: **Italy**
Director: **Aristide Massaccesi** (as Joe D'Amato)
Year: **1980** Time: **88m 14s** (VFP) **87m 57s** Video Shack
Video Label: **VFP** (Video Film Promotions) / Video Shack

Absurd: The sequel to '**Anthropophagous the Beast**', Absurd received an uncut video release around the same time it had been granted an '18' certificate (with 2m 32s of cuts) for theatrical exhibition. It was soon reissued on video with cuts, although it had never been granted a video classification certificate.

Anthropophagous the Beast: Released uncut on video, clips from this film have featured on 'The News at Ten', citing this as a 'Snuff Movie'. Just after it joined the banned list, Video Shack, a new video label, re-released a much softer version with self-imposed cuts made to some of the more excessive gore scenes. In addition to the cuts, the cover art was toned down to obscure the beast's face.

Axe: Although deemed obscene on video, it was granted a theatrical BBFC 'X' certificate after 2m 54s of cuts in April 1982, where it was screened under the title '**The California Axe Massacre**'.

Statement from the DPP, March 1987.

Following the Attorney General's statement in the House of Commons on 23 July 1984, a list of titles of video cassettes of the horror variety which have been the subject of prosecution under section 2 of the Obscene Publications Act, 1959 or advised as suitable for such projection is as follows:

Absurd
Anthropophagous the Beast
Axe
The Beast in Heat
Blood Bath
Blood Feast
Blood Rites
Bloody Moon
The Burning
Cannibal Apocalypse
Cannibal Ferox
Cannibal Holocaust
The Cannibal Man
Devil Hunter
Don't Go in the Woods... Alone!
The Driller Killer
Evilspeak
Exposé
Faces of Death,
Fight For Your Life
Frankenstein (Andy Warhol's)
Forest of Fear
The Gestapo's Last Orgy
The House by the Cemetery
House on the Edge of the Park
I Spit on Your Grave
Island of Death
The Last House on the Left
Love Camp 7
Madhouse
Mardi Gras Massacre
Night of the Bloody Apes
Night of the Demon,
Nightmares in a Damaged Brain
Snuff
SS Experiment Camp
Tenebrae
The Werewolf and the Yeti
Zombie Flesh-Eaters.

THE OFFICIAL NASTIES

1984 - Band Aid formed

A Charity formed by Bob Geldof and Midge Ure in December 1984 in response to the famine in Ethiopia. Geldof and Ure wrote the song Do They Know it's Christmas with all proceeds going to charity. It reached No 1 on 14 December 1984.

1982 - ABC enter charts with 'Lexicon of Love'

Stylish dance music with gold lamé suits.

Blood Bath
Original Title: **Reazione a catena**
Country: **Italy**
Director: **Mario Bava**
Time: **80m 54s** Year: **1971**
Video Label: **Hokushin**

Blood Feast
Original Title: **None**
Country: **USA**
Director: **Herschell Gordon Lewis**
Time: **64m 10s** Year: **1963**
Video Label: **Astra**

The Beast in Heat
Original Title: **La bestia in calore**
Country: **Italy**
Director: **Luigi Batzella** (as Ivan Katansky)
Year: **1976** Time: **85m 59s**
Video Label: **JVI**

Blood Bath: This precursor to the stalk and slash films of the 1980's was rejected outright when submitted to the BBFC for theatrical distribution in April 1972. This uncut version sneaked out on video in April 1983, and has since been re-released on video by Redemption Films under the title '**Bay of Blood**' with BBFC approved cuts totalling 43s.

The Beast in Heat: The actual on-screen title is '**Horrifying Experiments of S.S. Last Days**', and it's a miracle that this incredibly sleazy 'Ilsa' inspired obscurity ever found its way onto the banned list, as it is perhaps the single most hard to find of all the banned films. It was never advertised and received a very limited release from its Rochdale based distributor.

Blood Feast: The oldest of the 'nasties', and considered by many to be the first ever gore film, earning its director the 'Godfather of Gore' moniker. Featuring 'Playboy Playmate' Connie Mason, this was a huge hit on the US Drive-In circuit, and was swiftly followed by '**Two-Thousand Maniacs**' and '**The Gruesome Twosome**'.

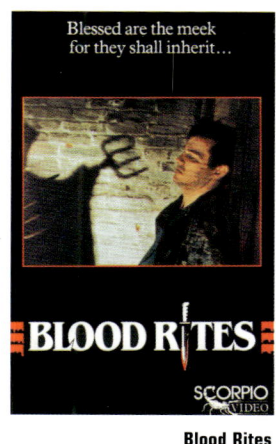

Blood Rites
Original Title: **The Ghastly Ones**
Country: **USA**
Director: **Andy Milligan**
Year: **1967** Time: **67m 22s**
Video Label: **Scorpio**

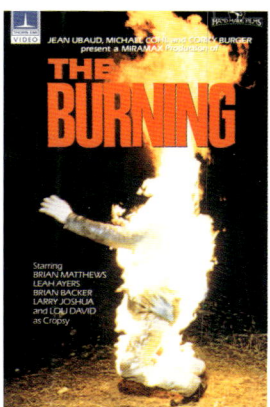

The Burning
Country: **USA**
Director: **Tony Maylam**
Year: **1980** Time: **87m 26s**
Video Label: **Thorn EMI**

Bloody Moon
Original Title: **Die Säge des Todes**
Country: **West Germany**
Director: **Jesús Franco**
Year: **1980** Time: **81m 35s**
Video Label: **Inter-Light**

1982 - The British National Party is formed

The BNP, an extreme right-wing party, was formed by John Tyndall as a breakaway group from the National Front. It was first known as the New National Front and from April 1982 as the BNP.

Blood Rites: A laughable excuse for a gore film from Staten Island based Milligan, who preferred to shoot period pieces so they wouldn't date. The UK release was inexplicably missing some 1m 35s of footage, which any viewer would have been thankful for.

Bloody Moon: Passed for theatrical distribution by the BBFC in a cut 'X' rated version in January 1982, this uncut version was released on tape just prior to this in November 1981. The uncut video release was later replaced with the 'X' rated cut version. It has subsequently been passed for video in an '18' rated version with cuts totalling 1m 20s.

The Burning: Although passed with slight cuts and an 'X' certificate for theatrical exhibition by the BBFC in September 1981, an uncut version was released in error by Thorn in November 1982. Red faced, they placed ads in the trade press appealing to dealers to return their uncut copies in exchange for the BBFC approved version, which was sent back to the dealer over taped with the cut version and a date stamped label. Surprisingly, most dealers kept the uncut version. This was Holly Hunter's first film role.

THE OFFICIAL NASTIES

1984 - British Telecom

BT becomes a public limited company in what was the largest ever stock flotation in the UK. Gross proceeds of the sale, through a share rights issue, amounted to some £3,900 million.

1984 - 'Blood and Guts in High School' published

Avant garde feminist and ex-42nd Street porn star Kathy Acker lauded as original literary punk. Reads like spilt ink.

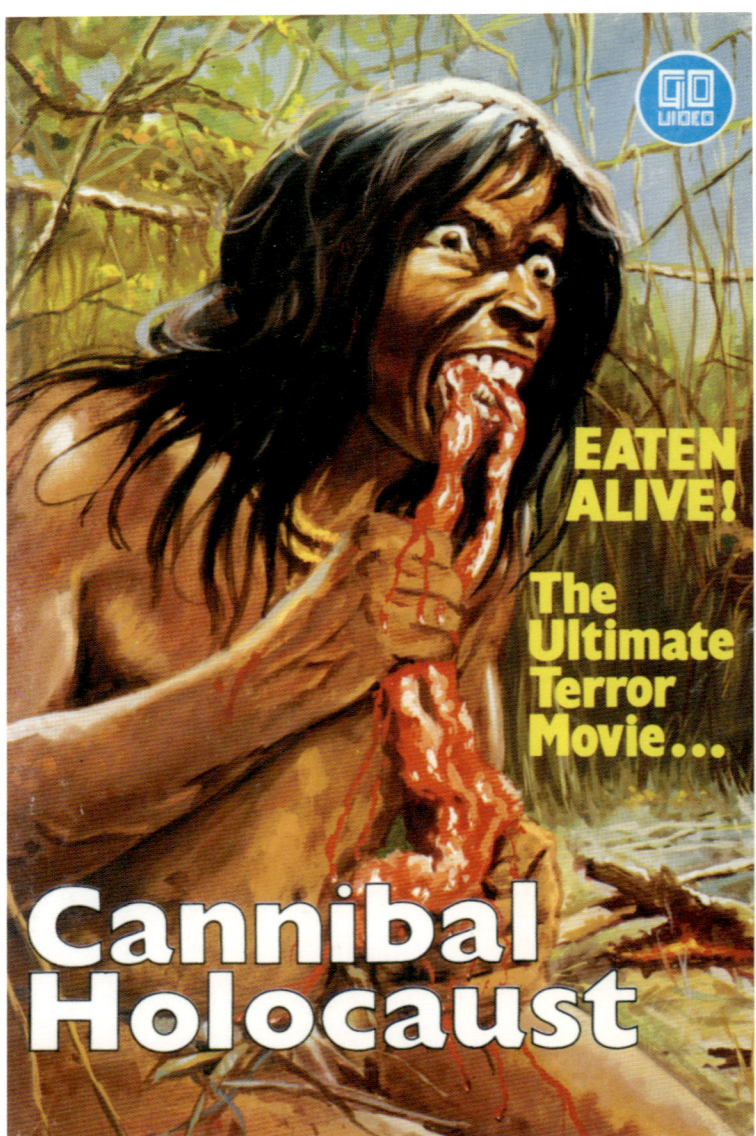

Cannibal Holocaust
Country: **Italy**
Director: **Ruggero Deodato**
Year: **1979**   Time: **85m 14s**
Video Label: **Go**

Cannibal Apocalypse
Original Title: **Apocalipse domani**
Country: **Italy**
Director: **Antonio Margheriti**
Time: **92m 06s**   Year: **1980**
Video Label: **Replay**

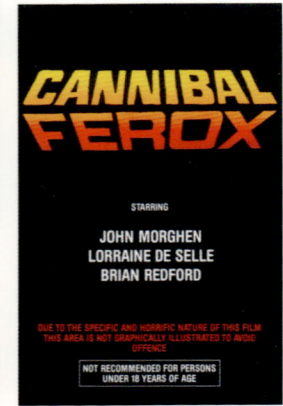

Cannibal Ferox
Country: **Italy**
Director: **Umberto Lenzi**
Time: **89m 08s**   Year: **1980**
Video Label: **Replay**

Cannibal Apocalypse: The 'Cannibal' films were among the first to join the so-called 'nasties' list. Never screened theatrically in the UK, this uncut version featuring cannibal Vietnam veterans was released in August 1982.

Cannibal Ferox: Released in the US as '**Make Them Die Slowly**', this was released on video here uncut in October 1982, and subsequently ended up on the banned list. It was re-released soon afterwards in new packaging with a very large (fake) '18' certificate on the cover, after numerous self-imposed cuts had been made by the distributor.

Cannibal Holocaust: The most notorious of all the cannibal movies and still considered by some (including certain Trading Standards officers) to be a real snuff movie! This appeared on the shelves of UK video stores way back in April 1982. Contrary to popular belief, it was not the uncut version, and had infact been cut prior to release by the distributors by 6m 24s. It was released on tape and laser disc uncut in Holland where it no doubt continues to sell to British tourists.

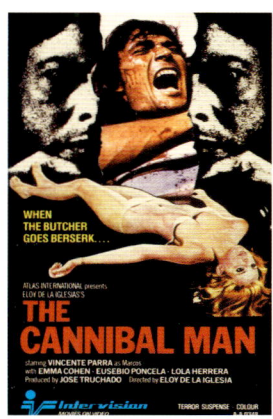

The Cannibal Man
Original Title: **La Semana del Asesino**
Country: **Spain**
Director: **Eloy De La Iglesia**
Year: **1972** Time: **94m 13s**
Video Label: **Intervision**

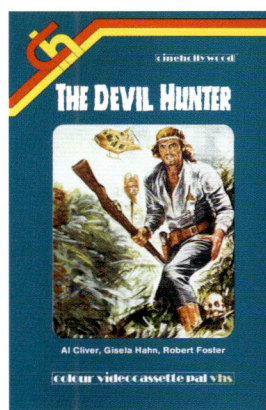

Devil Hunter
Original Title: **Sexo Canibal / Il cacciatore di uomini / Jungfrau unter Kannibalen**
Country: **Spain / Italy / West Germany**
Director: **Jesús Franco** (as Clifford Brown)
Year: **1980** Time: **85m 23s**
Video Label: **Cinehollywood**

Don't Go in the Woods…Alone!
Original Title: **Don't Go in the Woods**
Country: **USA**
Director: **James Bryan**
Year: **1980** Time: **78m 15s**
Video Label: **Video Network**

1983 - Paddy Ashdown enters the House of Commons

The future leader of the Liberal Democrats wins the hitherto safe Conservative seat of Yeovil.

1983 - 'Alice in Wonderland' club opens

Ultra trendy hippy-trippy night club opens on Monday nights playing a heady mixture of Hendrix and love drug tracks to psychedelic goths and '80's flower children.

The Cannibal Man: Not a cannibal movie at all, but a psychological study of a man's break down. Re-released with an '18' certificate with just 3s worth of cuts by Redemption Films.

Devil Hunter: The fact that this film made the banned list is a mystery - any jury forced to watch this mess would have probably fallen asleep whilst deciding its fate! Until its UK video premiere in November 1981, this was the first time it had been seen here.

Don't Go in the Woods…Alone!: Never released theatrically in the UK, this is another extremely low budget yarn which features a scene where a man in a wheelchair is decapitated whilst admiring the sunset! Certainly not worthy of its cult 'banned list' status.

THE OFFICIAL NASTIES

1982 - May 2, Argentinean battle cruiser the General Belgrano is sunk

British submarine HMS Conqueror sunk the Belgrano when it was on a heading 55.18S, 61.47W, taking it away from the British imposed exclusion zone. 323 are killed.

The Driller Killer
Country: **USA**
Director: **Abel Ferrara**
Year: **1979** Time: **85m 10s**
Video Label: **Vipco**

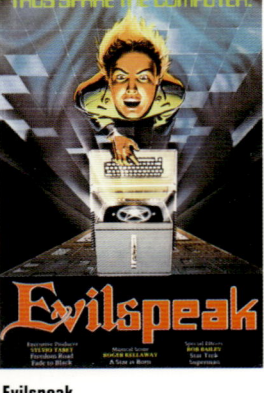

Evilspeak
Country: **USA**
Director: **Eric Weston**
Time: **99m 53s** Year: **1981**
Video Label: **Videospace / Filmtown**

Exposé
Original Title: **The House on Straw Hill**
Country: **Great Britain**
Director: **James Kenelm Clarke**
Time: **80m 16s** Year: **1975**
Video Label: **Intervision**

The Driller Killer: Released in the UK on April 1982 with perhaps the most over-the-top video cover ever seen in the UK. The film itself would probably be granted an '18' certificate with minor cuts if submitted today. More a New York art film than a nasty, this was clearly inspired by Polanski's Repulsion. Unfortunately the UK release was inexplicably missing a whole sequence totalling 6m 35s.

Evilspeak: Released uncut on video in August 1983, a cut version was also made available when this was banned. Re-released in the late 1980's by Apex video with cuts totalling 3m 34s courtesy of the BBFC.

Exposé: The only British film to make the 'nasties' list, this film was granted an 'X' certificate in November 1975 with minor cuts. One can only wonder why it was deemed obscene by the DPP. It was recently re-released on video and passed '18' with 51s of cuts.

20

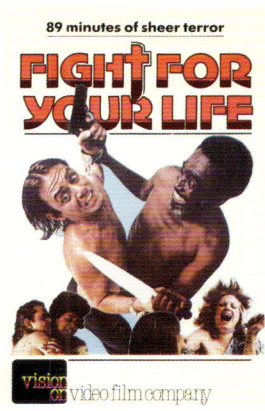

Fight For Your Life
Original Title: **I Hate Your Guts**
Country: **USA**
Director: **Robert A. Endelson**
Year: **1977** Time: **82m 11s**
Video Label: **Vision On**

Frankenstein (Andy Warhol's)
Original Title: **Il mostro e in tavola... barone Frankenstein / Chair pour Frankenstein**
Country: **Italy / France**
Director: **Paul Morrissey & Antonio Margheriti**
Year: **1973** Time: **88m 55s** (Vipco)
91m 10s (Video Gems)
Video Label: **Vipco / Video Gems**

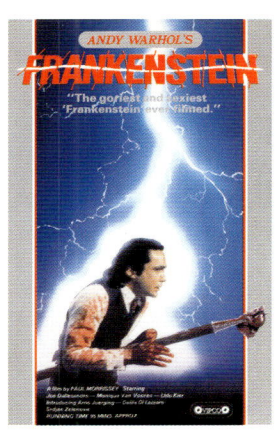

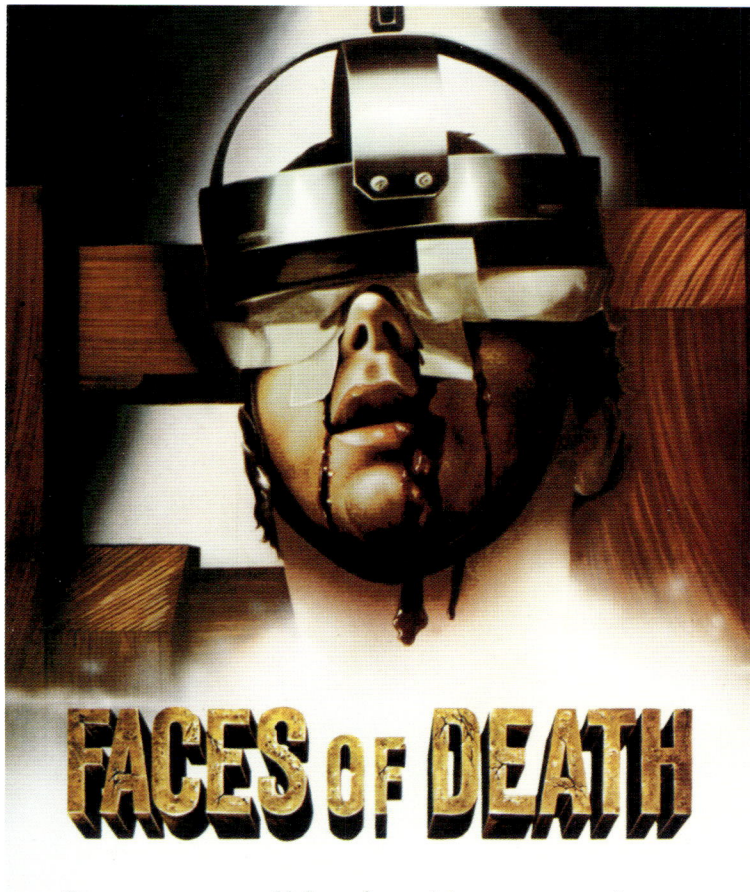

Faces of Death
Country: **USA**
Director: **Conan Le Cilaire**
Year: **1979** Time: **77m 56s**
Video Label: **Atlantis**

1984 - The IRA bomb a Brighton Hotel during the Conservative Party conference

October 1984, five people are killed in the explosion, which left Norman Tebbit, then Trade and Industry secretary, and his wife, seriously injured

THE OFFICIAL NASTIES

Faces of Death: Supposedly made for the Japanese market, this tasteless 'Mondo Film' appeared on tape in November 1982 in a version which deleted some 26m of footage. Hugely successful on video in America among the new breed of kids looking for real death footage, it was followed by four sequels and paved the way for numerous imitations.

Fight For Your Life: This tale of racial hatred, rape and revenge was rejected outright by the BBFC in October 1981. This uncut version appeared on video a year later. The racist thug was played by William J. Sanderson, who later appeared as J. F. Sebastian in '**Blade Runner**'.

Frankenstein (Andy Warhol's): Passed with an 'X' certificate by the BBFC in January 1975 as '**Flesh for Frankenstein**', this camp remake was made back-to-back with '**Blood for Dracula**', both starring Udo Kier and Joe Dallesandro. Two video releases of these were in circulation at the time this was banned, but it was only the American import release on Video Gems that was actually uncut. The Vipco release had had many of its gorier moments removed. It was recently re-released on video with 56s worth of cuts.

1983 - Gordon Brown enters House of Commons

The future Chancellor of the Exchequer is elected as Labour MP for Dunfermline.

1982/3 - Goth mecca the Batcave reigns

Wednesday nights in Dean Street Soho saw gatherings of post punk, pale individuals reeking of petuli oil, festooned with crucifix's and wearing black, gather at the Goths coolest watering hole run by Goth band 'Specimen'.

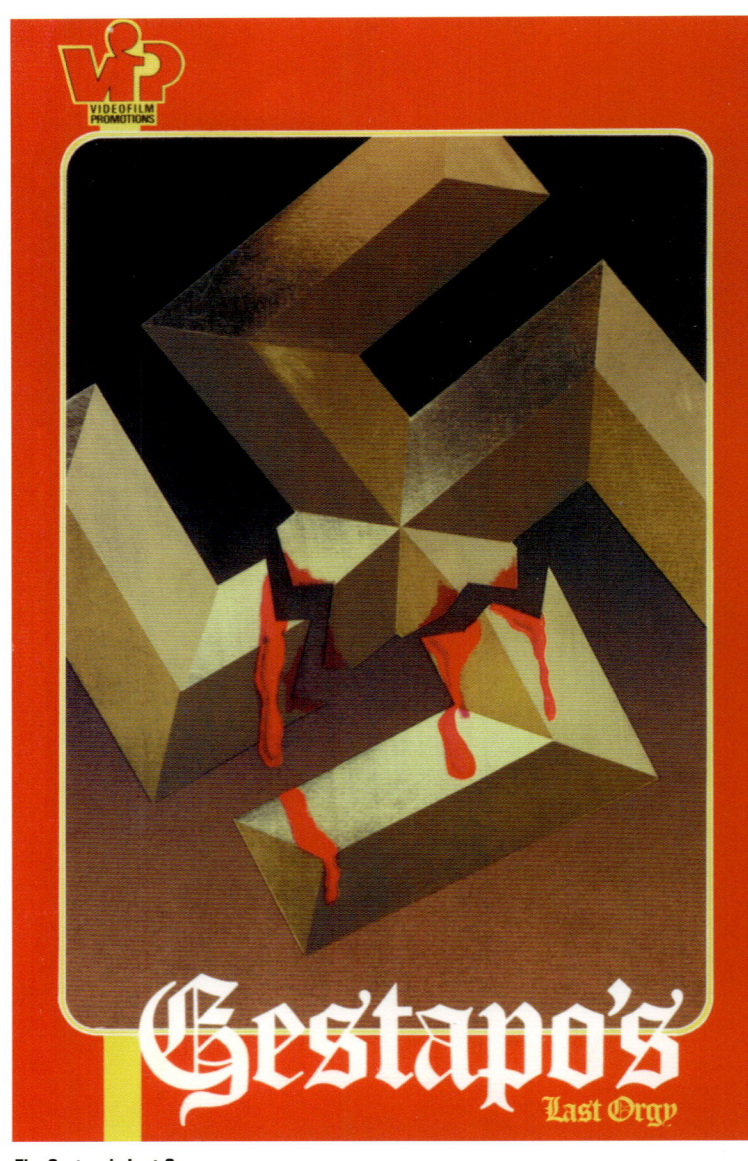

The Gestapo's Last Orgy
Original Title: **L'ultima orgia del III Reich**
Country: **Italy**
Director: **Cesare Canevari**
Year: **1976** Time: **80m 56s**
Video Label: **VFP** (Video Film Promotions) / Video Shack

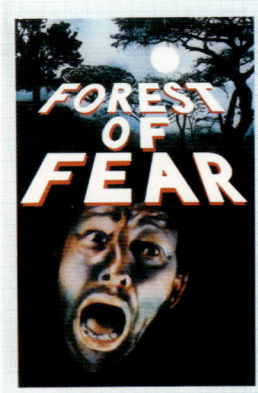

Forest of Fear
Original Title: **Blood Eaters**
Country: **USA**
Director: **Charles McCrann**
Time: **81m 05s** Year: **1979**
Video Label: **Monte**

The House by the Cemetery
Original Title: **Quella villa accanto al cimitero**
Country: **Italy**
Director: **Lucio Fulci**
Time: **81m 06s** Year: **1981**
Video Label: **Videomedia / Vampix**

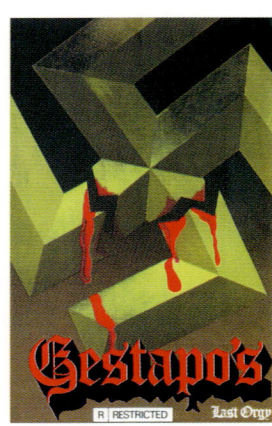

Forest of Fear: Yet another ultra low budget obscurity, non deserving of its banned list notoriety. This UK release inexplicably deletes the last 4 minutes of a man driving away in his car.

The Gestapo's Last Orgy: Perhaps the glossiest and best made of the Nazi death camp films, this one appeared on video in a watered down version with an entire 11 minute sequence deleted. The write-up on the back was later ammended to advise would be viewers of its explicit and violent nature. It received a very limited re-release by Video Shack around the time of its banning.

The House by the Cemetery: Another surprise addition to the banned list, this one had not long finished its theatrical run where it was granted an 'X' certificate in December 1981. The same BBFC approved 'X' version (with 4 cuts totalling 1m 21s) appeared on video in March 1983, where it subsequently joined the nasties list. When re-submitted to the BBFC by Elephant video in 1988 it was cut by over 4m, prompting its distributor never to repeat the experience.

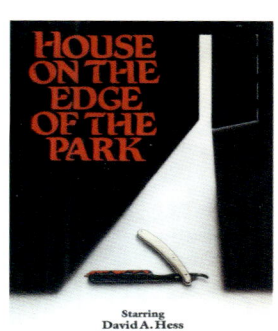

House on the Edge of the Park
Original Title: **La casa sperduta del parco**
Country: **Italy**
Director: **Ruggero Deodato**
Year: **1980** Time: **87m 48s**
Video Label: **Skyline**

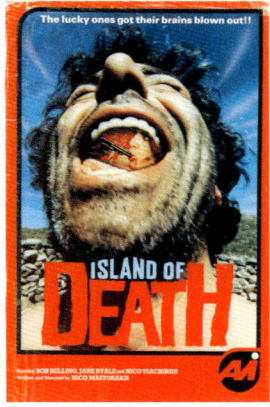

Island of Death
Original Title: **Island of Perversion**
Country: **Greece**
Director: **Nico Mastorakis** (as Nick Mastorakis)
Year: **1975** Time: **102m 39s**
Video Label: **AVI**

I Spit on Your Grave
Original Title: **Day of the Woman**
Country: **USA**
Director: **Meir Zarchi**
Year: **1978** Time: **96m 47s**
Video Label: **Astra**

House on the Edge of the Park: Released uncut on video in March 1983, this had previously been rejected outright by the BBFC back in March 1981 when submitted for theatrical distribution. No re-release is planned for this yuppies-in-peril epic from the maker of '**Cannibal Holocaust**'.

I Spit on Your Grave: Released on video in May 1982, this is perhaps the most famous of the 'nasties'. This one topped the UK rental charts when rumours of its imminent banning were publicised. It has recently been praised by women's groups as a true feminist movie.

Island of Death: Although the back of the video sleeve indicated that this was a BBFC approved 'X' version, this was far from the truth. This was in fact the full uncut version, which had been passed by the BBFC with cuts under the title 'A Craving for Lust' in April 1976. It was submitted for a video classification in 1987 under the bogus title '**Psychic Killer 2**', where it was rejected outright.

1982 - God's Banker is found hanged

June 1982, Roberto Calvi - God's banker, a member of the P-2 Masonic lodge, and president of the Italian Banco Ambrosiano, which was closely entwined with the Vatican Bank, was found hanging under Blackfriars Bridge. Foul play is suspected.

1982 - Blade Runner

Ridley Scotts' sci-fi classic of flashing neon, acid rain and replicants opens with grumpy detective Harrison Ford. A masterpiece.

THE OFFICIAL NASTIES

1982 - Hard-left Campaign Group launched

A group of Labour MP's including Tony Benn and Dennis Skinner establish a group to rally opposition to the expulsion of members of a militant tendency from the Labour Party.

Love Camp 7
Country: **USA**
Director: **Robert Lee Frost** (as R. L. Frost)
Year: **1968** Time: **91m 51s**
Video Label: **Abbey / Market**

The Last House on the Left
Country: **USA**
Director: **Wes Craven**
Time: **77m 23s** Year: **1972**
Video Label: **Replay**

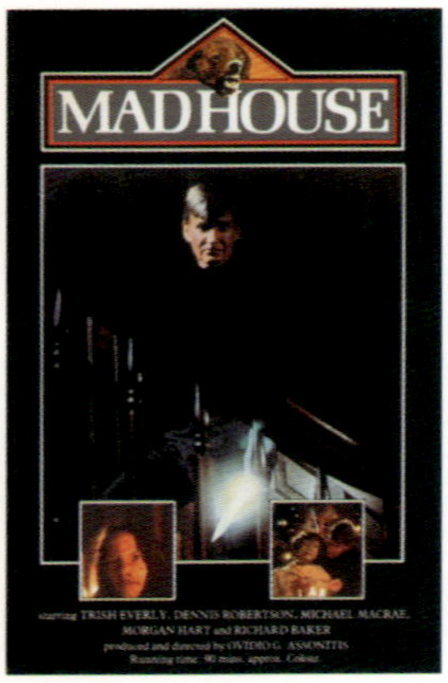

Madhouse
Original Title: **There was a Little Girl**
Country: **USA**
Director: **Ovidio G. Assonitis**
Time: **89m 16s** Year: **1981**
Video Label: **Medusa**

The Last House on the Left: From the director of '**Scream**', Craven's first feature was rejected outright by the BBFC in July 1974. This video release appeared in June 1982, and was promoted in various video magazines with an outrageous full page advertisement. Legend has it that a much stronger version was originally prepared, although most of this footage was trimmed prior to release at the request of Hallmark, the film's distributor. This UK video release deleted a sequence providing several minutes of comic relief. It has since been screened at London's National Film Theatre under the title '**Krug and Co**'.

Love Camp 7: Famous for being the very first in the wave of sleazy 'Nasty Nazi' movies, predating the Canadian 'Ilsa' and the notorious Italian 'death camp' movies. Never submitted to the BBFC for a theatrical or video certificate, although it was later (still pre-VRA) reissued by Market Video.

Madhouse: Not released theatrically in the UK, it was released in both cut and uncut versions by Medusa around the same time as '**Absurd**'. Featuring the only known scene of a (very fake) dog having its head drilled. This scene was unsurprisingly missing from the cut version.

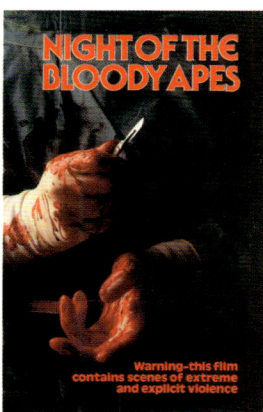

Night of the Bloody Apes
Original Title: **La Horriplante Bestia Humana**
Country: **Mexico**
Director: **Rene Cardona**
Year: **1968** Time: **79m 19s**
Video Label: **IFS** (Iver Film Services)

Night of the Demon
Country: **USA**
Director: **James C. Wasson**
Year: **1980** Time: **91m 54s**
Video Label: **IFS** (Iver Film Services)

Mardi gras Massacre
Country: **USA**
Director: **Jack Weis**
Year: **1981** Time: **91m 51s**
Video Label: **Derann / Goldstar / Market**

1984 - Capping introduced

The Government began imposing spending limits on local authorities, which proved highly controversial as councils blamed the spending limits for cut backs in services.

Mardi Gras Massacre: This makes the gore films of Herschell Gordon-Lewis look polished. Not released theatrically in the UK, this uncut version featuring graphic heart removals and bizarre rituals was actually re-released by another enterprising UK video company, Market Video. It remains unavailable in the UK to date.

Night of the Bloody Apes: Granted an 'X' certificate in March 1974 with cuts, who would have thought that a film featuring Mexican wrestling and a storyline dealing with a heart transplanted from a gorilla to a man could have been deemed 'nasty'? This is the UK guess, and anything can happen here. The gory operation footage probably got this one banned, but you can see far worse on television.

Night of the Demon: Not to be confused with Jacques Tourneur's 1957 classic, this was another obscure film which, if it hadn't featured the sleeve note 'Warning - this film contains scenes of extreme and explicit violence', would probably have slipped through the nasties net. See a Yeti spinning someone's entrails around and using them as a whip, after having ripped some poor guy's penis off during urination.

THE OFFICIAL NASTIES

1983 - Cruise missiles deployed

Highly controversial cruise missiles with nuclear warheads are deployed in Western Europe under sole US control.

1983 - Designers Body Map set UK fashion alight

Designers David Holah and Stevie Stewart win the Most Innovative Designer of the Year Award and put the fashion spotlight back on London

SS Experiment Camp
Original Title: **Lager SS adis kastrat kommandantur**
Country: **Italy**
Director: **Sergio Garrone**
Year: **1976** Time: **89m 54s**
Video Label: **Go**

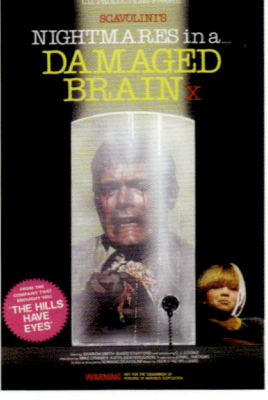

Nightmares in a Damaged Brain
Original Title: **Nightmare**
Country: **USA**
Director: **Romano Scavolini**
Time: **85m 51s** Year: **1981**
Video Label: **World of Video 2000**

Snuff
Original Title: **Slaughter**
Country: **Argentina / USA**
Director: **Roberta & Michael Findlay**
Time: **76m 39s** Year: **1976**
Video Label: **Astra**

Nightmares in a Damaged Brain: Passed 'X' with cuts in April 1982, a slightly longer version appeared on video just two months later, which resulted in its distributor, David Grant, being imprisoned for some twelve months. It's interesting to note that the supposedly uncut (hence 'obscene') version he released had been pre-cut by some 10 minutes removing some excessive gore. Apparently Grant promoted of this title at a video trade fair by featuring a brain in a jar and running a 'guess the weight of the brain' competition.

Snuff: Distributor Astra preferred to remain anonymous for this release, as no distributor's name is listed on the sleeve. Allegedly withdrawn on its day of release, it was available for one day only from a video trade fair. Obviously NOT a real 'Snuff' movie at all but a dull Argentinian effort which remained unreleased for several years until distributor Alan Shackleton came up with the idea of filming a new end sequence showing the alleged 'real killing' of the star (who was clearly a different girl).

SS Experiment Camp: Although Go Video decided to pre-cut their release of Cannibal Holocaust, they obviously thought this one was OK to release uncut. Rumours persist of a video shop in Cambridge doing a promotion for this title by featuring a window display of dummies dressed up in full Nazi attire.

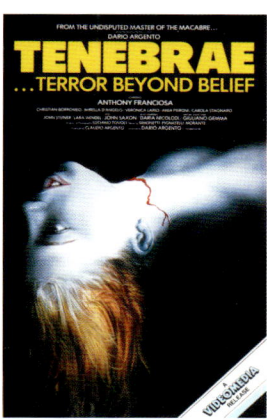

Tenebrae
Original Title: **Tenebre**
Country: **Italy**
Director: **Dario Argento**
Year: **1982** Time: **96m 48s**
Video Label: **Videomedia**

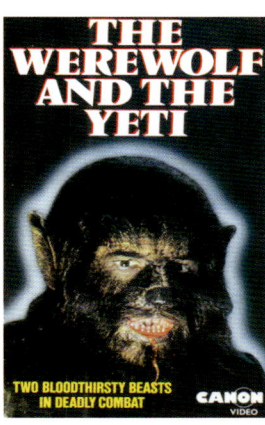

The Werewolf and the Yeti
Original Title: **La Maldicion de la Bestia**
Country: **Spain**
Director: **Miguel I. Bonns** (as M. I. Bonns)
Year: **1975** Time: **83m 43s**
Video Label: **Canon**

Zombie Flesh-Eaters
Original Title: **Zombi 2**
Country: **Italy**
Director: **Lucio Fulci**
Year: **1979** Time: **87m 01s**
Video Label: **Vipco** (Video Instant Picture Company Ltd)

1984 - Miners' strike starts

The bitter year-long strike by members of the National Union of Mineworkers, the NUM, began over plans for a drastic reduction in the size of the industry and pay. The key players Arthur Scargill and coal Chairman Sir Ian MacGregor, supported fully by Margaret Thatcher, were to clash bitterly, as were the miners and the police.

1982 - Culture Club enter charts with 'Do You Really Want to Hurt Me'

Boy George and crew shock the nation and 'gender bender' is coined by the tabloids

Tenebrae: Released onto video in August 1983, just shortly after it had finished its theatrical run where it had been passed 18 with just 3s of cuts (the cut scene featured a woman having her arm removed with an axe). It would seem that the DPP were clearly out to prosecute a BBFC approved title.

The Werewolf and the Yeti: An extremely obscure horror film, released in the US as 'Night of the Howling Beast' and starring ex-Spanish wrestler Paul Naschy (Jacinto Molina Alvarez). Another one of those 'why was this banned?' titles.

Zombie Flesh-Eaters: Originally released in its theatrical BBFC 'X' version (cut by 2 minutes) it was later re-released in a 'Strong Uncut Version' due to apparent public demand. It was re-released on video several years ago by the reformed Vipco in its original theatrical cut version (despite misleading sleeve notes which would indicate otherwise).

2 NASTIES ON PAROLE

34 films that the DPP (Director of Public Prosecutions) failed to get convictions on

The Beyond
Original Title: **L'aldila**
Country: **Italy**
Director: **Lucio Fulci**
Year: **1981** Time: **81m 59s**
Video Label: **Videomedia / Vampix**

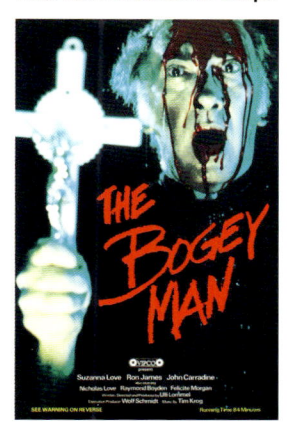

The Bogeyman
Original Title: **The Boogeyman**
Country: **USA**
Director: **Ulli Lommel**
Year: **1980** Time: **79m 24s**
Video Label: **Vipco** (Video Instant Picture Company Ltd)

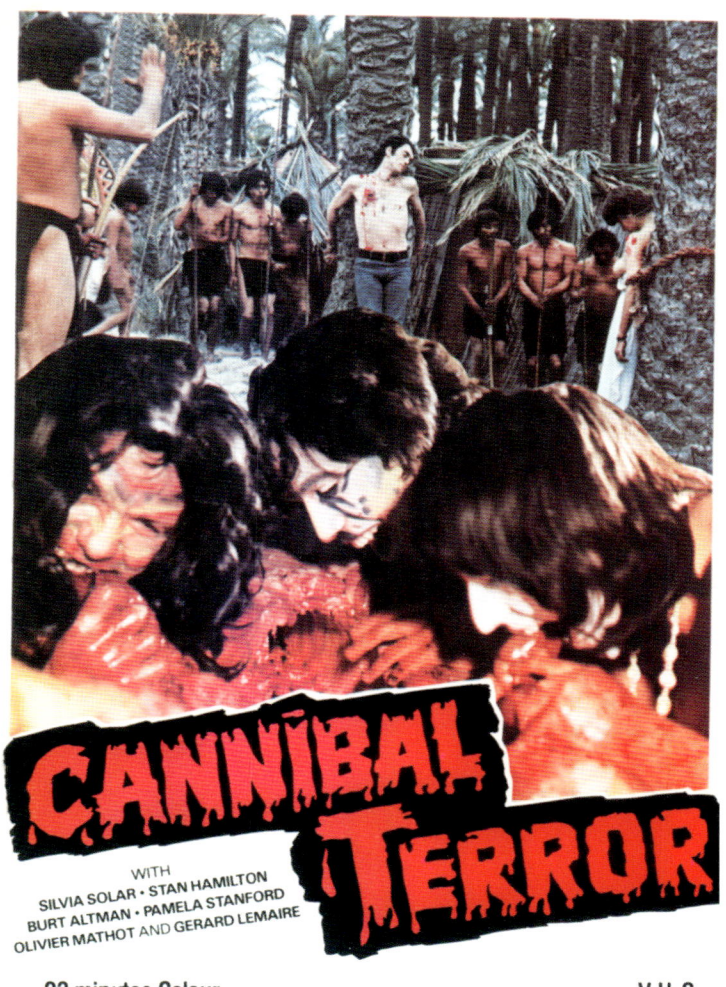

Cannibal Terror
Original Title: **Terror Caníbal / Terreur Cannibale**
Country: **Spain / France**
Director: **Julio Tabernero** (as Allan W. Steeve)
Year: **1980** Time: **89m 37s**
Video Label: **Modern**

The Beyond: This video release of the old BBFC 'X' version appeared in May 1982, after recently finishing its cinema run. It was reissued by Elephant Video in the same BBFC 'X' version, and more recently by the re-formed Vipco in a version which had been pre-cut by 1m 45s.

The Bogeyman: Arthouse director Lommel churned out this entertaining possession flick starring his then wife, Suzanna Love. Granted an 'X' certificate for the cinema, it has since been re-released on video with cuts totalling 44s.

Cannibal Terror: An appallingly bad movie, this film features some fake looking cannibalism sequences. More dull than nasty, it was most likely banned for its gory cover stills. It has since disappeared without trace.

1982 - De Lorean Motor Company collapses

After the De Lorean Company received nearly £80,000,000 from the UK government, it went into receivership amid allegations of serious irregularities.

1982 - Steve Strange opens new club The Camden Palace

April '82 Strange still basking in the success of 'Blitz', 'Hell' and 'Club for Heroes', opens mass new purpose built club. ('Slum it in style' was the place to be on Tuesday nights - for a while!)

NASTIES ON PAROLE

NASTIES ON PAROLE

1982 - Diana, Princess of Wales gives birth

In June 1982, Diana gives birth to her first son, William.

1983 - Goth rockers

Southern Death Cult eventually become The Cult. Sporting bits of dead turkeys, red indian togs and black cowboy hats, the Cult would become one of the '80's most successful rock bands.

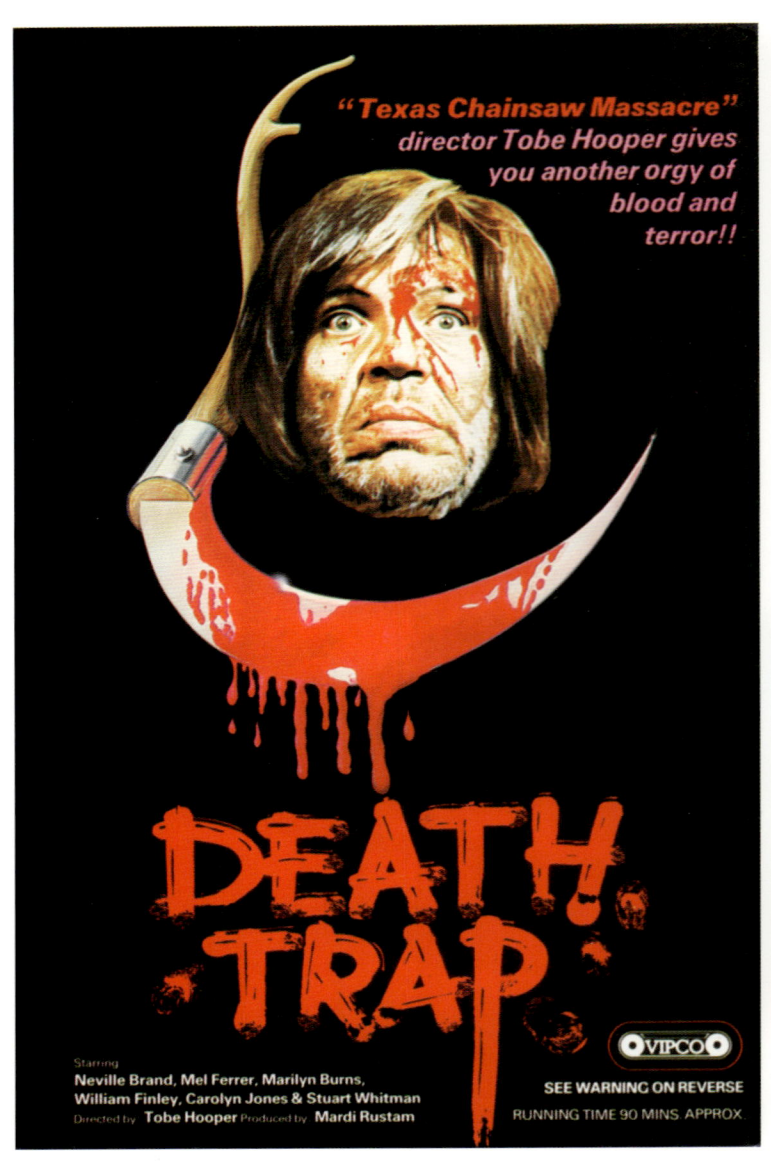

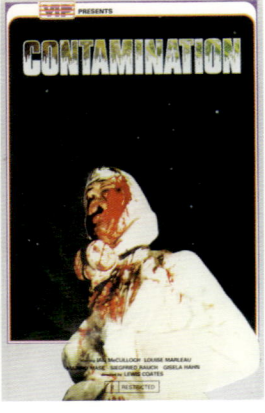

Contamination
Original Title: **Contaminazione alien arrive sulla terra / Astaron Brut des Schreckens**
Country: **Italy c West Germany**
Director: **Luigi Cozzi** (as Lewis Coates)
Year: **1980** Time: **85m 30s**
Video Label: **VIP** (Video Independent Productions Ltd)

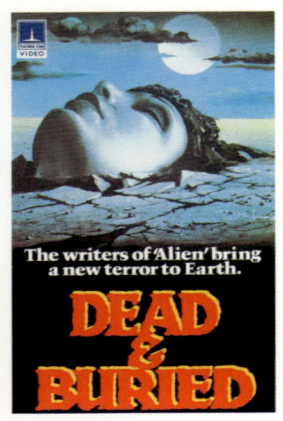

Dead & Buried
Country: **USA**
Director: **Gary A. Sherman**
Year: **1981** Time: **90m 18s**
Video Label: **Thorn EMI**

Death Trap
Original Title: **Eaten Alive**
Country: **USA**
Director: **Tobe Hooper**
Year: **1976** Time: **86m 06s** (Vipco) **82m 25s** (VCL)
Video Label: **Vipco** (Video Instant Picture Company Ltd) / **VCL**

Contamination: An Italian cash-in on '**Alien**', and promoted in some countries as '**Alien 2**', this gory unofficial 'sequel' was released on video in the UK in a shorter version than the rest of Europe, deleting some 5 mins of footage.

Dead & Buried: Passed 'X' by the BBFC in April 1981, this uncut video release followed in April 1983. From the maker of '**Death Line**', this film features a nasty syringe-in-the-eyeball sequence, but more notably includes an early appearance by Lisa Marie, the cute Martian girl from '**Mars Attacks**'. Re-released with 30s cut for an '18' certificate.

Death Trap: Hooper's follow up to **The Texas Chainsaw Massacre**' featured Robert Englund, who went on to play 'Freddy Krueger'. Released originally in 1981 by VCL Video in a cardboard box, this release was more complete and featured a front cover sticker boasting 'Strong Uncut Version'. Who could resist? This was the title Mary Whitehouse took personal exception to, although she had not actually viewed it.

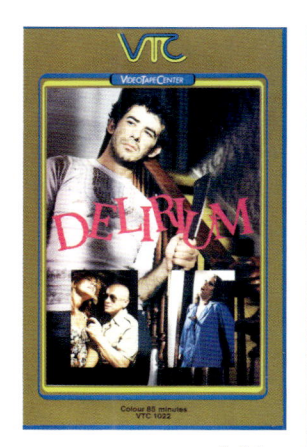

Delirium
Country: **USA**
Director: **Peter Maris**
Year: **1979** Time: **84m 29s**
Video Label: **VTC** (Video Tape Centre)

Don't Go in the House
Country: **USA**
Director: **Joseph Ellison**
Year: **1979** Time: **79m 01s**
Video Label: **Videospace / Arcade**

Deep River Savages
Original Title: **Il paese del sesso selvaggio**
Country: **Italy / Thailand**
Director: **Umberto Lenzi**
Year: **1972** Time: **89m 25s**
Video Label: **Derann**

1984 - Nigerian diplomat found in crate at Stanstead airport.

On 5 July 1984, Umaru Dikko a Nigerian politician was found drugged in a crate at Stanstead airport. With him, in three other crates, were three Israelis and another Nigerian politician, who were later charged with kidnapping and administering drugs.

Deep River Savages: This was rejected by the BBFC when submitted as 'Man from Deep River' in September 1975, so it was no wonder that it joined the nasties list after being released on video in an uncut form. From the makers of '**Cannibal Ferox**'.

Delirium: Another 'Vietnam veteran on the rampage' exploiter, this was re-released by Viz Movies as '**Psycho Puppet**' with 16s of BBFC cuts.

Don't Go in the House: Passed 'X' with cuts in November 1980, this was another title released onto video in both cut and uncut versions. The uncut release was the easier to find of the two, and included some extreme sequences of women being burned alive with a flame-thrower. It has since been re-released with cuts totalling 3m 07s.

NASTIES ON PAROLE

1983 - Labour finds Dream Ticket

Labour enter '83 election with the supposed winning dynamic duo of Neil Kinnock as leader and Roy Hattersley as deputy. Labour lost - horribly.

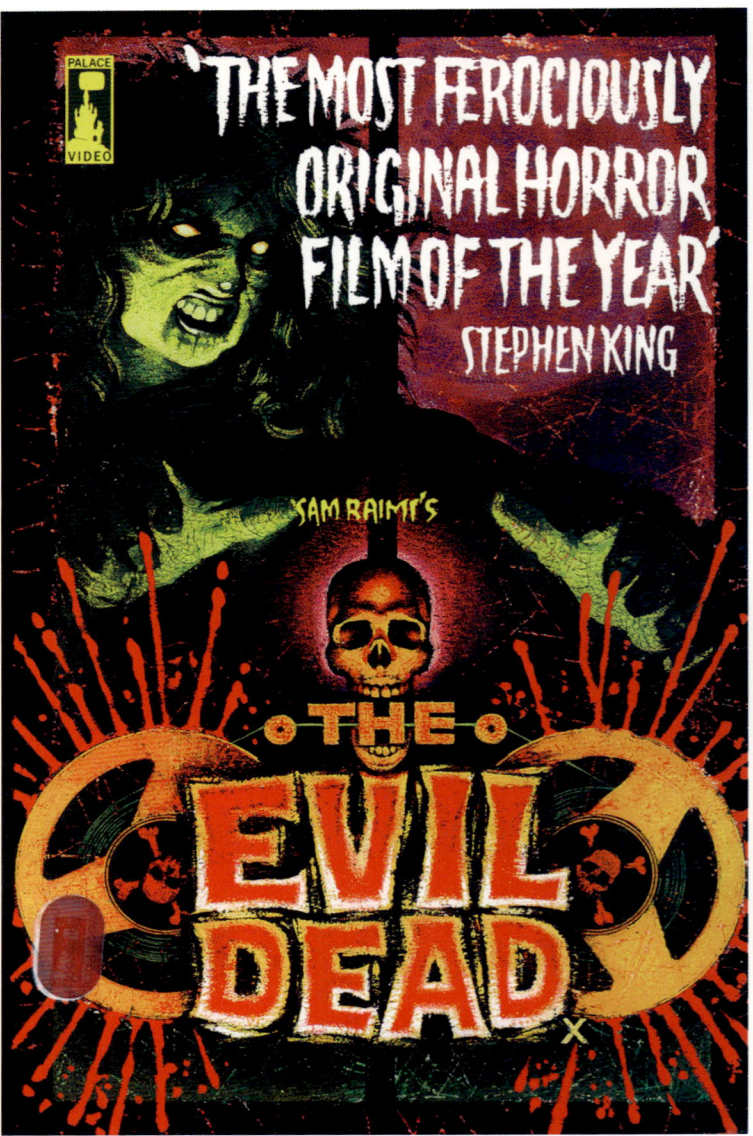

NASTIES ON PAROLE

The Evil Dead
Country: **USA**
Director: **Sam Raimi**
Year: **1982** Time: **80m 49s**
Video Label: **Palace**

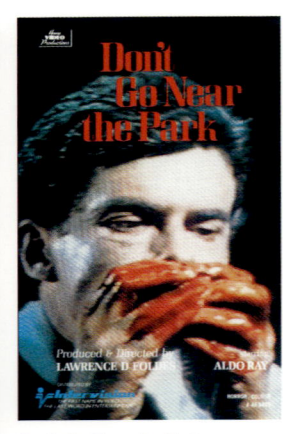

Don't Go Near the Park
Country: **USA**
Director: **Lawrence D. Foldes**
Year: **1979** Time: **80m 00s**
Video Label: **Intervision**

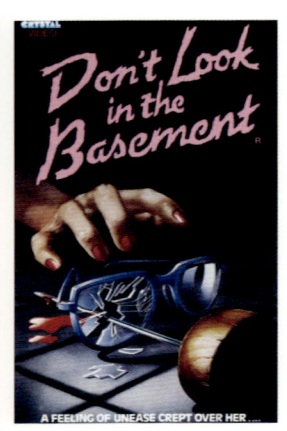

Don't Look in the Basement
Country: **USA**
Director: **S. F. Brownrigg**
Year: **1973** Time: **78m 43s**
Video Label: **Derann**

Don't Go Near the Park: An obscure low budget horror exploiter more famous perhaps for featuring Scream Queen Linnea Quigley in an early role, although it's doubtful anybody could have sat through this just to see her take her clothes off.

Don't Look in the Basement: Submitted to the BBFC for theatrical distribution in 1977, it was cut for the obligatory 'X' rating by just 2s. This video release sneaked out in an abridged version deleting some 6 mins.

The Evil Dead: Originally given a simultaneous video and theatrical release in February 1983 with 18 cuts totalling 56s (it has never been available in the UK in an uncut form), it soon became one of the most prosecuted titles on the original 'nasties' list. When re-released several years later by Palace, it was subjected to a further 23 cuts totalling 1m 6s, thus making 'The most ferociously original horror movie of the year' one of the most censored horror classics available in Britain today, with 41 cuts totalling 2m 02s.

Frozen Scream
Country: **USA**
Director: **Frank Roach**
Year: **1981** Time: **77m 00s**
Video Label: **Intervision**

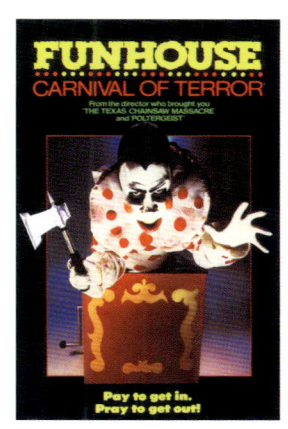

The Funhouse
Country: **USA**
Director: **Tobe Hooper**
Year: **1981** Time: **88m 44s**
Video Label: **CIC**

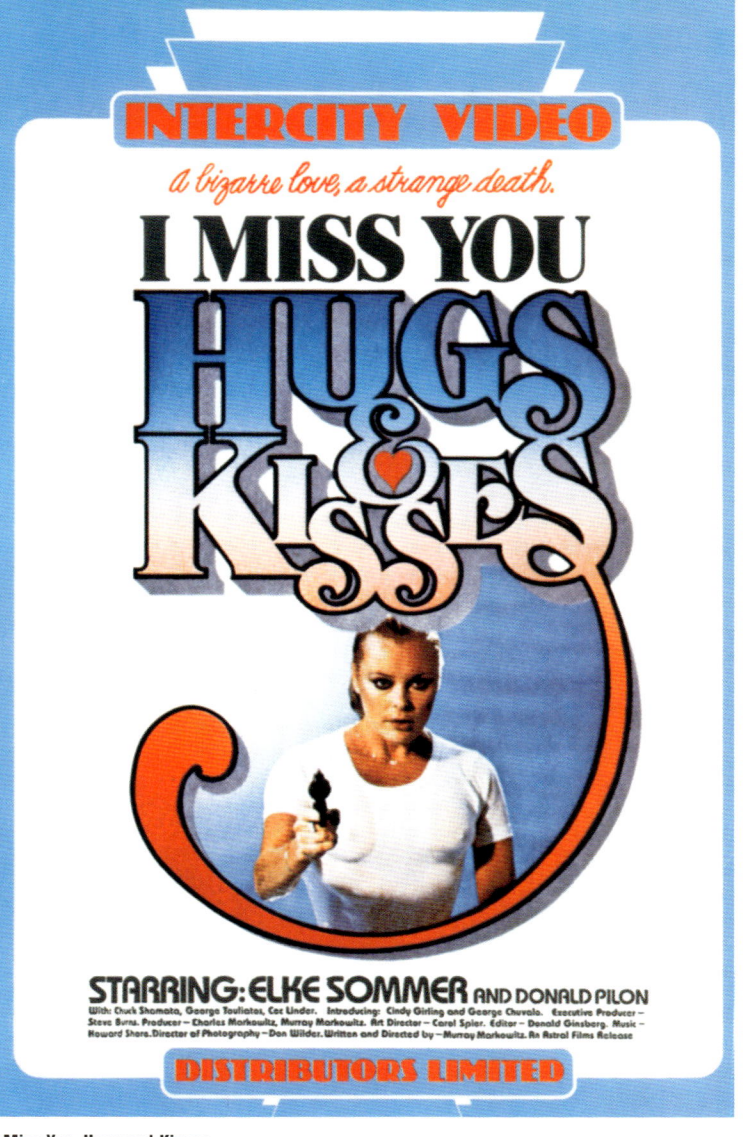

I Miss You, Hugs and Kisses
Country: **Canada**
Director: **Murray Markowitz**
Year: **1978** Time: **83m 24s**
Video Label: **Intercity**

1984-5 - The 'enemy within'
Prime Minister Margaret Thatcher claims subversive and clandestine elements were working to undermine the state.

1982 - ET phones home
Irresistable alien sprog makes the world weep in Spielberg sentimental megamillion cutesy about a stranded Extra Terrestrial. Also featured pre-naughty phase Drew Barrymore.

Frozen Scream: There is no reason at all to recommend this film to anybody. It's amazing somebody came to the conclusion that this should be banned without falling asleep. Luckily, it has not been re-released.

The Funhouse: Granted a BBFC 'X' certificate without cuts in February 1982, and probably banned on video due to hysterical police raids and its cover mentioning **The Texas Chainsaw Massacre**'.

I Miss You, Hugs and Kisses: This thriller starring Elke Sommer is another of those films that is allegedly based on a true story. Nevertheless, its hard to work out why this was banned, as there is nothing gratuitous in there at all. It has since been re-released under the title '**Drop Dead Dearest**', with cuts totalling 1m 6s.

2 · NASTIES ON PAROLE

35

1984-6 - Conservatives promote 'Enterprise Culture'

Praise from the government for the commitment to the free operation of market forces, privatization, the spread of investment in shares and a growth in home ownership.

NASTIES ON PAROLE

The Killer Nun
Original Title: **Suor omicidi**
Country: **Italy**
Director: **Giulio Berruti**
Year: **1978** Time: **80m 55s**
Video Label: **Techno Film / Fletcher**

Inferno
Country: **Italy**
Director: **Dario Argento**
Year: **1980** Time: **102m 08s**
Video Label: **CBS/Fox**

Late Night Trains
Original Title: **L'ultimo treno della notte**
Country: **Italy**
Director: **Aldo Lado**
Year: **1974** Time: **87m 58s**
Video Label: **World Of Video 2000**

Inferno: Passed by the BBFC with 10s of cuts for an 'X' certificate in March 1980, Argento's eagerly awaited follow up to '**Suspiria**' was available to rent on video and video disc uncut from September 1982. It has since been re-released with cuts totalling 28s, most notably to the sequence involving a cat eating a mouse.

The Killer Nun: Starring Anita Ekberg, this was allegedly based on a true story. Yeah, sure. The only reason I can imagine this one joining the banned list is for its cover shot, which looks like...well, go figure. Re-released by Redemption Films with 13s of cuts, as requested by the BBFC.

Late Night Trains: Actually an Italian remake of '**Last House on the Left**' but set aboard a train. Another title refused a BBFC certificate when submitted in July 1976, even though a much softer version had been prepared. This video version, with the on-screen title of '**Night Train Murders**', was slightly softer than the European release.

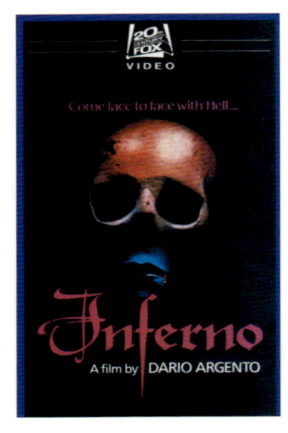

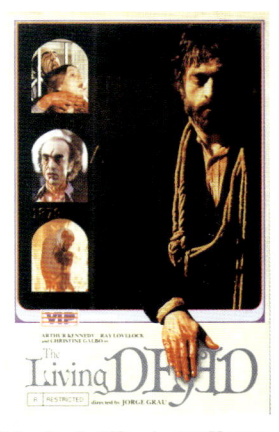

1983 - The Equal Pay (Amendment) Act

Permits claims for equal pay based on work of equal value; Its introduction by a reluctant Conservative Government only came after pressure from the European Commission.

The Living Dead at Manchester Morgue
Original Title: **Fin de Semana Para los Muertos / Non si deve profanare il sonno dei morti**
Country: **Spain / Italy**
Director: **Jorge Grau**
Year: **1974** Time: **88m 56s**
Video Label: **VIP** (Video Independent Productions Ltd)

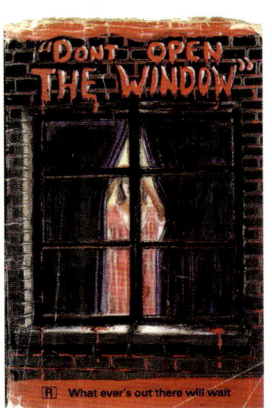

Nightmare Maker
Original Title: **Butcher, Baker, Nightmare Maker**
Country: **USA**
Director: **William Asher**
Year: **1981** Time: **92m 25s**
Video Label: **Atlantis**

The Living Dead at Manchester Morgue: A celebrated zombie film set in the Lake District, this had been granted a BBFC 'X' certificate in January 1975 with numerous cuts. This uncut video release reinstated many of the gorier highlights, although when re-released many years later by European Creative Films these scenes had been removed. A more obscure release of this film was also circulating in the UK during the early 1980's under the title '**Don't Open the Window**', which was the heavily trimmed American 'R' rated version.

Nightmare Maker: This film had allegedly been named 'Best Horror Film of 1982' by the Academy of Science Fiction, Fantasy & Horror, but this didn't stop it joining the queue for the UK nasties list. It was rejected when submitted for a video certificate under the title '**The Evil Protege**'. From the same director who gave us 1965's '**How to Stuff a Wild Bikini**'.

NASTIES ON PAROLE

1984 - WPC Yvonne Fletcher shot dead

WPC Fletcher was shot outside the Libyan embassy or 'people's bureau' on 17 April in a burst of gunfire from the embassy at a demonstration outside by opponents of the Gadafi regime.

1984 - Relax gets to Number 1

Frankie Goes to Hollywood storm the charts after Radio 1 DJ Mike Reid bans their single 'Relax' because of the line 'When you wanna come'.

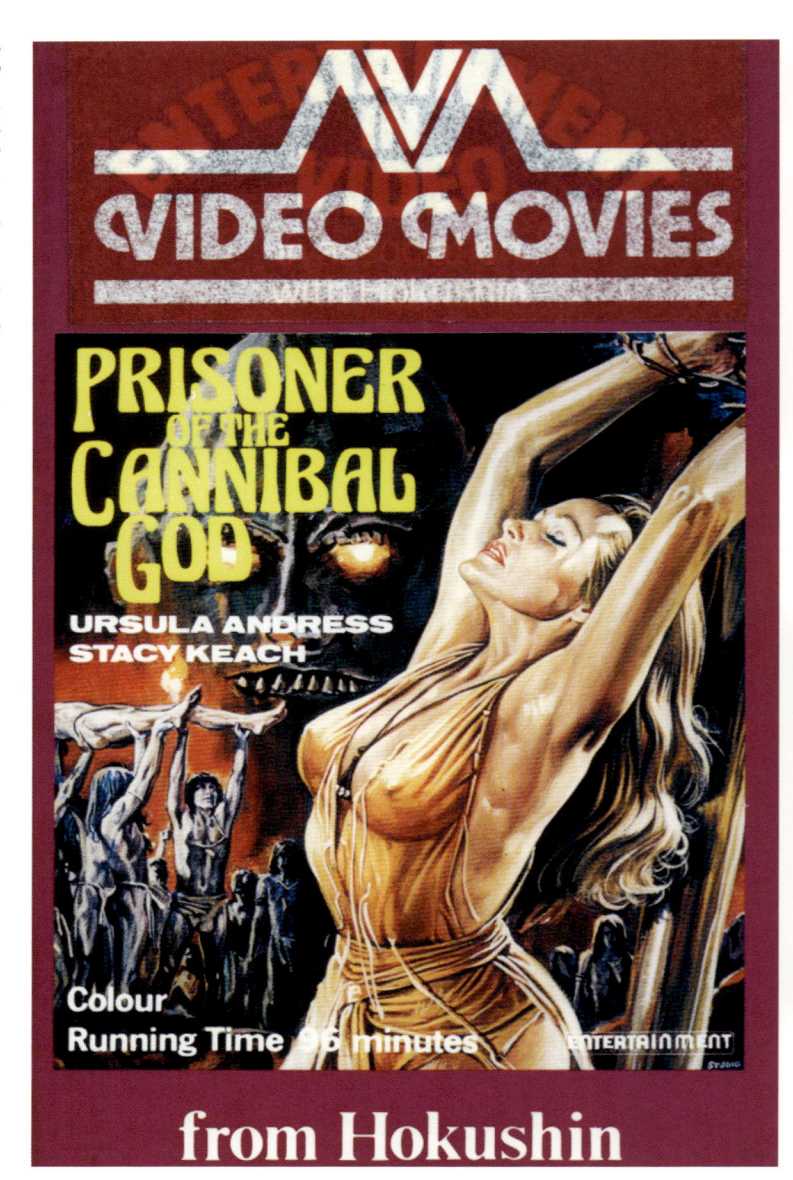

Possession
Country: **France / West Germany**
Director: **Andrzej Zulawski**
Year: **1981** Time: **118m 23s**
Video Label: **VTC** (Video Tape Centre)

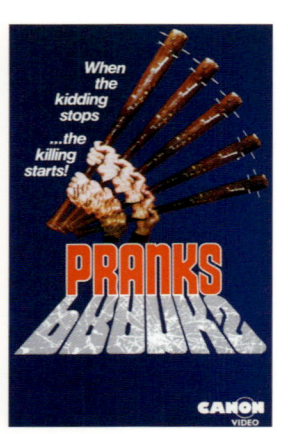

Pranks
Original Title: **The Dorm that Dripped Blood**
Country: **USA**
Director: **Jeffrey Obrow & Stephen Carpenter**
Year: **1981** Time: **81m 31s**
Video Label: **Canon**

The Prisoner of the Cannibal God
Original Title: **La montagna del dio cannibale**
Country: **Italy**
Director: **Sergio Martino**
Year: **1978** Time: **92m 17s**
Video Label: **Hokushin**

Possession: Actually an amazingly bizarre 'art' film starring Isabelle Adjani and Sam Neill, the inclusion of this title on the banned list clearly indicated the absurdity of the situation at the time. Passed uncut for the cinema in October 1981, the video release followed exactly one year later. Once dropped from the banned list, it was reissued with new cover art.

Pranks: Another cheap stalk and slash movie, following in the wake of '**Friday the 13th**'. Once this uncut version had been cleared from the shops, a new BBFC approved '18' certificate version was released by VPD (the original distributor of Canon's videos) with 10s worth of cuts.

The Prisoner of the Cannibal God: Who could have imagined that a film starring both Ursula Andress and Stacy Keach could end up on the nasties list? Passed by the BBFC with an 'X' certificate with around 3 mins of cuts in September 1976, it still featured some particularly nasty animal deaths. This video release contained the same cut-down version. Andress claims that her nude scenes were filmed using a stand-in.

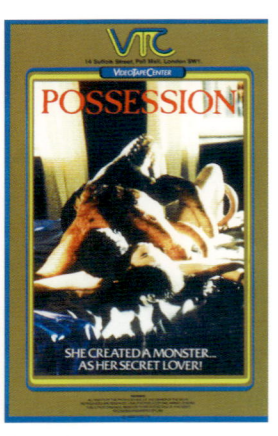

1981 - Green shoots of Recovery

The then Conservative Chancellor of the Exchequer, Norman Lamont claimed that the economy was on the mend with this opportunistic phrase, only to find that it suffered a further sharp downturn.

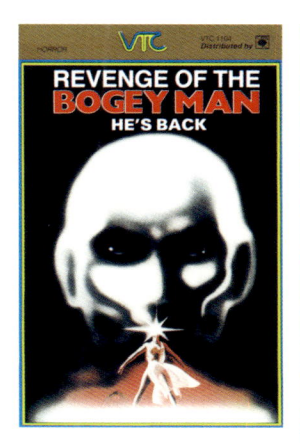

Revenge of the Bogeyman
Original Title: **Boogeyman 2**
Country: **USA**
Director: **Bruce Starr & Ulli Lommel** (uncredited)
Year: **1982** Time: **75m 39s**
Video Label: **VTC** (Video Tape Centre)

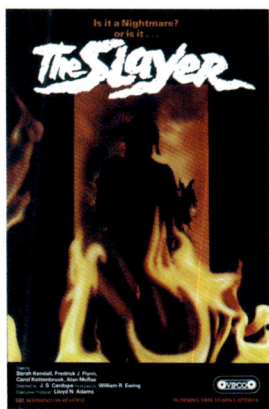

The Slayer
Country: **USA**
Director: **J. S. Cardone**
Year: **1981** Time: **86m 01s**
Video Label: **Vipco** (Video Instant Picture Company Ltd)

Shogun Assassin
Country: **USA**
Director: **Robert Houston**
Year: **1980** Time: **81m 31s**
Video Label: **Vipco** (Video Instant Picture Company Ltd)

Revenge of the Bogeyman: The sequel to '**The Bogeyman**', again starring Lommel's then wife, Suzanna Love. Presumably banned due to the inclusion of flashbacks to the first movie, it runs several minutes shorter than its listed running time.

Shogun Assassin: A combination of '**Lightning Swords of Death**' and '**Baby Cart at the River Styx**' and considered a classic among Martial Arts fans. This was passed 'X' in September 1981 with 37s of cuts. This uncut release soon became a much sought-after item when added to the nasties list. It was later re-released by the re-formed Vipco in its original cinema version. Listen out for the voice of comic Sandra Bernhard, who was among the dubbing crew.

The Slayer: A monster is killing holidaymakers in this rather mundane effort, originally released on video without cuts. Again, the newly re-formed Vipco decided to re-release this on video, and the BBFC passed it '18' with cuts totalling 14s.

2 · NASTIES ON PAROLE

1984 - FTSE - 100 Index starts

The Financial Times Stock Exchange index was introduced and quickly became the most avidly followed measure of share prices in the UK.

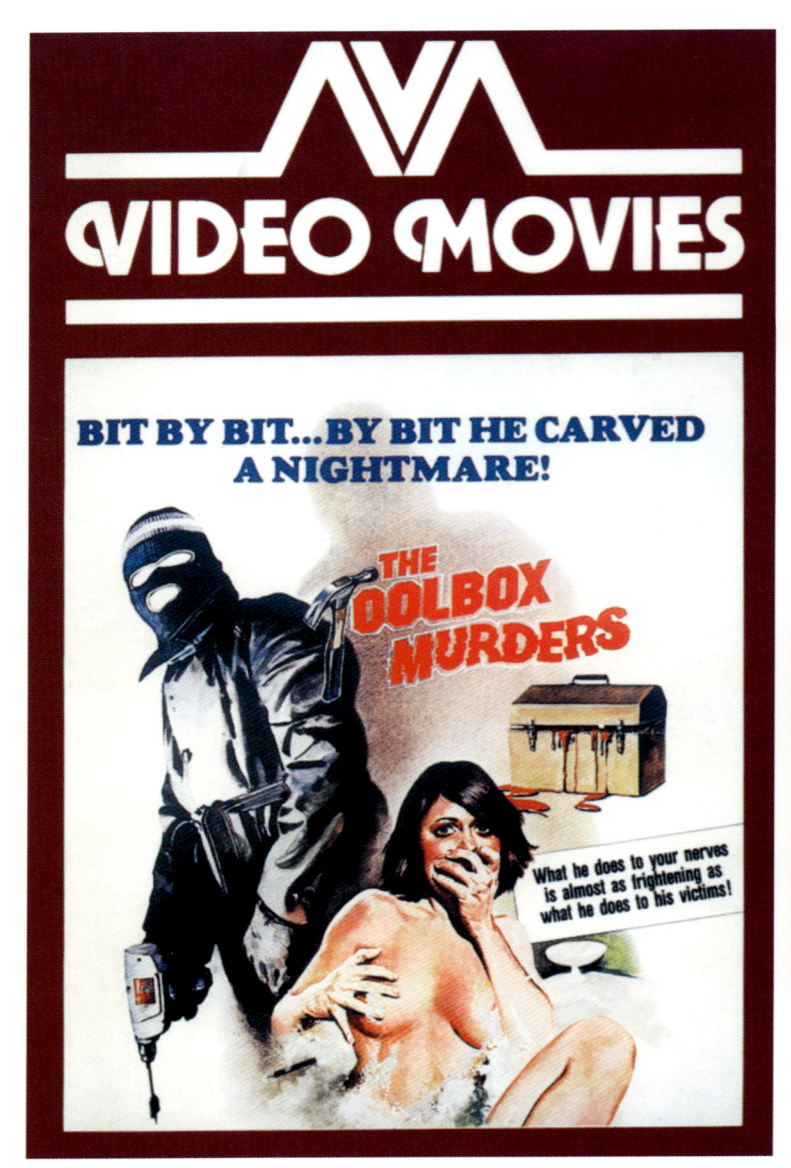

NASTIES ON PAROLE

The Toolbox Murders
Country: **USA**
Director: **Dennis Donnelly**
Year: **1977** Time: **83m 56s**
Video Label: **Hokushin**

Terror Eyes
Original Title: **Night School**
Country: **USA**
Director: **Kenneth Hughes**
Year: **1980** Time: **84m 56s**
Video Label: **Guild**

Unhinged
Country: **USA**
Director: **Don Gronquist**
Year: **1982** Time: **76m 08s**
Video Label: **Avatar**

Terror Eyes: Director Hughes had previously directed '**Casino Royale**' (1967) and '**Chitty Chitty Bang Bang**' (1968), so it must have come as something of a surprise to discover he had also churned out a video nasty! Starring British actress Rachel Ward, this film was released in both cut and uncut versions. Granted an 'X' certificate with cuts totalling 5s in March 1981, the uncut release appeared on tape in February 1983.

The Toolbox Murders: Yet another previously BBFC approved title to find its way onto the banned list, this was just the plain old 'X' version which had already done the rounds at the cinema around the end of 1979, deleting around 6 mins of footage. One censored scene showed porn star Kelly Nichols masturbating in the bath and then being chased around her flat by Cameron Mitchell, subsequently meeting a nasty death courtesy of a nail gun to the head.

Unhinged: Another dull 'stalk and slash' film, which was probably one of the first titles to be dropped from the list as it had previously been passed uncut by the BBFC with an '18' certificate for theatrical distribution in May 1983.

1982 - Channel 4 Starts

Channel 4 starts broadcasting and within four weeks is accused of 'bad language, political bias and many other undesirable qualities' by the Conservative Party Home Secretary William Whitelaw.

1982 - Mad Jodie Foster fan attempts to asssinate Reagan

Nutter John Hinckley tries to kill President Reagan citing the influence of the actress's role in the film Taxi Driver

Visiting Hours
Country: **Canada**
Director: **Jean Claude Lord**
Year: **1981** Time: **99m 24s**
Video Label: **CBS/Fox**

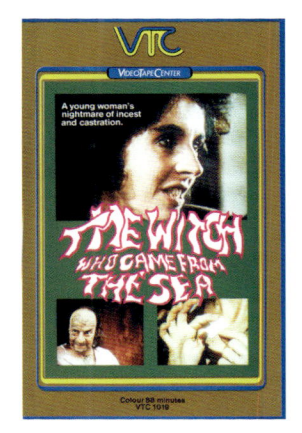

The Witch Who Came from the Sea
Country: **USA**
Director: **Matt Cimber**
Year: **1976** Time: **84m 05s**
Video Label: **VTC** (Video Tape Centre)

Women Behind Bars
Original Title: **Des Diamants pour L'Enfer**
Country: **France / Spain**
Director: **Jesús Franco** (as Rick Deconnink)
Year: **1975** Time: **75m 12s**
Video Label: **Go**

Visiting Hours: Starring William 'Captain Kirk' Shatner and passed by the BBFC with an 'X' rating in January 1982 with 1m 9s of cuts, the video release appeared a year later in the same cut version. When televised by London's ITV during the late 1980's, the uncut version was shown in error, prompting numerous complaints.

The Witch Who Came from the Sea: Starring Millie Perkins from 'The Diary of Anne Frank' in a bizarre role in which she castrates two men with a razor blade during one gruelling scene. This obscurity appeared on video in September 1982, and has not been re-issued.

Women Behind Bars: More sleaze from those folks at Go Video, this 'Women in Prison' film packs in sex, violence and gratuitous nudity. Not to be confused with the play of the same name, which stars divine.

NASTIES ON PAROLE

41

NASTIES ON PAROLE

1982 - Grandmaster gets the Message

Rapper Grandmaster Flash (with his Furious Five), releases one of the decade's most important tracks - 'The Message', one of the first social consciousness hip hop records.

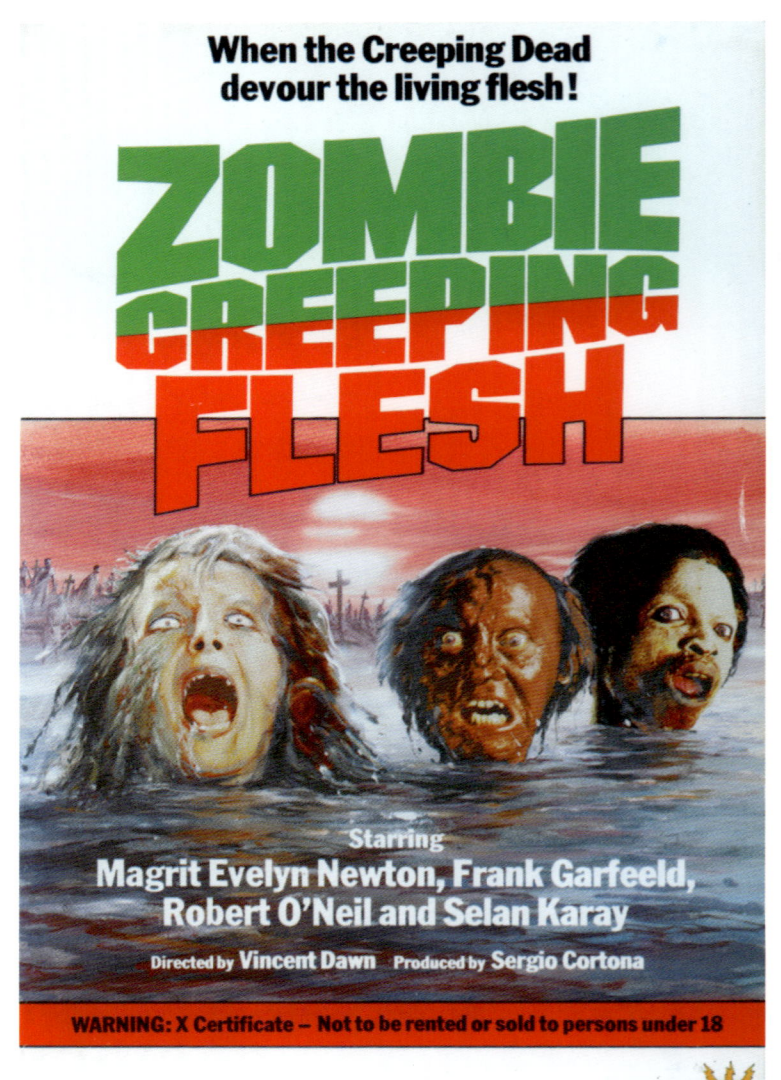

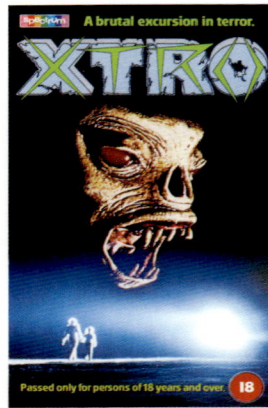

Xtro
Country: **Great Britain**
Director: **Harry Bromley Davenport**
Year: **1982** Time: **82m 03s**
Video Label: **Polygram / Spectrum**

Zombie Creeping Flesh
Original Title: **Inferno dei morti viventi / Apocalypsis Caníbal**
Country: **Italy / Spain**
Director: **Bruno Mattei** (as Vincent Dawn)
Year: **1981** Time: **81m 35s**
Video Label: **Merlin**

Xtro: Cashing in on the success of '**Alien**' comes this low budget sci-fi shocker, which had already been screened at the cinema, and had been granted a BBFC '18' in December 1982 without cuts. The video release was made available just five months later, in the same uncut version. Several poor sequels followed.

Zombie Creeping Flesh: Released in America as '**Night of the Zombies**', and passed here with an 'X' rating in May 1982. This video release appeared just five months later, and deleted an incredible 14 minutes of footage. During one particularly memorable sequence, (not included in this version!) a hand is pushed into one unfortunate girl's mouth, squeezing her eyeballs out of their sockets. Tasteful stuff indeed.

42

The following three sections feature a variety of video releases, some of which were decidedly dodgy, and all of which would have had problems either with the DPP or the VPRC (Video Packaging Review Committee).

3 NASTIES - THE ONES THAT GOT AWAY

Serious nasties that avoided prosecution by the DPP (Director of Public Prosecutions)

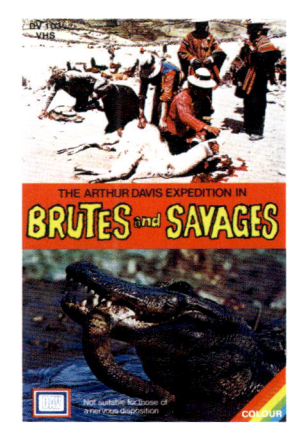

1984 - The IRA Bomb Harrods

On 17 December a huge car bomb outside Harrods kills two police officers and three civilians, and injures a further 100 people.

Brutes and Savages
Country: **USA**
Director: **Arthur Davis**
Year: **1977** Time: **87m 03s**
Video Label: **Derann**

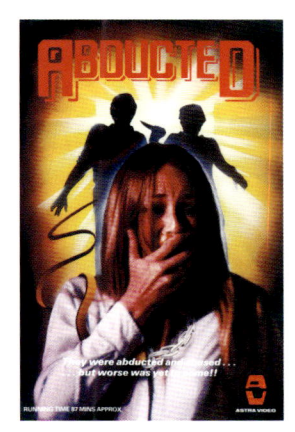

Abducted
Original Title: **Schoolgirls in Chains**
Country: **USA**
Director: **Don Jones**
Year: **1973** Time: **85m 43s**
Video Label: **Astra**

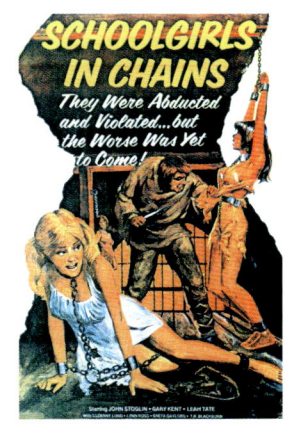

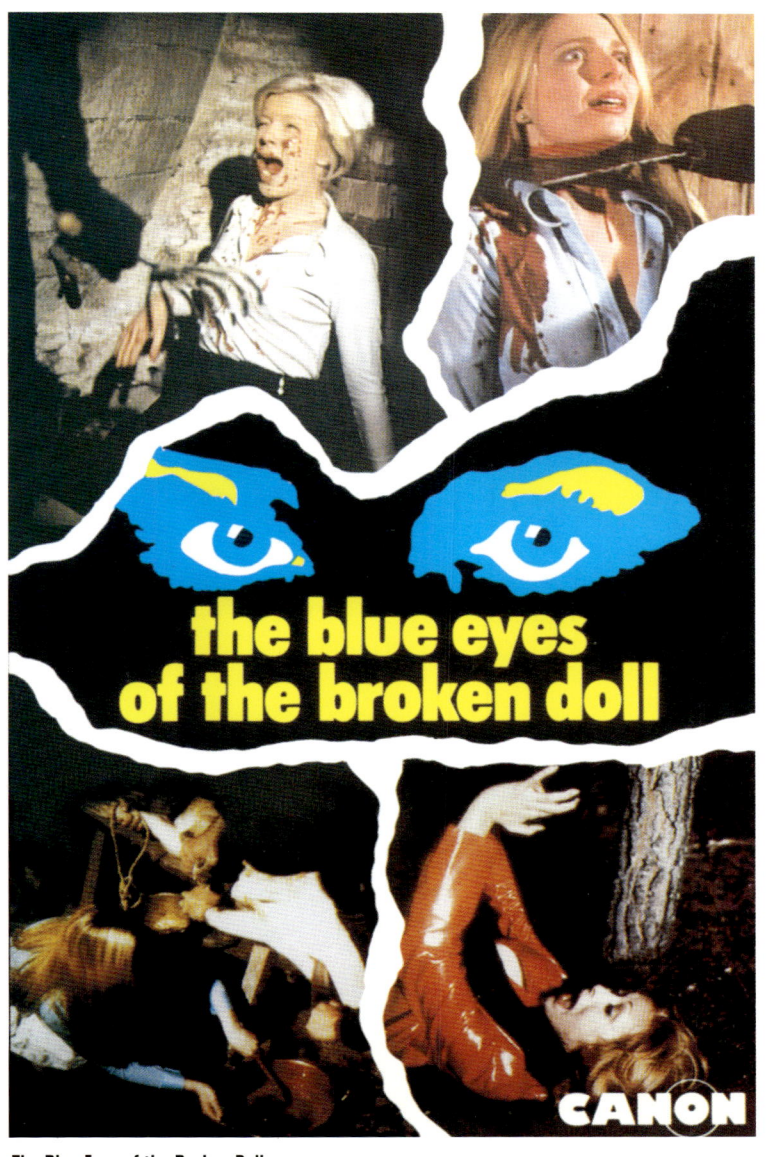

The Blue Eyes of the Broken Doll
Original Title: **Los Ojos Azules de la Muñeca Rota**
Country: **Spain**
Director: **Carlos Aured**
Year: **1973** Time: **85m 03s**
Video Label: **Canon**

Abducted: Re-titled to divert unwanted attention, this wasn't submitted to the BBFC for theatrical or video classification. Curiously though, it did apparently receive a limited release, under its original title, from another distributor. You won't be seeing this film on tape in Britain again.

The Blue Eyes of the Broken Doll: Although widely available on video during the early 1980's this was never singled out for banning, which is surprising considering some of the titles that did end up on the list. Features the unpleasant death of a pig, and a woman who gets a meat cleaver in the neck.

Brutes and Savages: Another 'Mondo' film featuring cruelty to animals among other things. It wasn't released theatrically in the UK.

THE ONES THAT GOT AWAY

1982 - Barbican Centre opened

Elizabeth II opens the Barbican Centre for Arts and Conferences. The Barbican Art Gallery formally opens with 'Aftermath', an exhibition of post-1945 French art.

Cataclysm
Original Title: **The Nightmare Never Ends**
Country: **USA**
Director: **Tom McGowan, Greg Tallas & Philip Marshak**
Year: **1980** Time: **88m 04s**
Video Label: **Video Unlimited**

City of the Living Dead
Original Title: **Paura nella città dei morti viventi**
Country: **Italy**
Director: **Lucio Fulci**
Year: **1980** Time: **87m 51s**
Video Label: **Intervision**

Confessions of a Blue Movie Star (The Evolution of Snuff)
Original Title: **Snuff**
Country: **West Germany**
Director: **Karl Martine**
Year: **1976** Time: **79m 08s**
Video Label: **Intervision**

Cataclysm: This one did apparently end up on some banned lists up and down the country, but it never made the official DPP list of titles.

City of the Living Dead: Granted a BBFC certificate for its theatrical release in December 1981 with 45s of cuts, the video version was available to rent soon after. Gorier than many of the other titles that ended up on the banned list, the video release was missing only a gruesome drill through the head sequence. Many other scenes were trimmed for its '18' rated video release some years later courtesy of Elephant Video, who were instructed to remove 2m 21s.

Confessions of a Blue Movie Star (The Evolution of Snuff): A pseudo documentary about actress Claudia Fielers, who apparently committed suicide as a result of her involvement in the porn industry. The end sequence involves a man disguised with a paper bag over his head talking about his involvement in the snuff movie industry, interspersed with gory highlights from '**Last House on the Left**'. Even the trailer for this was rejected by the BBFC. The eventual '18' rated video release deleted this end sequence in its entirety.

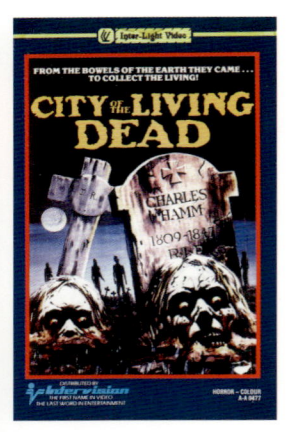

48

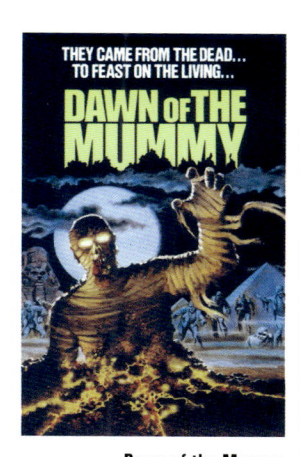

Dawn of the Mummy
Country: **USA / Italy / Egypt**
Director: **Farouk Agrama** (as Frank Agrama)
Year: **1981** Time: **88m 16s**
Video Label: **Videospace / Filmtown**

Death Wish
Country: **USA**
Director: **Michael Winner**
Year: **1974** Time: **89m 17s**
Video Label: **CIC**

Demented
Country: **USA**
Director: **Arthur Jeffreys**
Year: **1980** Time: **88m 02s**
Video Label: **Media**

1984 - Live Aid

Massive pop concerts organised by the Band Aid charity were held simultaneously throughout the world on 13 July. By 17 July over £50 million had been raised towards famine relief in Ethiopia.

Dawn of the Mummy: This ridiculous 'mummy gore film' was originally released in both cut and uncut versions. The '18' rated re-release was cut by 1m 43s.

Death Wish: Passed uncut with an 'X' certificate at the time of its cinema release, and released onto home video in the same version during the early 1980's. It is extremely unlikely the BBFC would now consider granting this one a video certificate, despite censored television screenings.

Demented: A sleazy rape / revenge exploiter featuring porn star Harry Reems. The video re-release was cut by 1m 19s for an '18' certificate.

1984 - Hill Street Blues

Highly intelligent US television police series arrives to mass critical acclaim and is an immediate success

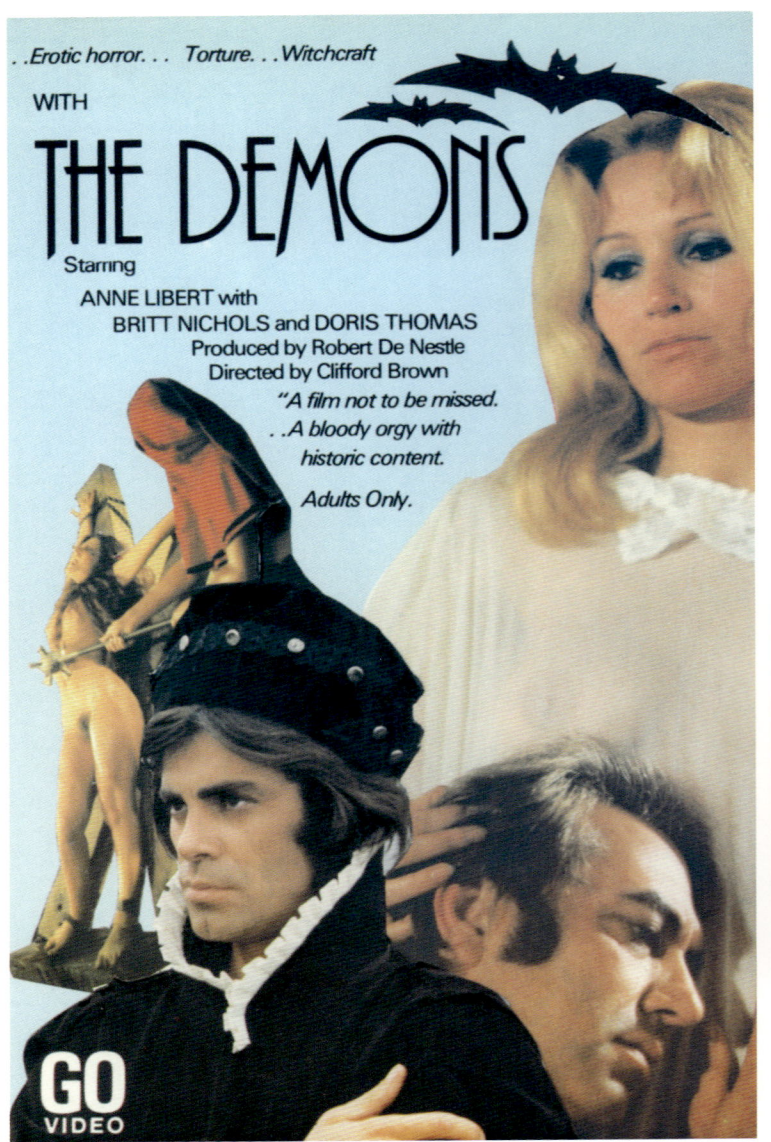

THE ONES THAT GOT AWAY

Deported Women of the SS Special Section
Original Title: **Le deportate della sezione speciale SS**
Country: **Italy**
Director: **Rino Di Silvestro**
Year: **1976** Time: **93m 34s**
Video Label: **VTI**

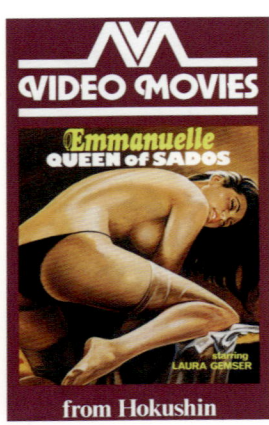

Emanuelle Queen of Sados
Original Title: **Mavri Emmanouella**
Country: **Greece / Italy**
Director: **Ilias Milonakos**
Year: **1979** Time: **87m 21s**
Video Label: **Hokushin**

The Demons
Original Title: **Les Demons / Los Demonios**
Country: **France / Portugal**
Director: **Jesús Franco** (as Clifford Brown)
Year: **1972** Time: **79m 28s**
Video Label: **Go**

The Demons: Go Video surely deserve some kind of award for releasing some of the trashiest, sleaziest films on video in the UK, including this re-enactment of the 17th century witch trials. It was rejected when submitted to the BBFC in 1972.

Deported Women of the SS Special Section: A remarkably sleazy film, this was another reject at BBFC H.Q. in November 1977 when submitted by Border Films as '**Deported Women**'. The director is probably best known for '**Werewolf Woman**'.

Emanuelle Queen of Sados: Another cash-in on the original Emmanuelle series, all of which deleted one of the 'm's from the spelling to avoid any legal problems. Strangely, the original spelling was used on this one's cover art. Released theatrically as '**Emanuelle Queen Bitch**' in a truncated 'X' rated print, this video release runs around 8 mins longer than most other known video releases.

50

1983 - HIV the virus that causes AIDS is discovered by French scientists

AIDS (Acquired Immune Deficiency Syndrome), then a little known sexually transmitted disease, attacks the human immune system leaving the body vulnerable to death from opportunistic infection. At this stage it was mainly contained within the homosexual community giving rise to it being termed the 'gay plague'.

Hell Prison
Original Title: **Femmine infernali / El Infierno de las Mujeres**
Country: **Italy / Spain**
Director: **Eduardo Mulargia** (as Edward G. Muller)
Year: **1979** Time: **88m 33s**
Video Label: **KM**

Ilsa, Harem Keeper of the Oil Sheiks
Country: **Canada**
Director: **Don Edmonds**
Year: **1975** Time: **83m 45s**
Video Label: **VTI**

Farewell Africa
Original Title: **Africa addio**
Country: **Italy**
Director: **Gualtiero Jacopetti & Franco Prosperi**
Year: **1966** Time: **111m 40s**
Video Label: **Techno Film / Fletcher**

Farewell Africa: Granted a BBFC 'X' certificate way back in June 1968 with cuts, there is no way they'd consider passing this one now. Released in America as '**Africa Blood and Guts**', this is full of animal killings, massacres and executions etc. A film guaranteed to offend anybody, it was followed by '**Mondo Cane**' and '**Goodbye Uncle Tom**'.

Hell Prison: 'Women in Prison' sleaze featuring sex-change Ajita Wilson. The re-release was cut by 3m 46s for an '18' certificate.

Ilsa, Harem Keeper of the Oil Sheiks: Its unclear whether this sequel to '**Ilsa, She-Wolf of the SS**' was officially released on tape in the UK at all, but even so it did make its way onto the shleves of some video stores, despite the Arabic subtitles. Although missing 2 minutes of sleazy footage, it can still be considered a miracle that it wasn't added to the list.

1982 - Bow Wow Wow

Malcolm McLaren's prodigys reach No 7 in the charts with 'Go Wild in the Country'.

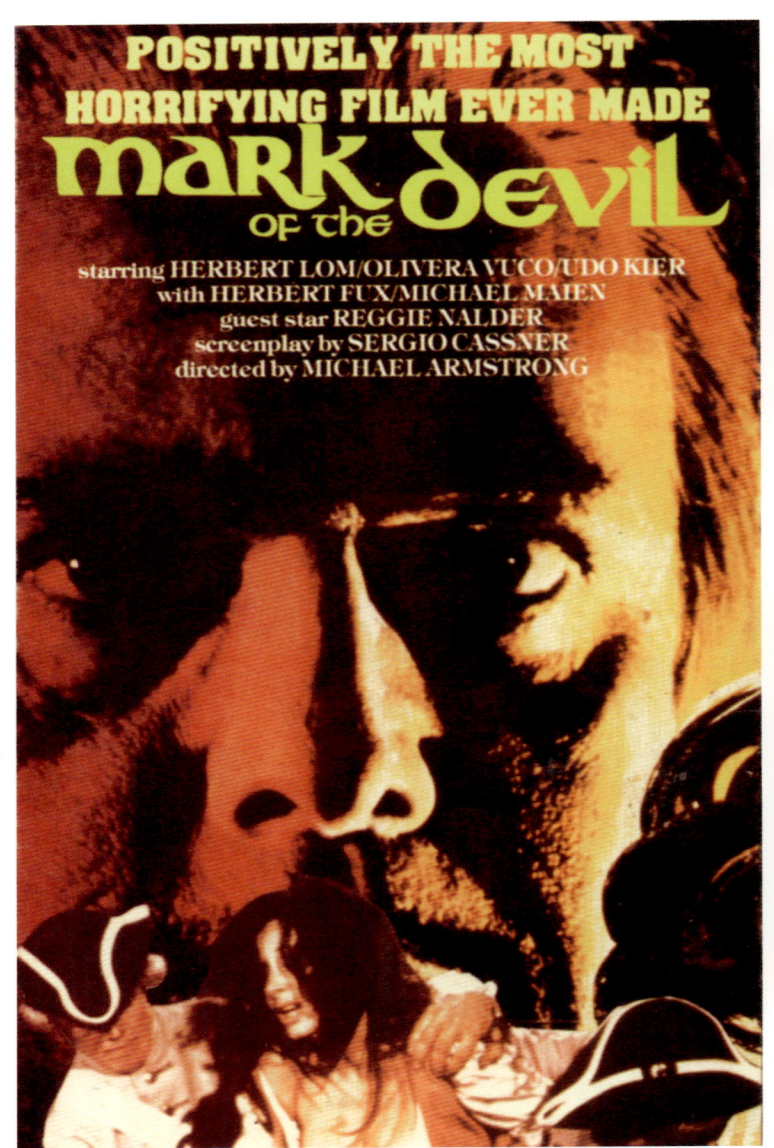

THE ONES THAT GOT AWAY

3

In the Realm of the Senses
Original Title: **Ai No Corrida**
Country: **Japan / France**
Director: **Nagisa Oshima**
Year: **1976** Time: **97m 26s**
Video Label: **Virgin**

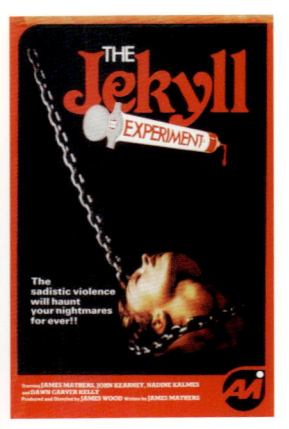

The Jekyll Experiment
Original Title: **Dr Jekyll's Dungeon of Death**
Country: **USA**
Director: **James Wood**
Year: **1982** Time: **88m 18s**
Video Label: **AVI**

Mark of the Devil
Original Title: **Hexen bis aufs Blut Gequält**
Country: **West Germany**
Director: **Michael Armstrong**
Year: **1969** Time: **92m 27s**
Video Label: **Intervision**

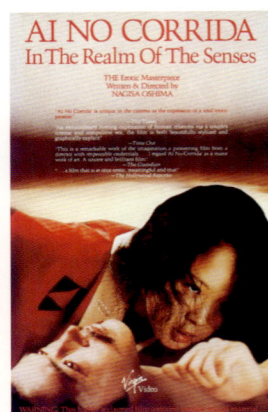

In the Realm of the Senses: Considered an arthouse classic and re-released theatrically with an '18' certificate several years ago, one scene had to be re-framed in order to comply with the Protection of Children Act. No video re-release is planned for this one.

The Jekyll Experiment: Another video re-title, disguising its high sleaze factor. Would probably be rejected if submitted to the BBFC today.

Mark of the Devil: This graphic account of the witch-hunting trials of the 1700's was released uncut on video during November 1981. Its subsequent re-release on Redemption Films had 4m 27s cut at the request of the BBFC.

52

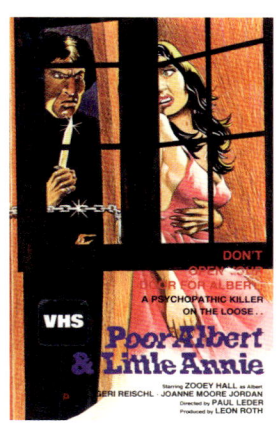

Poor Albert & Little Annie
Country: **USA**
Director: **Paul Leder**
Year: **1972** Time: **81m 46s**
Video Label: **Intervision**

Pink Flamingos
Country: **USA**
Director: **John Waters**
Year: **1972** Time: **88m 17s**
Video Label: **Palace**

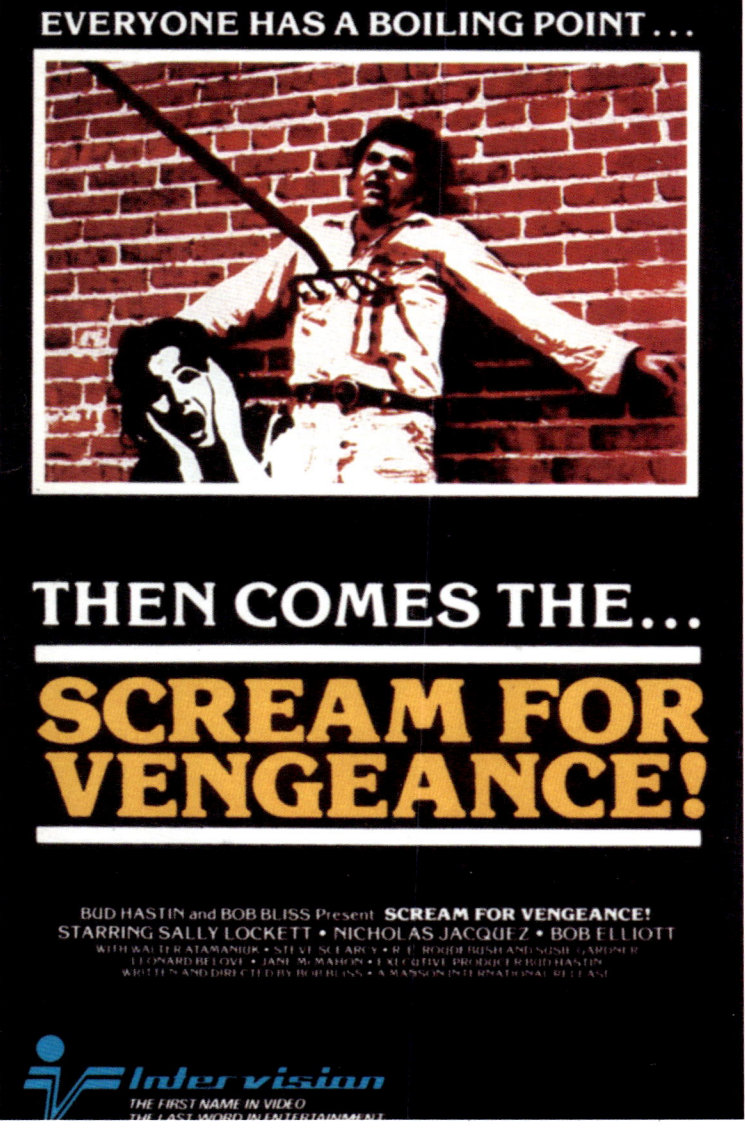

Scream for Vengeance!
Country: **USA**
Director: **Bob Bliss**
Year: **1979** Time: **89m 19s**
Video Label: **Intervision**

1984 - Ted Hughes appointed Poet Laureate

Hughes succeeds John Betjemin, who died on 19 May

1983 - Cecil Parkinson admits affair

Trade and Industry Secretary Parkinson owns up to shagging his secretary, Sara Keays

Pink Flamingos: This surfaced here on tape in November 1981 fully uncut, and could be obtained by simply sending a blank tape and some cash to Palace Video and they'd send you the film by return post. It was never submitted to the BBFC for theatrical screenings as it plainly would stand no chance of being granted a certificate. The re-release was cut 3m 4s and had some scenes substituted. It was recently re-released in America in a special 25th Anniversary edition.

Poor Albert & Little Annie: Albert, who thinks all women are whores, escapes from a sanatorium and develops a rather dubious friendship with an eleven year old girl. They sure don't make them like this anymore, so forget trying to rent this one from your local Blockbuster store.

Scream for Vengeance!: A disturbed man taunts a couple and their daughter with sex threats. He proceeds to rape the daughter, then shoots her. Another title never submitted to the BBFC. I wonder why?

1983 - Michael Foot resigns
Foot resigns as Labour Party leader

1983 - Shoot-to-Kill
December 4, allegations of a 'Shoot-to-Kill' policy are raised after the deaths of two IRA gunmen in an SAS ambush

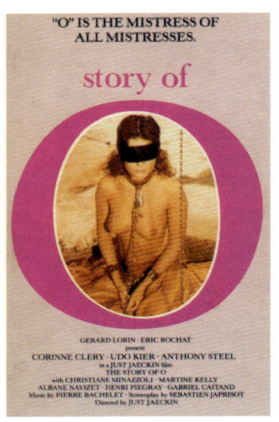

THE ONES THAT GOT AWAY

Story of O
Original Title: **Histoire d' O**
Country: **France / West Germany**
Director: **Just Jaeckin**
Year: **1975** Time: **92m 46s**
Video Label: **Intervision**

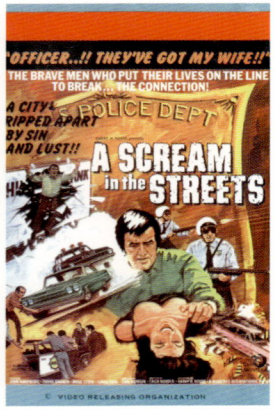

A Scream in the Streets
Country: **USA**
Director: **Carl Monson**
Year: **1972** Time: **86m 24s**
Video Label: **Video Network / LVC**

Straw Dogs
Country: **Great Britain**
Director: **Sam Peckinpah**
Year: **1971** Time: **112m 20s**
Video Label: **Guild**

A Scream in the Streets: Considering that this was cut by nearly 15 mins for an '18' certificate some years back, it's a miracle that this uncut version, featuring some incredibly explicit and violent sex scenes, didn't wind up falling foul of the Obscene Publications Act. Released by the same company with two different covers.

Story of O: Rejected by the BBFC in November 1975 and further rejected by the GLC in 1976, this glossy S&M tale soon found its way onto the home video market during the early 1980's. Considering that the rather tame sequel was rejected for video some years back, there seems no chance of this ever being re-released in the UK.

Straw Dogs: Although granted a theatrical 'X' certificate back in November 1971 after trims during the rough-cut stage, this uncut release appeared on video in November 1980. It remained on the market after the introduction of the Video Recordings Act, until its legally required withdrawal date. There is still no sign of a video re-release scheduled.

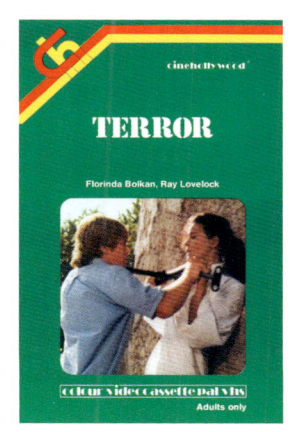

Terror
Original Title: **La settima donna**
Country: **Italy**
Director: **Franco Prosperi**
Year: **1978** Time: **85m 24s**
Video Label: **Cinehollywood**

Terror Express!
Original Title: **La ragazza del vagone letto**
Country: **Italy**
Director: **Ferdinando Baldi**
Year: **1979** Time: **80m 57s**
Video Label: **Techno Film / Fletcher**

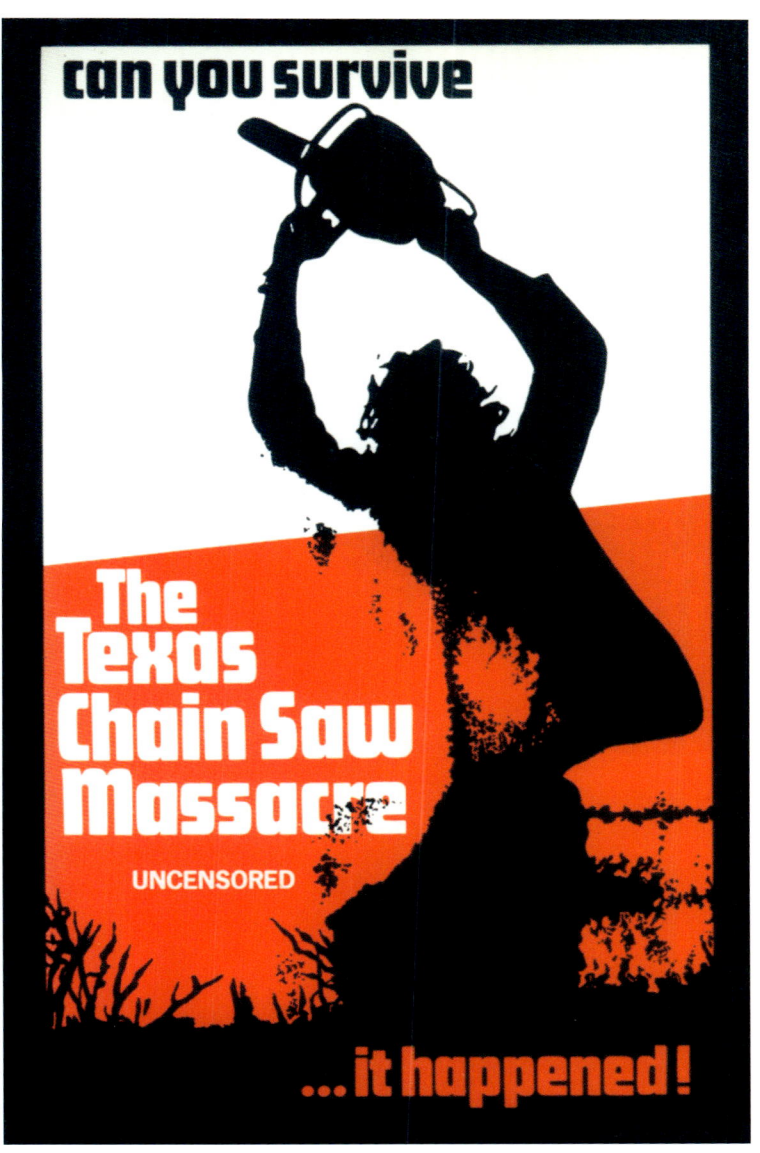

The Texas Chainsaw Massacre
Country: **USA**
Director: **Tobe Hooper**
Year: **1974** Time: **79m 29s**
Video Label: **IFS** (Iver Film Services)

Terror: A group of girls and a nun are held hostage and victimised by a group of bank robbers. Another UK video release never submitted to the BBFC.

Terror Express!: It's amazing this slipped through the net. Like '**Late Night Trains**' it features an unpleasant trio of rich kids terrorising a carriage of people. Never submitted to the BBFC.

The Texas Chainsaw Massacre: Rejected by the BBFC in March 1975 when submitted for a cinema release, it was later granted an 'X' certificate by London's GLC (with warning notices). The uncut video release was widely available, and could be found in almost every video rental store until the introduction of the Video Recordings Act in 1984 which effectively banned it. Even today it's highly unlikely it would be passed by the BBFC, which is unfortunate considering it is regarded as a classic of the horror genre. It received several video releases in the UK, all of which were intact.

1983 - Shergar is kidnapped

February 9, Epsom and Derby winner horse, the £10 million Shergar, is stolen. A £2 million ransom is demanded - the IRA are suspected

---

3. THE ONES THAT GOT AWAY

55

4 NICE AND SLEAZY DOES IT

Not nasty and certainly not pretty, the sleaze epics from the halcyon days of pre-certificate heaven

1983 - US Attacks

Commonwealth member Grenada is invaded by the United States after alleged infiltration by Marxist Cubans

Adventures of a Teenage Tramp
Original Title: **Teenage Tramp**
Country: **USA**
Director: **Anton Holden**
Year: **1975** Time: **74m 26s**
Video Label: **Midas**

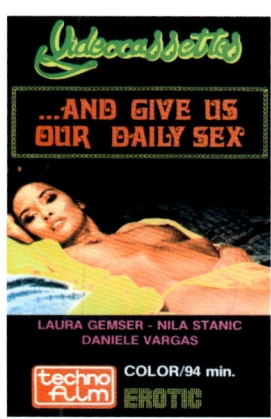

And Give Us Our Daily Sex
Original Title: **El Periscopio / Malizia erotica**
Country: **Spain / Italy**
Director: **José Ramon Larraz**
Year: **1979** Time: **84m 32s**
Video Label: **Techno Film / Fletcher**

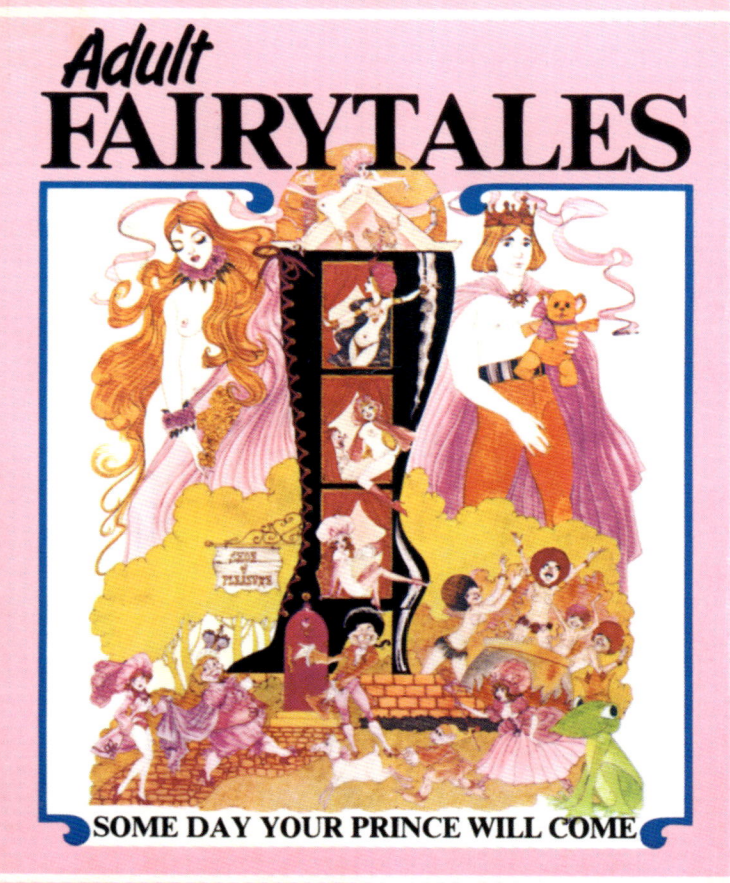

Adult Fairytales
Original Title: **Fairytales**
Country: **USA**
Director: **Harry Hurwitz** (as Harry Tampa)
Year: **1978** Time: **72m 52s**
Video Label: **Inter-Ocean**

Adult Fairytales: A musical-sex comedy. Lead actor Don Sparks now appears in TV sitcoms like Frasier and Cheers. Passed by the BBFC with an 'X' certificate with cuts in June 1979.

Adventures of a Teenage Tramp: All Midas' video releases were re-titled and marketed under the 'adventures' monicker. This one was re-released on video with 49s of cuts for an '18' certificate. Director Holden now works as a sound editor.

And Give Us Our Daily Sex: Laura Gemser stars in this ridiculous but fun sex comedy. It was granted an 'X' rating with cuts when submitted to the BBFC for a theatrical release in August 1980. This video release is a much more sexually explicit version.

4 NICE AND SLEAZY DOES IT

59

1984 - Cool Sadism

The beautiful and stylish singer Sade has her first hit with 'Your Love is King'

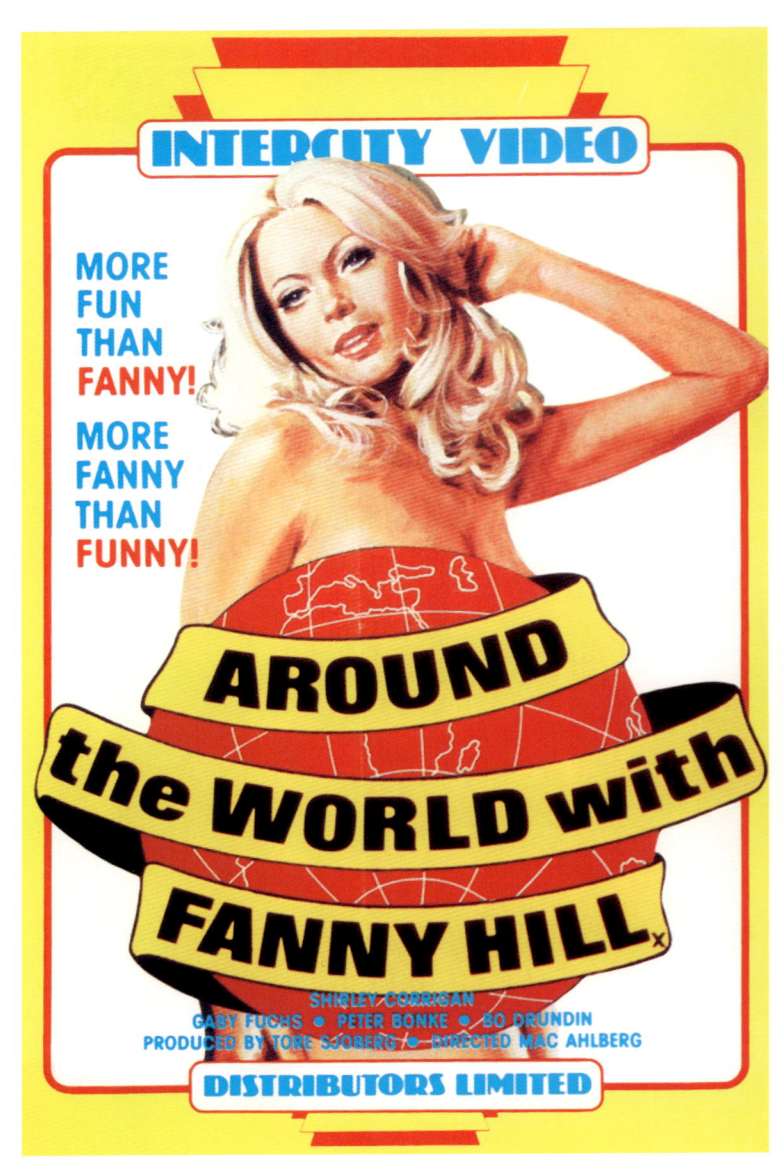

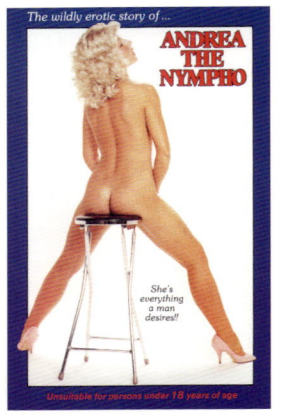

Andrea the Nympho
Original Title: **Andrea Wie ein Blatt auf nackter Haut**
Country: **West Germany**
Director: **Hanns Schott-Schöbinger**
Year: **1968** Time: **83m 20s**
Video Label: **Market**

Assault
Country: **Great Britain**
Director: **Sidney Hayers**
Year: **1970** Time: **86m 46s**
Video Label: **Rank**

Around the World with Fanny Hill
Original Title: **Jorden runt med Fanny Hill**
Country: **Sweden**
Director: **Mac Ahlberg**
Year: **1973** Time: **84m 18s**
Video Label: **Intercity**

Andrea the Nympho: Dagmar Lassander stars as 'Andrea', the real title of this film, cleverly spiced up by the distributors. Perhaps they should have mentioned that it had previously been rejected by both the BBFC and the GLC in 1969.

Around the World with Fanny Hill: Starring Euro babes Christina Lindberg and Shirley Corrigan, this was directed by noted cinematographer Ahlberg. It was passed for the cinema with an 'X' certificate in August 1974 without cuts.

Assault: This was passed 'X' by the BBFC without cuts in October 1970. It starred Suzy Kendall and Frank Finlay, and is notable for the debut appearance of Leslie-Anne Down, who went on to do TV's 'Upstairs Downstairs'.

1982 - Kinski Purrs

Nastassja Kinski sets pulses racing as she crawls naked in a stylish remake of 1940's 'Cat People'

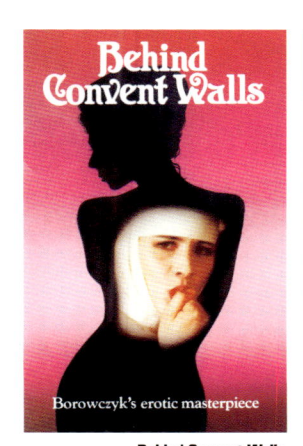

Behind Convent Walls
Original Title: **Interno di un convento / Unmoralische Novizzinnen**
Country: **Italy / W. Germany**
Director: **Walerian Borowczyk**
Year: **1977** Time: **90m 18s**
Video Label: **Canon**

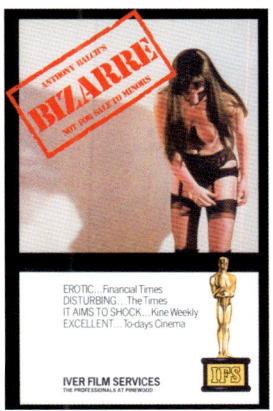

Bizarre
Original Title: **Secrets of Sex**
Country: **Great Britain**
Director: **Antony Balch**
Year: **1969** Time: **88m 14s**
Video Label: **IFS (Iver Film Services)**

The Best of Sex and Violence
Country: **USA**
Director: **Ken Dixon**
Year: **1981** Time: **76m 03s**
Video Label: **Wizard**

Behind Convent Walls: More 'nunsploitation' from the maker of '**Immoral Tales**'. Passed 'X' in June 1978 and re-issued with 24s of cuts by Redemption Films.

The Best of Sex and Violence: A compilation of sleazy movie trailers introduced by actor John Carradine and his sons, Keith and David. Featured trailers include '**I Spit on Your Grave**', '**Zombie Flesh-Eaters**', '**The Boogeyman**', **Dolemite** and '**The Human Tornado**'.

Bizarre: From maverick director and distributor Balch, and passed 'X' with cuts in August 1970. This much sought-after release is the full uncut version.

NICE AND SLEAZY DOES IT

61

1984 - Adams Shot

Sinn Féin leader Gerry Adams is shot by loyalists

Black Deep Throat
Original Title: **Gola profonda nera**
Country: **Italy**
Director: **Guido Zurli** (as Albert Moore)
Year: **1976** Time: **83m 28s**
Video Label: **Intervision**

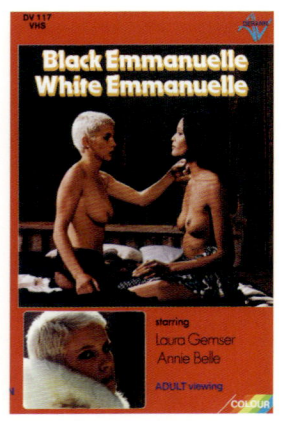

Black Emanuelle White Emanuelle
Original Title: **Velluto nero**
Country: **Italy**
Director: **Brunello Rondi**
Year: **1976** Time: **79m 21s**
Video Label: **Derann**

Blood Vengeance
Original Title: **Emanuelle e Françoise "Le sorelline"**
Country: **Italy**
Director: **Aristide Massaccesi** (as Joe D'Amato)
Year: **1975** Time: **91m 10s**
Video Label: **Walton**

Black Deep Throat: Starring sex-change porn star Ajita Wilson, this uncut release appeared around 1981, and although never a hardcore film, this version was uncut. It was later re-released on video as Queen of Sex with cuts totalling 4m 5s for the obligatory '18' certificate.

Black Emanuelle White Emanuelle: This was the censored theatrical BBFC 'X' version, which was re-released with additional cuts totalling 1m 52s for an '18' certificate.

Blood Vengeance: This release featured the BBFC 'X' censored version, although it would stand little chance of getting a certificate nowadays. Could anybody ever imagine this cover art being approved by the Video Packaging Review Committee?

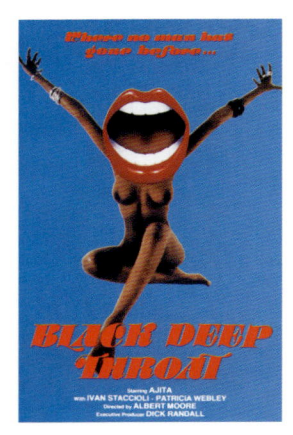

1984 - Working Women

New US magazine aimed at career women is launched in the UK. Despite Stateside success, the title was closed within two years

Blue Belle
Original Title: **La fine dell' innocenza**
Country: **Great Britain / Italy**
Director: **Massimo Dallamano**
Year: **1975** Time: **81m 25s**
Video Label: **Derann**

Caged Women
Original Title: **Frauen-Gefängnis**
Country: **Switzerland**
Director: **Jesús Franco**
Year: **1975** Time: **60m 02s**
Video Label: **Vipco**

Bloodrage
Original Title: **Never Pick Up a Stranger**
Country: **USA**
Director: **Joseph Bigwood**
Year: **1979** Time: **78m 05s**
Video Label: **AVI**

Bloodrage: A rather obscure sexploitation film produced by Joseph Zito who, two years later, went on to produce the ultra-violent '**Rosemary's Killer**' (aka The Prowler).

Blue Belle: This sleazy Harry Alan Towers production starred Annie Bell and Felicity Devonshire. It was passed 'X' with cuts in July 1976.

Caged Women: Originally rejected by the BBFC outright when submitted in October 1976, it was eventually passed 'X' with around 18 minutes of wall-to-wall sex and sleaze trimmed. This release contains that very same theatrical version.

NICE AND SLEAZY DOES IT

63

1983 - 'There Ain't No Flies on Me'

'Lord of the Flies' author William Golding receives Nobel prize for literature

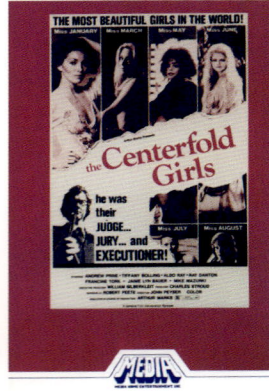

NICE AND SLEAZY DOES IT

The Centerfold Girls
Country: **USA**
Director: **John Peyser**
Year: **1974** Time: **88m 32s**
Video Label: **Media**

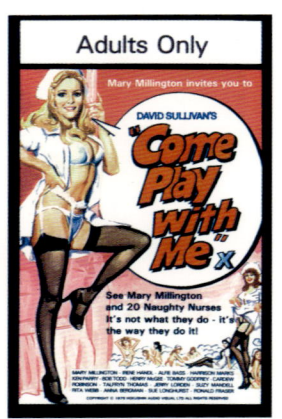

Come Play With Me
Country: **Great Britain**
Director: **George Harrison Marks**
Year: **1977** Time: **89m 29s**
Video Label: **Hokushin**

Celestine
Original Title: Celestine, Bonne à Tout Faire
Country: **France**
Director: **Jesús Franco**
Year: **1974** Time: **93m 56s**
Video Label: **Go**

Celestine: Passed 'X' with cuts by the BBFC in October 1974, Go Video released this scarce uncut version.

The Centerfold Girls: This sleazefest about a psychopath murdering his way through calendar girls was originally passed 'X' with cuts by the BBFC in December 1975. This release was uncut, and would probably have problems at the BBFC if submitted.

Come Play With Me: One of the more famous British sex comedies With Mary Millington, it was passed 'X' with cuts by the BBFC in January 1977. This release featured the same cinema version.

64

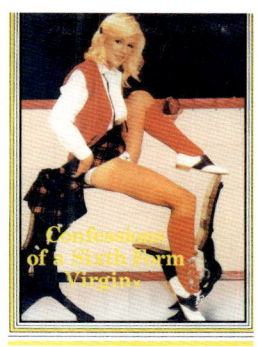

Confessions of a Sixth Form Virgin
Original Title: **Die Schulmädchen vom Treffpunkt Zoo**
Country: **West Germany**
Director: **Walter Boos**
Year: **1979** Time: **82m 34s**
Video Label: **World of Video 2000**

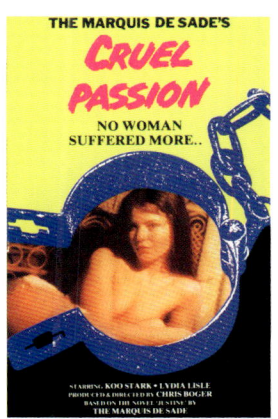

Cruel Passion
Country: **Great Britain**
Director: **Chris Boger**
Year: **1977** Time: **92m 00s**
Video Label: **Intervision**

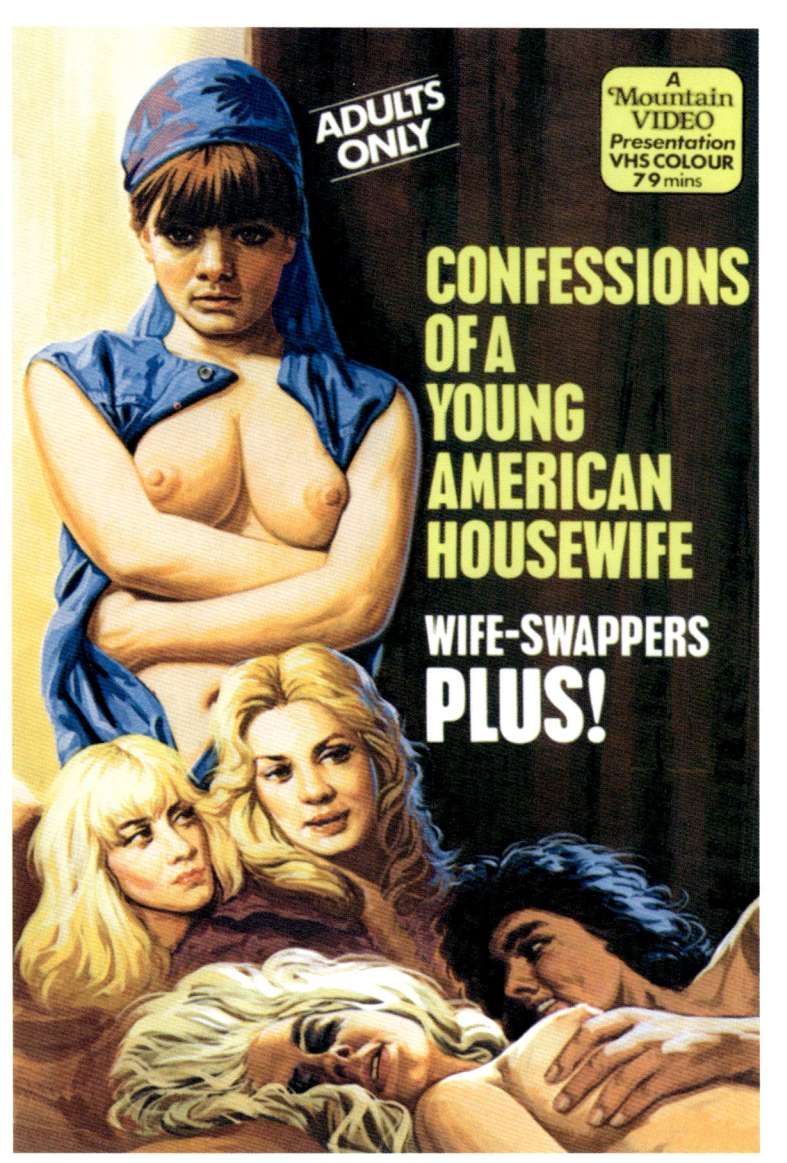

Confessions of a Young American Housewife
Country: **USA**
Director: **Joe Sarno**
Year: **1978** Time: **80m 27s**
Video Label: **Mountain**

1983 - First Order

New Order's classic dance track 'Blue Monday' enters the charts for the first time

Confessions of a Sixth Form Virgin: This video release was much more complete than the theatrical release, which did the rounds of selected UK cinemas under the less salubrious title of '**Confessions of a Campus Virgin**'.

Confessions of a Young American Housewife: This obscure release runs a whole 10 minutes longer than the sanitised BBFC 'X' version which was played here theatrically.

Cruel Passion: Koo Stark and Martin Potter star in this adaptation of De Sade's '**Justine**'. This version contained the 'X' rated cinema release, and has since been re-released by Jezebel Films in a version running 3 mins longer.

NICE AND SLEAZY DOES IT

1983 - Tony Blair enters House of Commons

The future leader of the Labour Party and Prime Minister is elected as Labour MP for Sedgefield

Deadly Weapons
Country: **USA**
Director: **Doris Wishman**
Year: **1974** Time: **72m 00s**
Video Label: **Intervision**

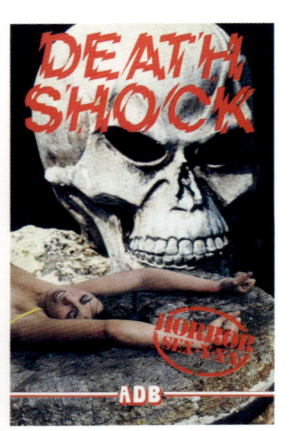

Death Shock
Country: **Great Britain**
Director: **Lindsay Honey** (uncredited)
Year: **1981** Time: **47m 10s**
Video Label: **ADB**

Devil's Nightmare
Original Title: **Au Service du Diable / La terrificante notte del demonio**
Country: **Belgium / Italy**
Director: **Jean Brismée**
Year: **1971** Time: **84m 01s**
Video Label: **Go**

Deadly Weapons: Starring the legendary Chesty Morgan, this was made back-to-back with the equally inept (but fun) Double Agent 73. In this one she suffocates her victims with her breasts! It was cut by 24s for its re-release.

Death Shock: An early shot-on-video sex film, followed by a series of out-takes, entitled "It will be alright on the bed!" Made by, and starring, the undisputed king of British sleaze, Mr. Ben Dover.

Devil's Nightmare: A classic piece of Euro-horror featuring Daniel Emilfork and the delectable Erika Blanc. This was released theatrically in the UK with an 'X' rating after minor cuts, in a version which was more complete than this release.

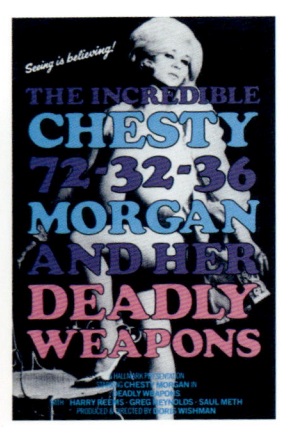

Diary of a Sinner
Country: **Canada**
Director: **Ed Hunt**
Year: **1968** Time: **74m 21s**
Video Label: **Champion**

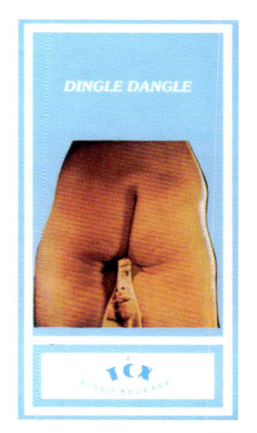

Dingle Dangle
Country: **USA**
Director: **Bobby Davis**
Year: **1972** Time: **61m 26s**
Video Label: **TCX**

The Dirty Mind of Young Sally
Country: **USA**
Director: **Bethel Buckalew**
Year: **1972** Time: **91m 18s**
Video Label: **TCX**

1983 - Maze prison breakout

38 prisoners escape from the Maze prison near Belfast, killing a prison officer in the process. Half of them were recaptured within days, and most over the years, but some remain at liberty

Diary of a Sinner: Champion went all-out in putting together their cover quotes on this one!

Dingle Dangle: A very obscure sex film with an incredibly strange choice of cover image. Try finding this one in reference books.

The Dirty Mind of Young Sally: Another title rejected outright by the BBFC, it was eventually passed by the GLC with an 'AA' certificate. Originally released uncut on video, the re-release was pre-cut by its distributors.

1983 - ZTT Record label formed

Paul Morley, Trevor Horn and wife Jill Sinclair set up a new label, taking the name from a Futurist poem

Elsa Fraulein SS
Country: **France**
Director: **Patrice Rohm** (as Mark Stern)
Year: **1977** Time: **81m 10s**
Video Label: **Modern**

Double Agent 73
Country: **USA**
Director: **Doris Wishman**
Year: **1974** Time: **69m 54s**
Video Label: **Replay**

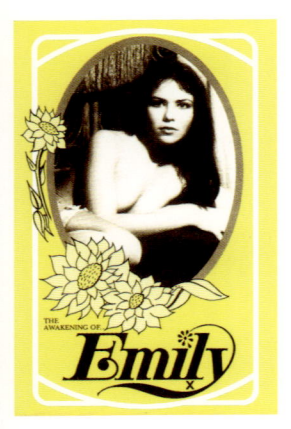

Emily
Country: **Great Britain**
Director: **Henry Herbert**
Year: **1976** Time: **83m 11s**
Video Label: **Videospace**

Double Agent 73: The companion piece to '**Deadly Weapons**', again featuring Chesty Morgan's alleged 73 inch breasts. It was cut by 26s for an '18' certificate for its video re-release.

Elsa Fraulein SS: More 'Ilsa' inspired Nazi sleaze, this time from France, cobbled together from various other films. Unfortunately, this one is very dull.

Emily: Made a year before '**Cruel Passion**', Koo Stark again stars in this classic slice of British erotica which was passed uncut with an 'X' rating in November 1976.

1983 - TV-am starts

Amid much nullabaloo ITV launch breakfast television. The 'star' line up of presenters was short lived

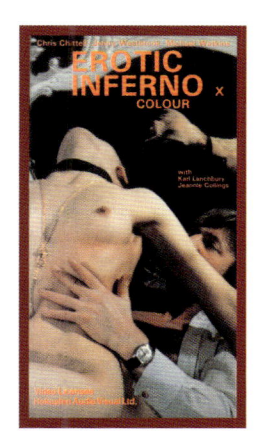

Erotic Inferno
Country: **Great Britain**
Director: **Trevor Wrenn**
Year: **1975** Time: **85m 43s**
Video Label: **Hokushin**

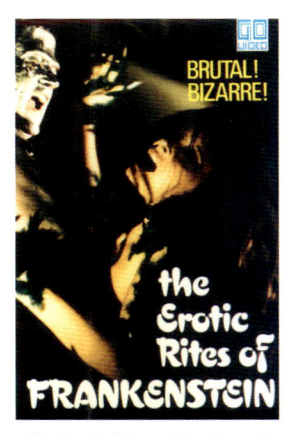

The Erotic Rites of Frankenstein
Original Title: **La Maldición de Frankenstein / Les Experiences Erotique de Frankenstein**
Country: **Spain / France**
Director: **Jesús Franco**
Year: **1972** Time: **70m 47s**
Video Label: **Go**

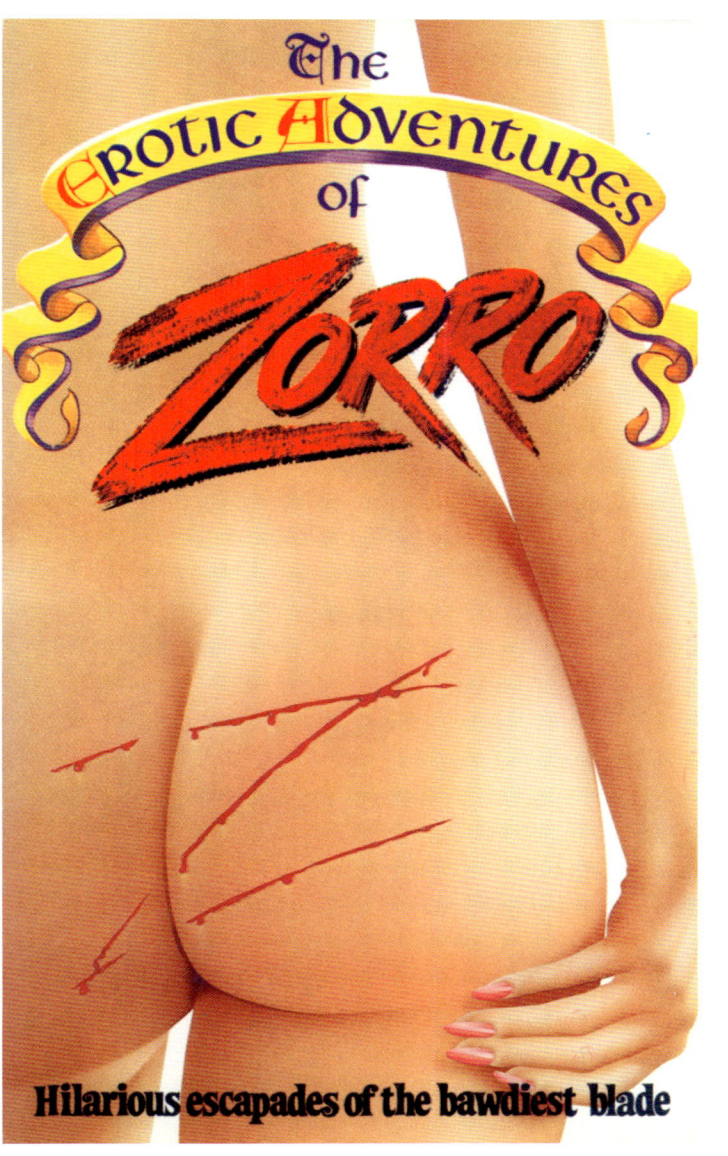

The Erotic Adventures of Zorro
Original Title: **Zorro und seine lüsternen Mädchen**
Country: **USA / West Germany / France**
Director: **William Allen Castleman** (as Col Robert Freeman)
Year: **1971** Time: **98m 25s**
Video Label: **Derann**

The Erotic Adventures of Zorro: This incredibly sleazy film was co-produced by the legendary king of exploitation, David F. Friedman. It was originally released here uncut, although the re-release was cut by an amazing 9m 45s for an '18' certificate.

Erotic Inferno: This 'X' rated British sex film starred the familiar face (and naked body) of Chris Chittell, who later turned up in TV soap '**Emmerdale**' as Eric Pollard!

The Erotic Rites of Frankenstein: An incredible slice of Euro-trash from the master himself, Jess Franco. This one features a silver coloured Frankenstein and a bizarre whipping sequence. Not released theatrically in the UK, this was the uncut Euro version.

4 NICE AND SLEAZY DOES IT

69

1982 - The Young Ones

Anarchic TV series The Young Ones debuts to great acclaim. The exploits of four revolting students living in a filthy house set the style for future 'alternative' comedy

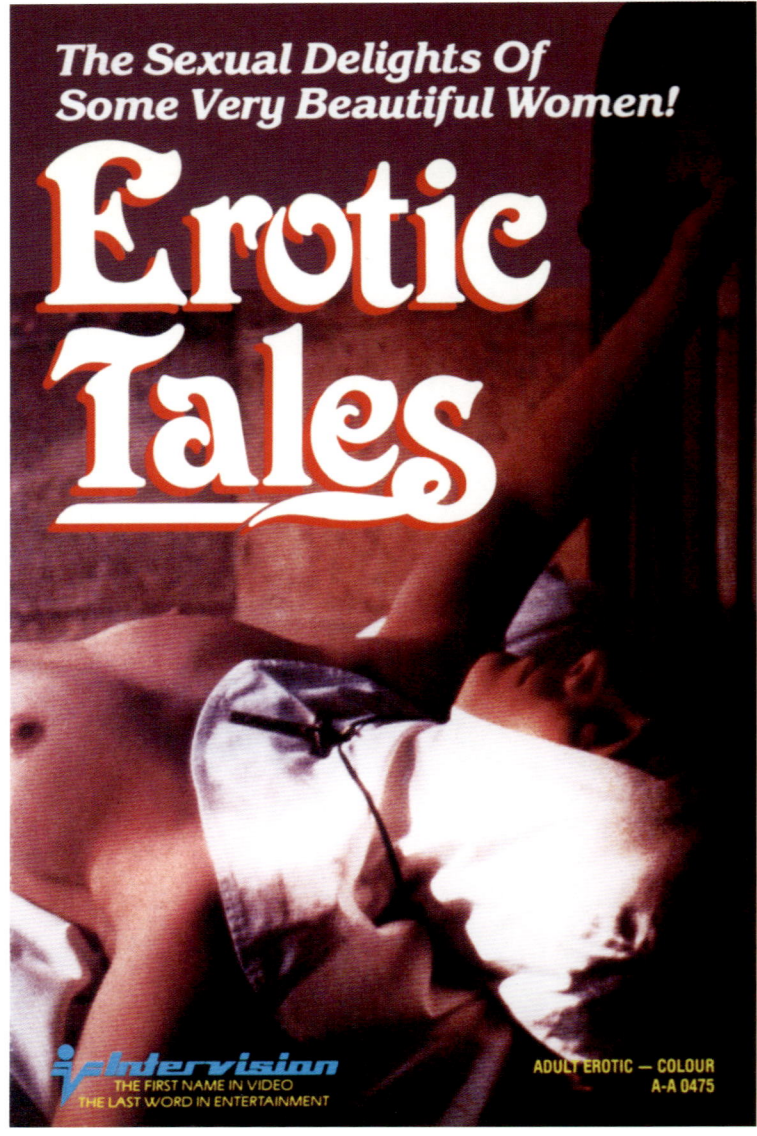

NICE AND SLEAZY DOES IT

Erotic Tales
Original Title: **Contes Pervers / Ragazze in affitto**
Country: **France / Italy**
Director: **Regine Deforges**
Year: **1980** Time: **79m 57s**
Video Label: **Intervision**

Evil Come, Evil Go
Country: **USA**
Director: **Walt Davis**
Year: **1972** Time: **66m 16s**
Video Label: **Mercury**

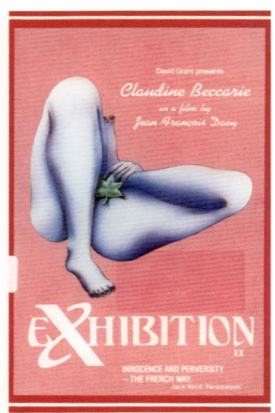

Exhibition
Country: **France**
Director: **Jean-Francois Davy**
Year: **1976** Time: **90m 45s**
Video Label: **World of Video 2000**

Erotic Tales: More European erotica starring Carina Barone, who now appears in television productions. This was released theatrically in the same 'X' rated cut version.

Evil Come, Evil Go: With an appearance by famed porn actor John Holmes, this twisted and perverse religious themed flick is from the same man who gave us the hardcore horror sicko '**Widow Blue**' (aka 'Sex Psycho').

Exhibition: This pseudo-documentary on the making of a porn film was rejected outright by the BBFC in March 1976, but was eventually granted a local GLC 'X' certificate.

70

1984 - The 'Yuppie' is born

First coined in connection with the Presidential Campaign of Baby Boomer candidate Gary Hart, the 'Yuppie' was an all-purpose name tag for the new breed of successful, monied, and upwardly mobile youngsters

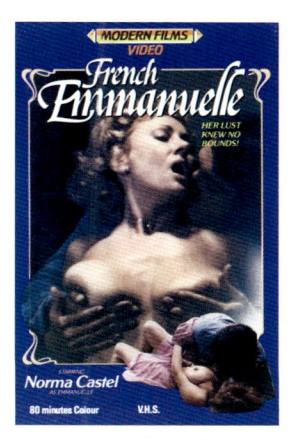

French Emanuelle
Original Title: **Des Frissons sur la Peau**
Country: **France**
Director: **Jesús Franco** (as J. P. Johnson)
Year: **1973** Time: **75m 06s**
Video Label: **Modern**

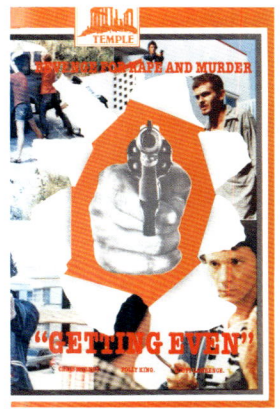

Getting Even
Original Title: **Deadbeat**
Country: **USA**
Director: **Harry E. Kerwin**
Year: **1976** Time: **80m 54s**
Video Label: **Temple**

Frauleins in Uniform
Original Title: **Eine Armee Gretchen**
Country: **Switzerland**
Director: **Erwin C. Dietrich**
Year: **1973** Time: **87m 08s**
Video Label: **Derann**

Frauleins in Uniform: Dietrich was the king of Euro sleaze, who produced and directed some of the most outrageous examples of the genre during the Seventies. This slice of Nazi kinkiness was the 'X' rated version, which had received numerous cuts in November 1974.

French Emanuelle: Hiding behind this re-title is a cut version of '**Tender and Perverse Emanuelle**', which has since been re-released by Redemption Films with 1m 11s of cuts, as requested by the BBFC.

Getting Even: Another sleazy rape / revenge exploiter which didn't get a UK cinema release. It has even less chance of getting a video re-release in the UK.

4 · NICE AND SLEAZY DOES IT

1983 - Westwood's Buffalo Collection

Vivienne Westwood launches her Buffalo collection, which features underwear as outer wear

Girls Come First
Country: **Great Britain**
Director: **Joseph McGrath** (as Croisette Meubles)
Year: **1975** Time: **43m 19s**
Video Label: **World of Video 2000**

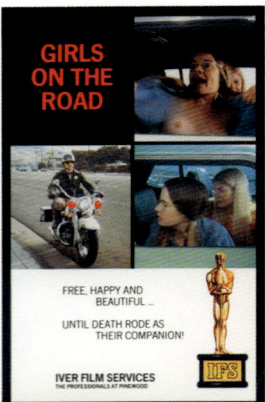

Girls on the Road
Country: **USA**
Director: **Thomas J. Schmidt**
Year: **1972** Time: **76m 06s**
Video Label: **IFS** (Iver Film Services)

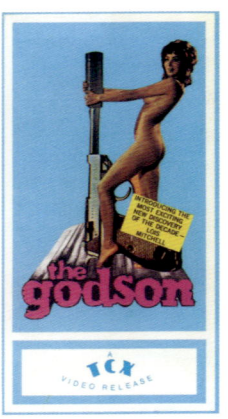

The Godson
Country: **USA**
Director: **William Rotsler**
Year: **1968** Time: **87m 27s**
Video Label: **TCX**

Girls Come First: This British sex film stars TV actor Bill Kerr, although it is more notable for its nude scenes with Hazel O'Connor. It was passed at 'X' for the cinema, and this tape features that same version.

Girls on the Road: Showing the many perils of picking up hitch-hikers, this obscurity stars Michael Ontkean, who went on to play the sheriff in 'Twin Peaks'.

The Godson: Super-vixen Uschi Digart appears in this obscure sexploitation film, which was made around the same time as Rotsler's more famous '**Mantis in Lace**'.

1984 Onwards - Safe Sex

Once it was obvious that Aids was here to stay, Condoms come into their own, so to speak, and become a major part of the sex scene

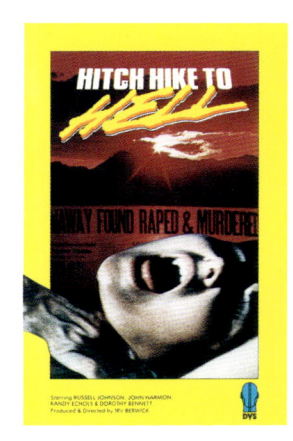

Hitch Hike to Hell
Original Title: **Kidnapped Co-Ed**
Country: **USA**
Director: **Irvin Berwick**
Year: **1976** Time: **84m 07s**
Video Label: **Video Network / DVS**

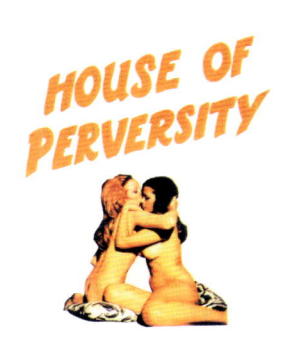

House of Perversity
Original Title: **La Tango de la Perversion**
Country: **Belgium / France**
Director: **Charles Lecoq** (as Pierre-Claude Garnier)
Year: **1974** Time: **83m 53s**
Video Label: **Go**

The Horrible Sexy Vampire
Original Title: **El Vampiro de la Autopista**
Country: **Spain**
Director: **José Luis Madrid**
Year: **1970** Time: **85m 27s**
Video Label: **Mercury**

Hitch Hike to Hell: Another video re-title, this sleazy tale would be a definite contender for the BBFC's 'rejected' list if ever submitted.

The Horrible Sexy Vampire: There's no doubting that this is a great title for an otherwise so-so horror flick. This obscurity was passed 'X' for British cinemas without cuts in February 1976.

House of Perversity: Passed by the BBFC with cuts for the obligatory 'X' rating under the title '**Sex Crazy**', this is perhaps Go Video's most obscure release.

4 · NICE AND SLEAZY DOES IT

73

1984 - Careless Whispers

George Michael has a massive Number 1 hit with 'Careless Whisper'

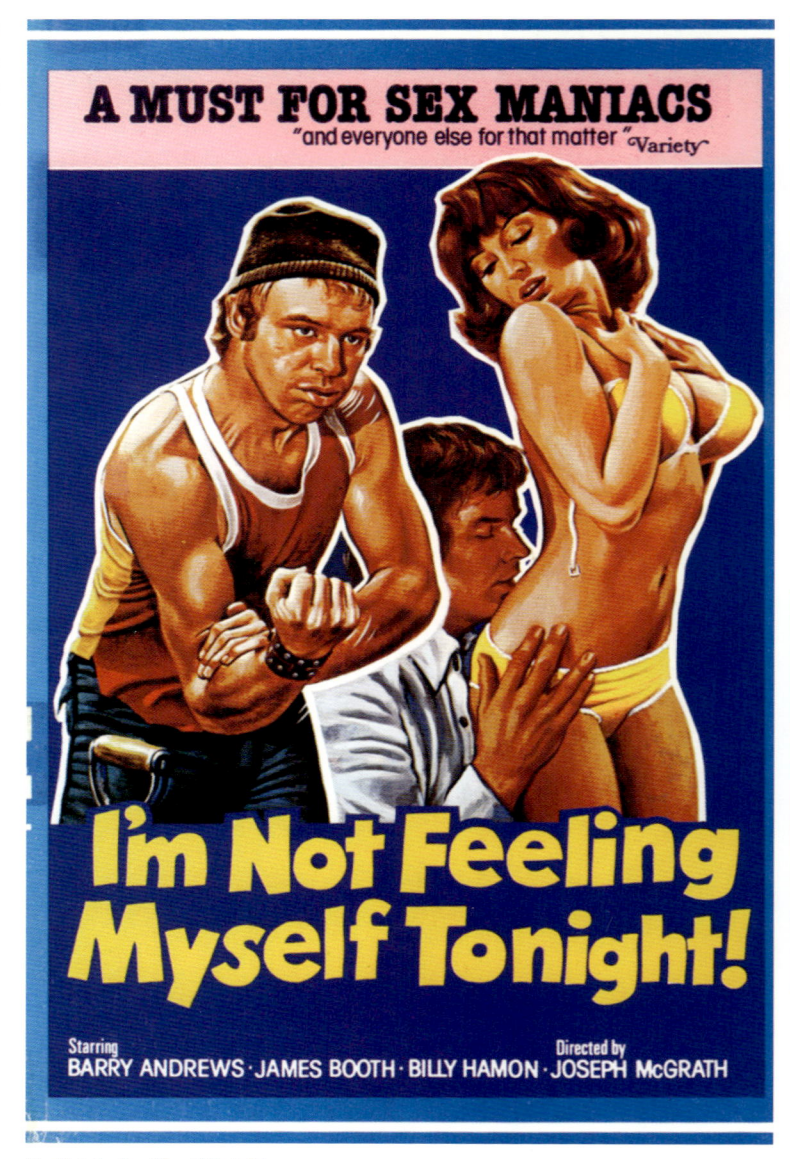

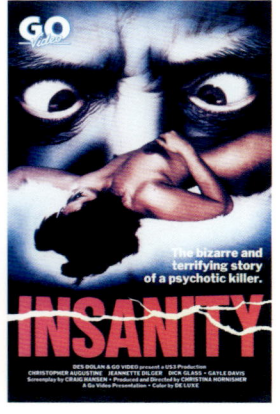

I'm Not Feeling Myself Tonight
Country: **Great Britain**
Director: **Joseph McGrath**
Year: **1975** Time: **60m 39s**
Video Label: **World of Video 2000 / Jaguar**

Insanity
Original Title: **Unknown**
Country: **USA**
Director: **Christina Hornisher**
Year: **Unknown** Time: **73m 50s**
Video Label: **Go**

Jailbait Babysitter
Country: **USA**
Director: **John Hayes**
Year: **1977** Time: **89m 27s**
Video Label: **Cyclo**

I'm Not Feeling Myself Tonight: Surely Britain's most famous sex film title, it featured a whole slew of familiar British faces including those of James Booth, Sally Faulkner and Brian Murphy. It was released theatrically with an 'X' rating.

Insanity: Lead actress Jeanette Dilger appeared with Johnny Legend in rock 'n' roll porno flick '**Teenage Cruisers**'.

Jailbait Babysitter: A trailer for this obscure sex comedy appeared on the US '**Sleazemania**' compilation. Yes, it's as tacky as you would expect.

1983 - Baby Stewart

Veteran singer Rod Stewart gets to Number 1 with 'Baby Jane'

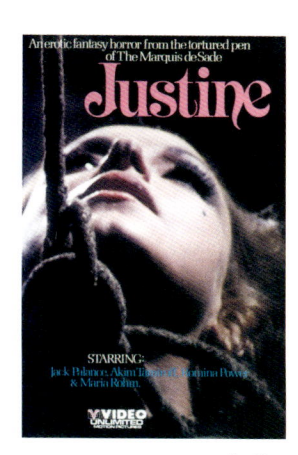

Justine
Original Title: **Justine & Juliette / De Sade les Infortunes de la Vertu**
Country: **Great Britain / West Germany / Italy**
Director: **Jesús Franco** Year: **1968**
Time: **119m 00s** Video Label: **Video Unlimited**

Keep it Up Jack!
Country: **Great Britain**
Director: **Derek Ford**
Year: **1973** Time: **84m 04s**
Video Label: **Replay**

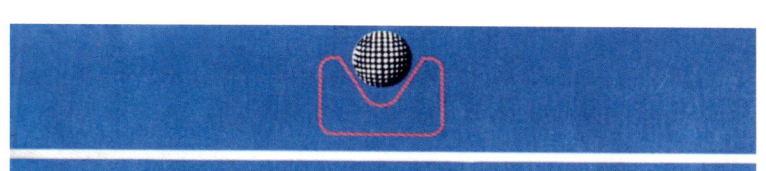

Title: Killer's Moon
Country: **Great Britain**
Director: **Alan Birkinshaw**
Year: **1978** Time: **88m 23s**
Video Label: **Inter-Ocean**

Justine: Romina Power stars in the title role, with support from Klaus Kinski, Howard Vernon and Jack Palance. Another title rejected by the BBFC when submitted in 1975 under the title '**Justine & Juliette**', it was released on video uncut in April 1982.

Keep it Up Jack!: More star-studded sex from Britain's major exponent of smut, Derek Ford. This one features appearances by Mark Jones, Frank Thornton and Queenie Watts.

Killer's Moon: This must surely be one of the sleaziest British movies ever made, featuring a group of schoolgirls being chased and ravaged by a trio of mentally disturbed psychos. Unbelievably, it was passed 'X' without cuts in August 1978, but would no doubt be rejected if submitted to the BBFC now.

4 · NICE AND SLEAZY DOES IT

1983 - Police Breath

The Police get to Number 1 with ' 'Every Breath You Take'

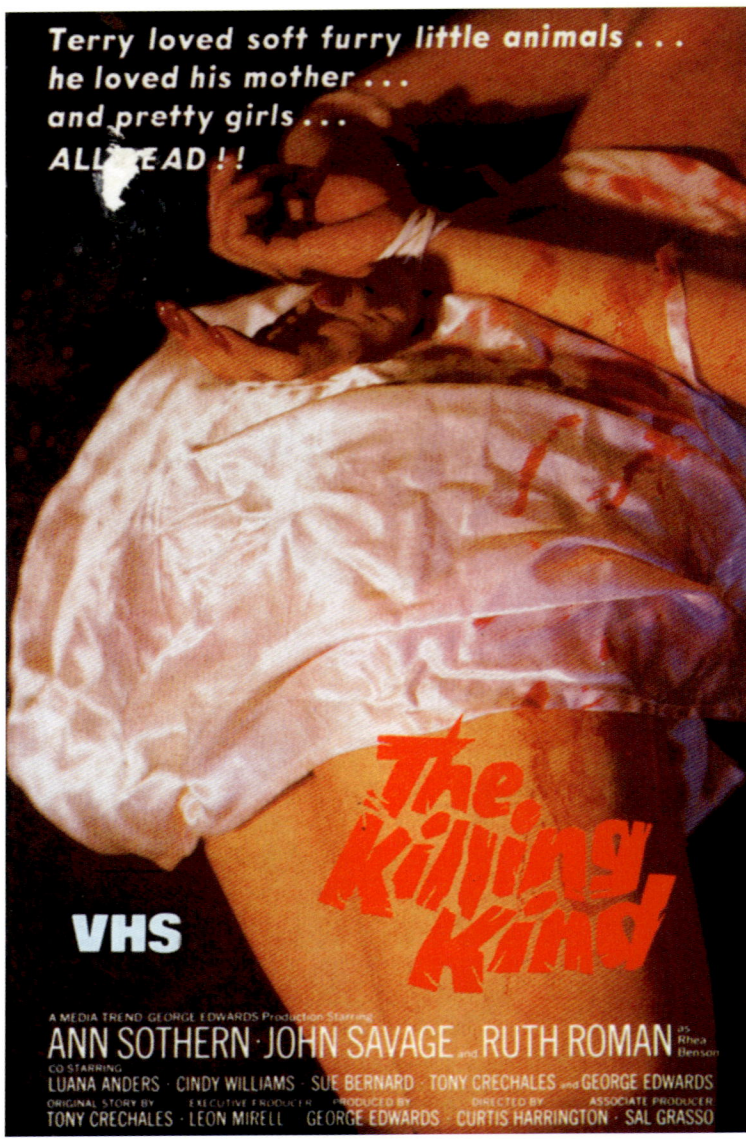

NICE AND SLEAZY DOES IT

The Killing Kind
Country: **USA**
Director: **Curtis Harrington**
Year: **1973** Time: **91m 13s**
Video Label: **Intervision**

Knife for the Ladies
Country: **USA**
Director: **Larry G. Spangler**
Year: **1973** Time: **51m 42s**
Video Label: **IFS** (Iver Film Services)

The Last Horror Film
Country: **USA**
Director: **David Winters**
Year: **1982** Time: **83m 24s**
Video Label: **Intervision**

The Killing Kind: The ad line for this one read "Terry loved soft, furry, little animals, he loved his mother, he loved pretty girls.... ALL DEAD!" Enough said?

Knife for the Ladies: Judging it by its cover, you could be forgiven for thinking that this was a 'stalk and slash' film. It is in fact a dull western which mixes in horror elements.

The Last Horror Film: Filmed during the 1982 Cannes film festival, this features **Maniac**'s Joe Spinell and British scream queen Caroline Munro. You don't see covers like this anymore!

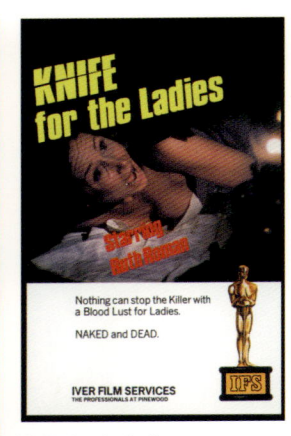

76

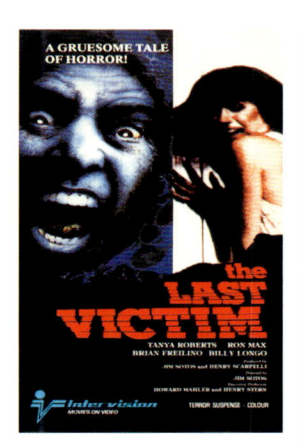

The Last Victim
Country: **USA**
Director: **Jim Sotos**
Year: **1975** Time: **82m 20s**
Video Label: **Intervision**

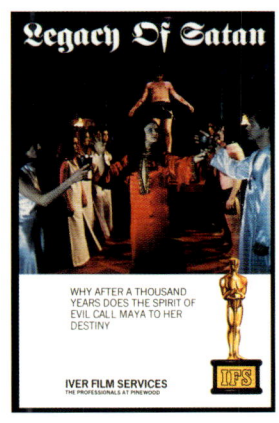

Legacy of Satan
Country: **USA**
Director: **Gerard Damiano**
Year: **1973** Time: **56m 52s**
Video Label: **IFS** (Iver Film Services)

Let Me Die a Woman
Country: **USA**
Director: **Doris Wishman** (uncredited)
Year: **1978** Time: **75m 11s**
Video Label: **Derann**

1982-3 - Sons of Glyndwr

A group of stroppy Welsh nationalists claim responsibility for fire bomb attacks on homes belonging to English people

The Last Victim: Rejected by the BBFC when submitted as '**Forced Entry**' in June 1982. With Tanya Roberts and Nancy Allen.

Legacy of Satan: From the maker of '**Deep Throat**' and '**Devil in Miss Jones**' comes this mixture of sex and Satanic worship.

Let Me Die a Woman: This exploitative sex-change documentary was originally rejected by the BBFC when submitted in March 1980. It was eventually passed in May 1982 with over 10 minutes of cuts. The video release was intact.

1983 - Gerry Adams elected

Republican Gerry Adams is elected leader of the IRA's political wing Sinn Féin

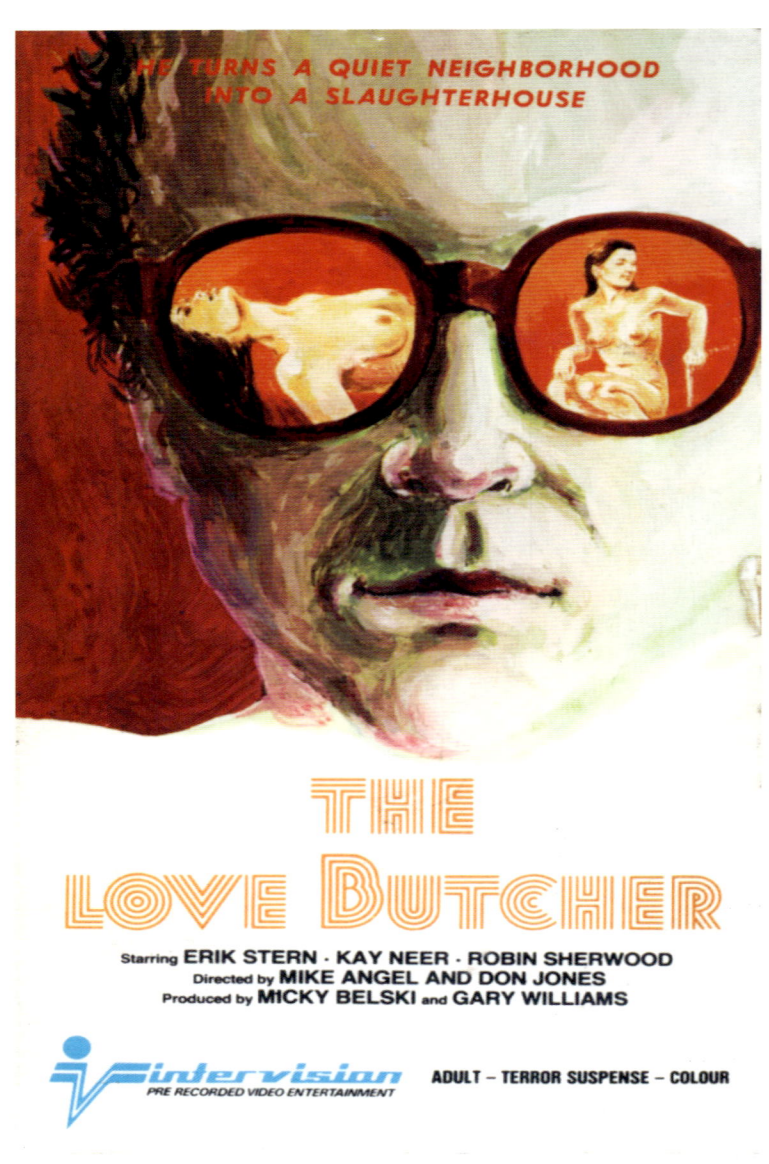

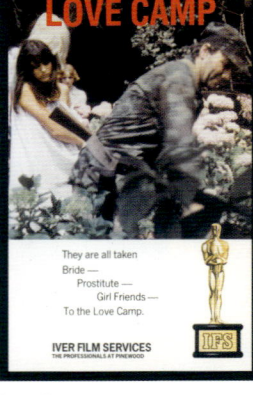

The Love Butcher
Country: **USA**
Director: **Mikel Angel & Don Jones**
Year: **1975** Time: **81m 07s**
Video Label: **Intervision**

Love Camp
Original Title: **Frauen im Liebeslager**
Country: **Switzerland / West Germany**
Director: **Jesús Franco** (as Jess Franco)
Year: **1977** Time: **69m 33s**
Video Label: **IFS** (Iver Film Services)

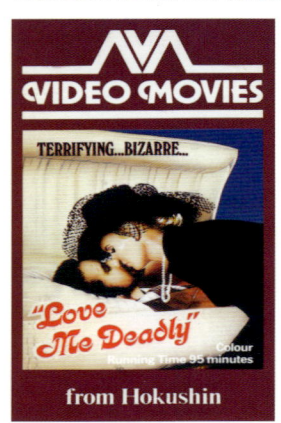

Love Me Deadly
Country: **USA**
Director: **Jacques LaCerte**
Year: **1972** Time: **89m 49s**
Video Label: **Hokushin**

The Love Butcher: Don Jones had recently churned out the equally dubious '**Schoolgirls in Chains**' before turning his hand to this strange psycho movie.

Love Camp: Another of Franco's extreme women in prison films, cut by around 6 mins to secure an 'X' rating, and released on video in the same cut-down version by Iver.

Love Me Deadly: Another BBFC reject passed 'X' by London's GLC, although it apparently turned them 'green' whilst viewing it. This uncut video release appeared on tape in February 1981.

My Friends Need Killing
Country: **USA**
Director: **Paul Leder**
Year: **1976** Time: **73m 37s**
Video Label: **Vision On**

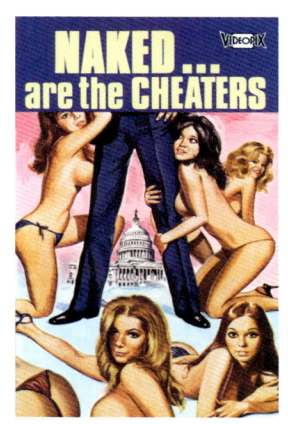

Naked... are the Cheaters
Country: **USA**
Director: **Derek Ashburne**
Year: **1971** Time: **66m 55s**
Video Label: **Videopix**

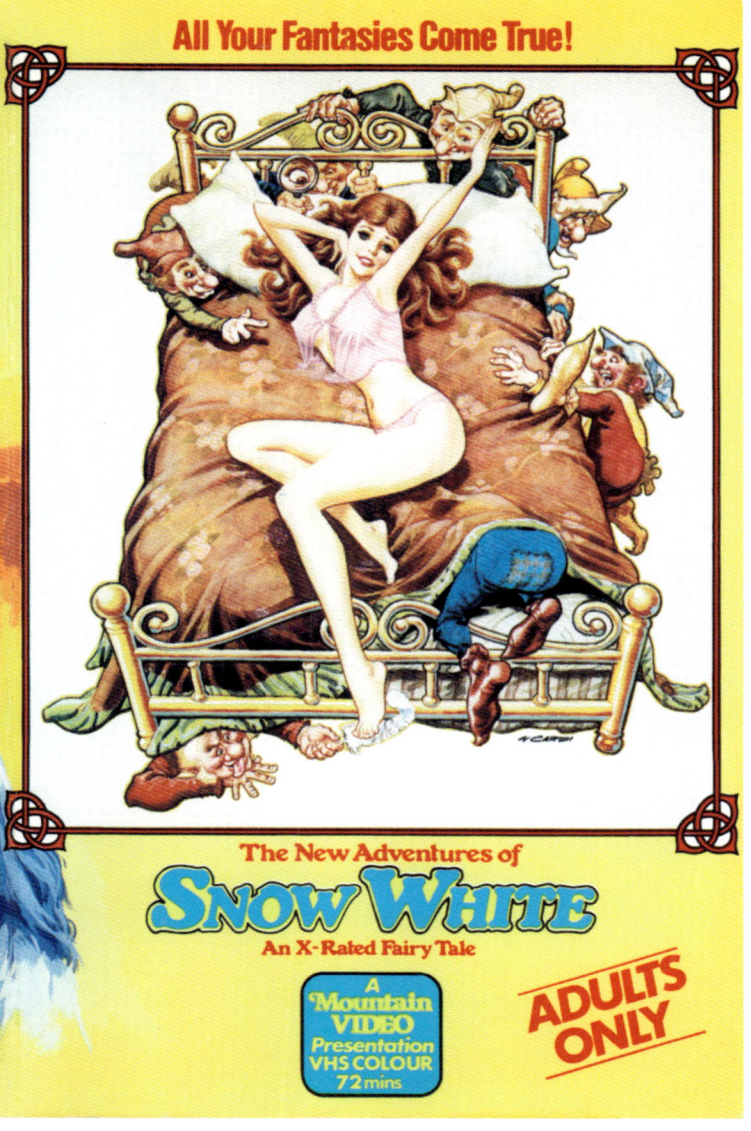

The New Adventures of Snow White
Original Title: **Grimms Märchen von lüsternen Pärchen / Grimm's Fairy Tales for Adults**
Country: **West Germany / USA**
Director: **Rolf Thiele**
Year: **1969** Time: **71m 51s**
Video Label: **Mountain**

My Friends Need Killing: More excess from the maker of '**Poor Albert and Little Annie**' - this is a nasty tale of a Vietnam vet on a killing spree. Again, it's hard to believe that this played UK cinemas.

Naked... are the Cheaters: Also known as '**The Politicians**', this sex film received a very limited video release.

The New Adventures of Snow White: Actress Marie Liljedahl appears as Snow White, fresh from starring with Christopher Lee in Jess Franco's '**Eugenie... the Story of Her Journey into Perversion**'.

1984 - Divorce changes

New legislation allows couples to petition for divorce on their first wedding anniversary

NICE AND SLEAZY DOES IT

79

1982 - New York Rips

Italian gore maestro Lucio Fulci directs the ultra nasty 'New York Ripper'. It induces vomiting at the BBFC and is banned outright

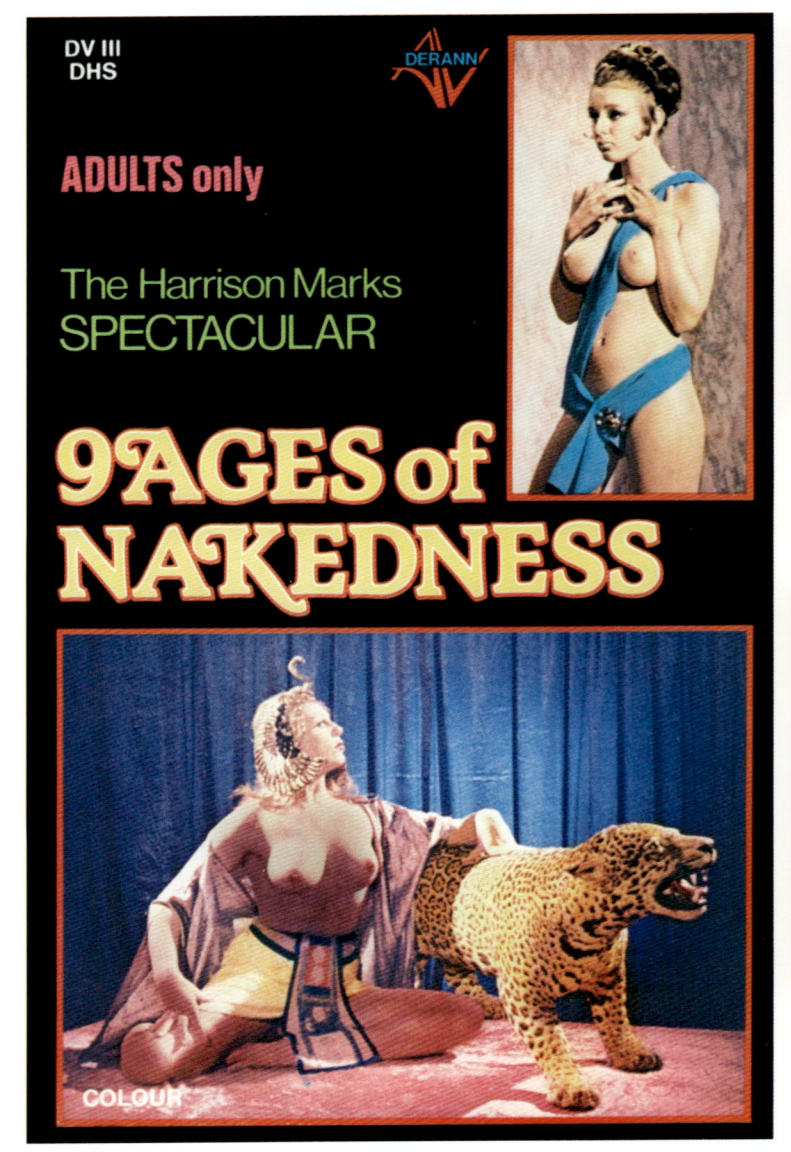

NICE AND SLEAZY DOES IT

Night, After Night, After Night
Country: **Great Britain**
Director: **Lindsay Shonteff** (as Lewis J. Force)
Year: **1969** Time: **84m 41s**
Video Label: **Vision On**

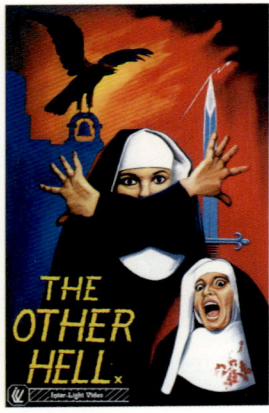

The Other Hell
Original Title: **L'altro inferno**
Country: **Italy**
Director: **Bruno Mattei** (as Stefan Oblowsky)
Year: **1980** Time: **84m 43s**
Video Label: **Inter-Light**

The Nine Ages of Nakedness
Country: **Great Britain**
Director: **George Harrison Marks**
Year: **1969** Time: **84m 35s**
Video Label: **Derann**

Night, After Night, After Night: A homicidal drag-queen is on a murdering spree in this film from the maker of the '**Big Zapper**' movies. This was released theatrically with cuts and an 'X' certificate.

The Nine Ages of Nakedness: British glamour girl June Palmer makes an appearance in this film from the maker of Naked as Nature Intended. Another title which did the rounds of UK cinemas at the end of the Sixties.

The Other Hell: Stoppi, fresh from appearing in Joe D'Amato's extremely unpleasant '**Beyond the Darkness**', makes an appearance in this nunsploitation epic from the director of '**SS Girls**'. Re-released by Redemption Films, with 19s cut at the behest of the BBFC.

80

1983 - 99 Balloons

German punkette, Nena, gets to the Number 1 spot with 99 Red Balloons

Part-Time Wife
Country: **USA**
Director: **Arthur Marks**
Year: **1974** Time: **91m 25s**
Video Label: **Films International**

Pleasure Shop on 7th Avenue
Original Title: **Il pornoshop della settima strada**
Country: **Italy**
Director: **Aristide Massaccesi** (as Joe D'Amato)
Year: **1979** Time: **77m 37s**
Video Label: **Intercity**

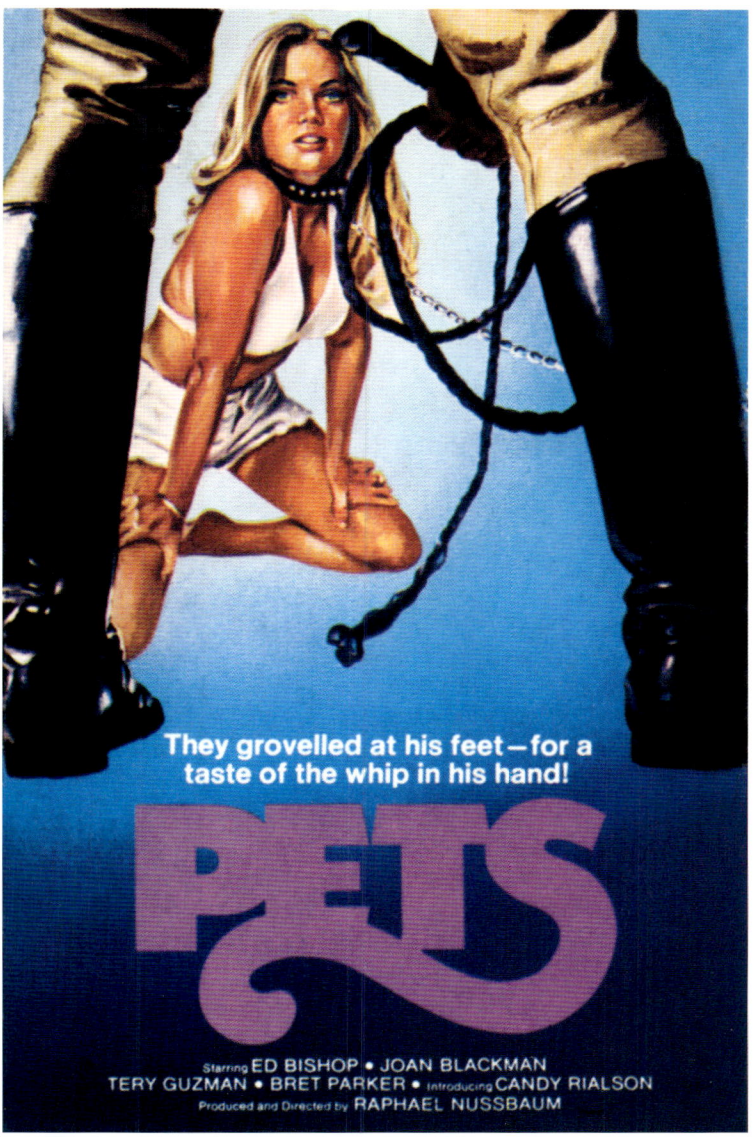

Pets
Country: **USA**
Director: **Raphael Nussbaum**
Year: **1973** Time: **97m 37s**
Video Label: **Intervision**

Part-Time Wife: Marks went on to direct several Blaxploitation films including '**Friday Foster**' with Pam Grier, whilst lead actor Andy Robinson had previously appeared in '**Dirty Harry**' alongside Clint Eastwood.

Pets: Ed Bishop and Candice Realson appeared in this incredible sexploitation film. Released theatrically in Britain as '**Submission**', after being passed 'X' in June 1975 with cuts.

Pleasure Shop on 7th Avenue: A group of sex-crazed bank robbers take refuge in a porno shop and sexually abuse the female staff. This is one very sleazy movie. This was the censored 'X' rated cinema release, but it still retained its high sleaze factor.

4 - NICE AND SLEAZY DOES IT

81

1984 - Lethal Hazards

The dumping of nuclear waste at sea is covered by moratorium under the 1972 London Dumping Convention, but the UK continue dumping until 1984

Poor White Trash
Original Title: **Poor White Trash Part II**
Country: **USA**
Director: **S. F. Brownrigg**
Year: **1974** Time: **80m 17s**
Video Label: **Intervision**

Provocation
Original Title: **Provokation**
Country: **Greece**
Director: **Omiros Efstratiades**
Year: **1970** Time: **90m 41s**
Video Label: **Inter-City**

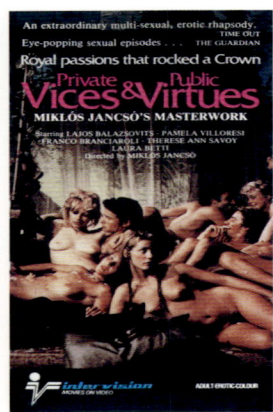

Private Vices, Public Virtues
Original Title: **Vizi privati, pubbliche virtù**
Country: **Italy / Yugoslavia**
Director: **Miklós Jancsó**
Year: **1976** Time: **99m 02s**
Video Label: **Intervision**

Poor White Trash: Not to be confused with the 1957 original starring Peter Graves, Intervision chose to illustrate this sequel with perhaps the goriest moment from the film.

Private Vices, Public Virtues: This much sought after piece of arty erotica features an early appearance by Iloner Staller, who later became Cicciolini. In much need of a video re-release, this was passed 'X' uncut in October 1976.

Provocation: Another scarce video release, this sexy Greek drama stars Udo Kier, fresh from his appearance in '**Mark of the Devil**'.

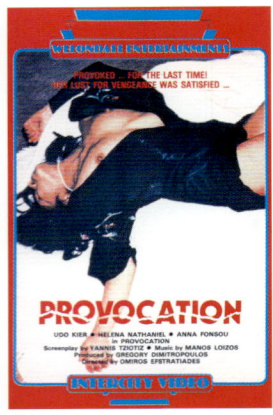

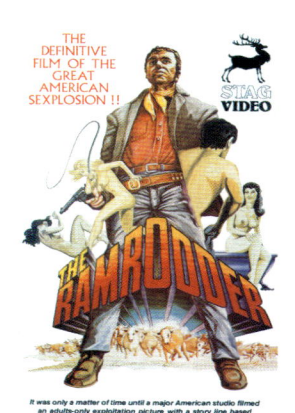

The Ramrodder
Country: **USA**
Director: **Van Guylder**
Year: **1969** Time: **85m 06s**
Video Label: **Stag**

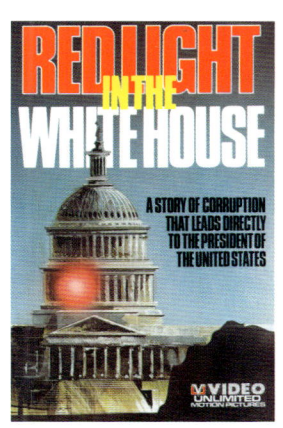

Red Light in the Whitehouse
Country: **USA**
Director: **Paul Leder**
Year: **1977** Time: **89m 17s**
Video Label: **Video Unlimited**

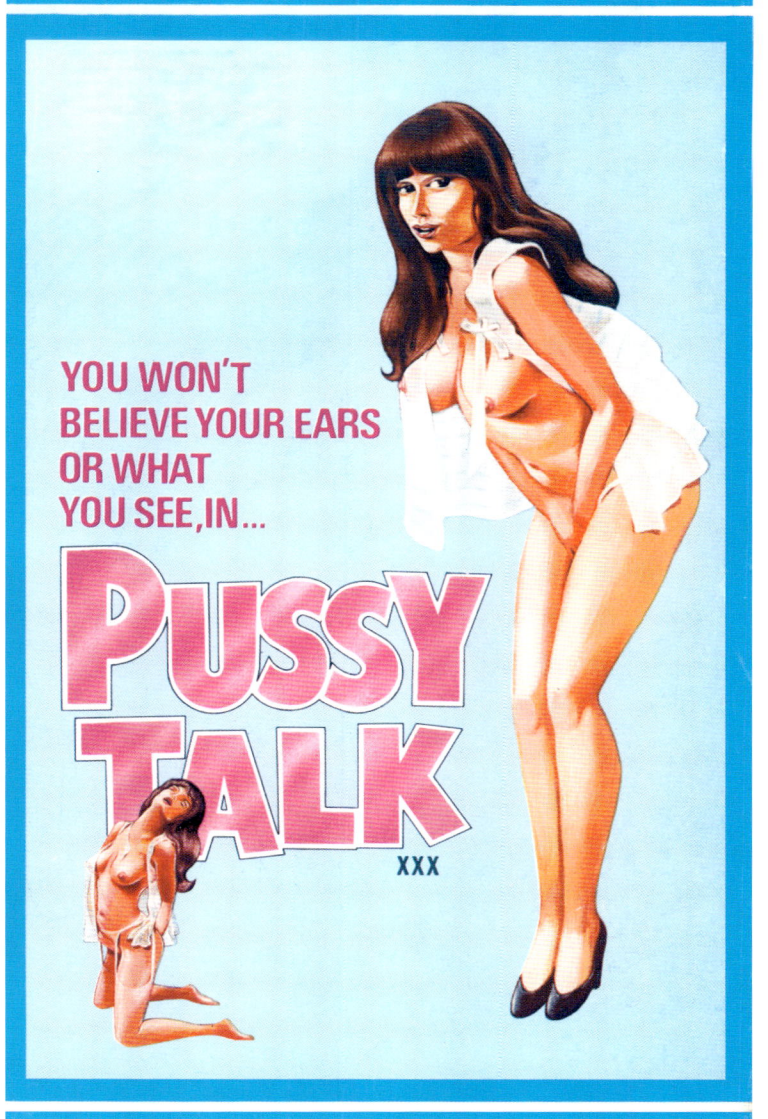

1984 - The Death of Love

Publisher IPC announces the closure of teeny-bop titles 'True' and 'Hers'.

Pussy Talk
Original Title: **Pussy Talk - Le Sexe qui Parle**
Country: **France**
Director: **Claude Mulot** (as Frédéric Lansac)
Year: **1975** Time: **70m 11s**
Video Label: **World of Video 2000**

Pussy Talk: A truly bizarre sex comedy about a talking vagina, which was passed 'X' with cuts by London's GLC, after being rejected by the BBFC.

The Ramrodder: Manson Family member Bobby Beausoleil appears in this sex film, which was rejected by the BBFC in November 1973.

Red Light in the Whitehouse: Sleaze is nothing new in the Whitehouse! This was banned on video in Australia, perhaps for political reasons. From the maker of '**My Friends Need Killing**'.

1982 - Tatler bought

Tatler, the bible of the aristocratic socialite is sold to Vogue publisher, Conde Nast

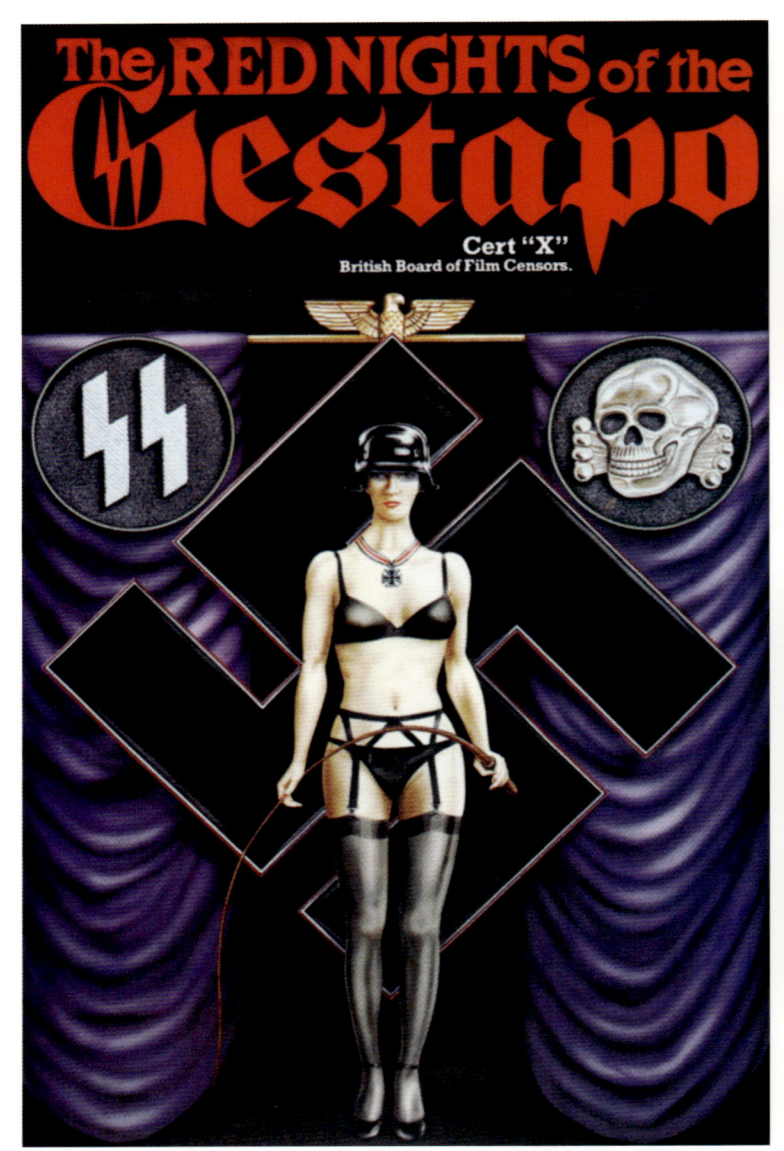

NICE AND SLEAZY DOES IT

The Red Nights of the Gestapo
Original Title: **Le lunghe notti della Gestapo**
Country: **Italy**
Director: **Fabio De Agostini**
Year: **1977** Time: **79m 27s**
Video Label: **VCL** (Video Cassette Library)

The Reluctant Virgin
Original Title: **No... sono vergine**
Country: **Italy**
Director: **Norman Schwartz & Cesare Mancini**
Year: **1973** Time: **80m 39s**
Video Label: **Market**

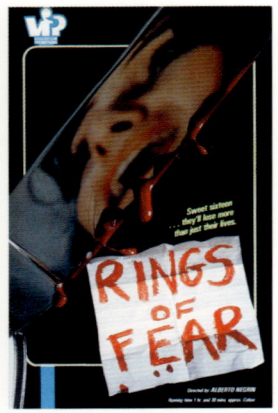

Rings of Fear
Original Title: **Enigma rosso / Orgie des Todes / Trafico de Menores**
Country: **Italy / West Germany / Spain**
Director: **Alberto Negrin**
Year: **1978** Time: **81m 07s**
Video Label: **VFP** (Video Film Promotions)

The Red Nights of the Gestapo: Originally rejected by the BBFC in December 1979, it was granted an 'X' certificate in March 1981 after cuts totalling 12 minutes were made. It is this version which appeared on video in January 1983.

The Reluctant Virgin: Fulvio Mingozzi (better known for his roles in at least five Argento films) appears in this sex comedy.

Rings of Fear: Passed 'X' with cuts and released theatrically as '**Red Rings of Fear**', this video release was uncut. The video re-release entitled '**Virgin Terror**' received BBFC cuts totalling 14s.

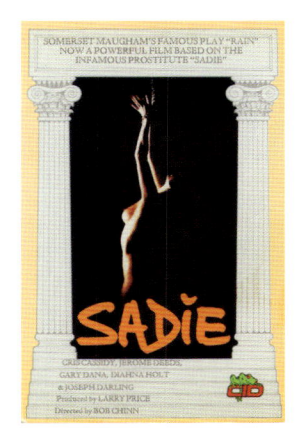

1984 - Gremlins

A parody of ET in which mad foot-high creatures with attitude, plague a small US town causing havoc. Spielberg is Executive Producer.

Sadie
Country: **USA**
Director: **Robert C. Chinn**
Year: **1980** Time: **71m 48s**
Video Label: **CID** (Cinema Indoors)

Scream Bloody Murder
Country: **USA**
Director: **Marc B. Ray**
Year: **1972** Time: **82m 15s**
Video Label: **Intervision**

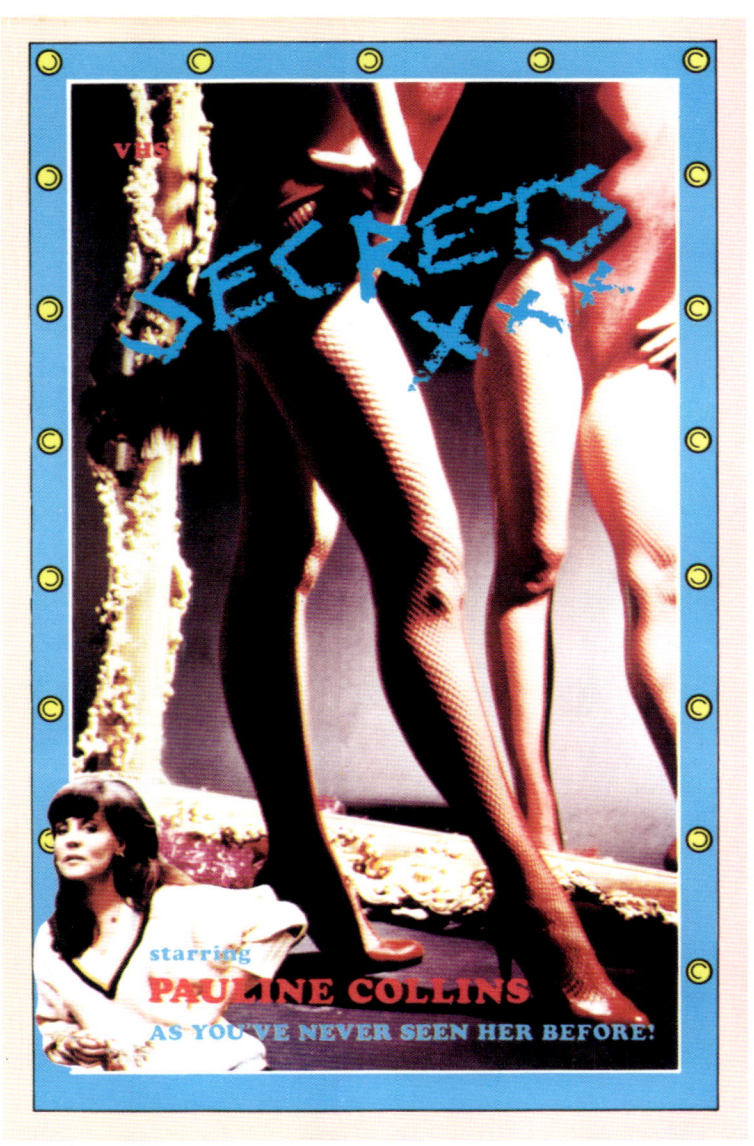

Secrets
Original Title: **Secrets of a Windmill Girl**
Country: **Great Britain**
Director: **Arnold Louis Miller**
Year: **1966** Time: **82m 28s**
Video Label: **Portland / Top Hat**

Sadie: Celebrated porn director Chinn teamed up with regular porn actress Chris Cassidy for this obscure sexploitation quickie.

Scream Bloody Murder: Whilst murdering his father, a boy loses his hand. He later becomes a hook wielding psycho-killer. Filmed in 'violent vision and gory colour'.

Secrets: A very obscure release starring Pauline Collins, this one is set at London's famous striptease venue The Windmill Theatre.

1982 - Save Me

Smooth as a couple of rhinestone Shell Suits the dulcet duo Renée and Renato reach Number 1 with 'Save Your Love'

4 NICE AND SLEAZY DOES IT

Secrets of a Door-to-Door Salesman
Country: **Great Britain**
Director: **Wolf Rilla**
Year: **1973** Time: **79m 05s**
Video Label: **World of Video 2000**

Seven Dangerous Girls
Original Title: **Sette ragazze di classe / Siete Chicas Peligros**
Country: **Italy / Spain**
Director: **Pedro Lazaga**
Year: **1978** Time: **83m 42s**
Video Label: **Market**

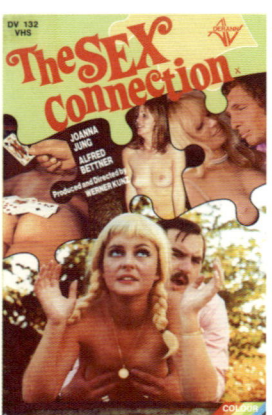

The Sex Connection
Original Title: **Unknown**
Country: **Switzerland**
Director: **Charles Ferrer**
Year: **1969** Time: **81m 15s**
Video Label: **Derann**

Secrets of a Door-to-Door Salesman: The director of 1954 TV series The Scarlet Pimpernel turned his hand to sex comedies during the early seventies. The opening credit sequence was directed by '**The Silence of the Lambs**' Jonathan Demme.

Seven Dangerous Girls: Janet Agren starred in this spy spoof before appearing in notorious gore films '**City of the Living Dead**' and '**Eaten Alive!**'

The Sex Connection: This sex comedy was also released as '**The Pleasure Machine**'. Producer Kunz also financed '**The Sexy Dozen**'.

86

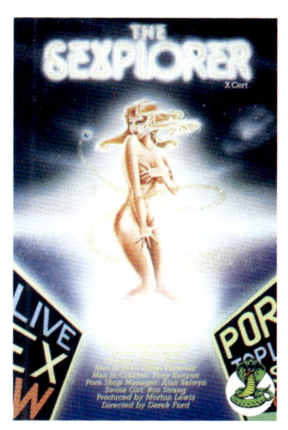

Sexplorer
Country: **Great Britain**
Director: **Derek Ford**
Year: **1975** Time: **81m 54s**
Video Label: **Cobra**

The Sexy Dozen
Original Title: **Charley's Tante - Nackt**
Country: **Switzerland**
Director: **Norbert Terry & Max Sieber**
Year: **1969** Time: **93m 42s**
Video Label: **Derann**

Sexorcist
Original Title: **L'ossessa**
Country: **Italy**
Director: **Mario Gariazzo**
Year: **1974** Time: **82m 17s**
Video Label: **Tobyward**

1981-3 - 'On Yer Bike'

Employment Secretary, Norman Tebbit, exhorts the unemployed following riots, when he recalled his father's experiences in the 1930's: "he didn't riot - he got on his bike and looked for work"

Sexorcist: Stella Carnacina plays Danilla, a girl possessed, who brings a statue of Christ to life by rubbing her naked body against it in this sexy '**Exorcist**' rip-off. This is perhaps the most re-released title or video in the UK, and has even been sold via mail order as a hardcore film!

Sexplorer: Released Stateside as '**The Girl from Starship Venus**', this is a favourite of Quentin Tarantino, who has introduced it at film festivals.

The Sexy Dozen: Another silly sex comedy featuring Vincent Gauthier, who also appeared in '**The Good Little Girls**'.

1984 - Mirror, Mirror on the Wall

Disgraced tycoon, Robert Maxwell, buys the Daily Mirror newspaper for £113.4 million

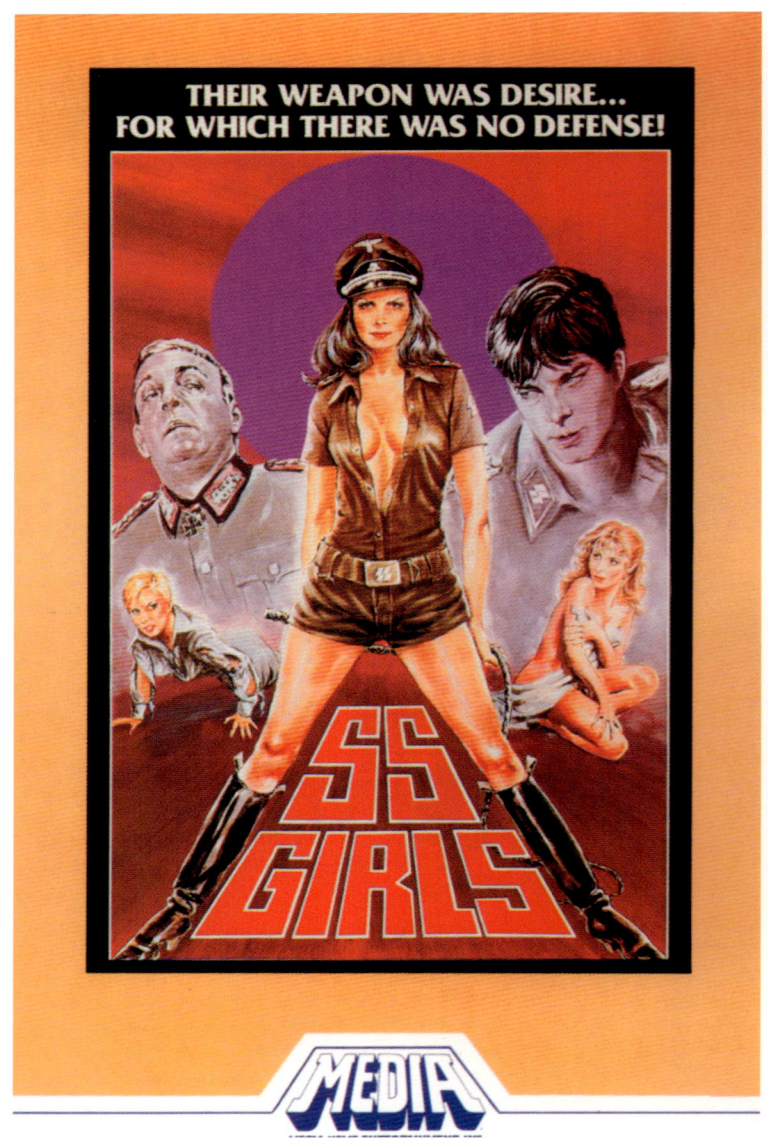

NICE AND SLEAZY DOES IT

SS Girls
Original Title: **La casa privata per le SS**
Country: **Italy**
Director: **Bruno Mattei** (uncredited)
Year: **1976** Time: **78m 24s**
Video Label: **Media**

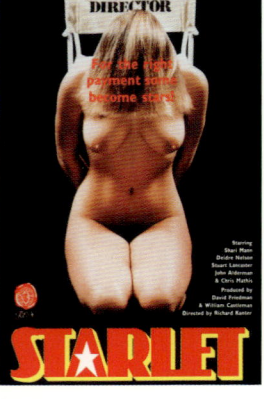

Starlet!
Country: **USA**
Director: **Richard Kanter**
Year: **1969** Time: **96m 05s**
Video Label: **Rex**

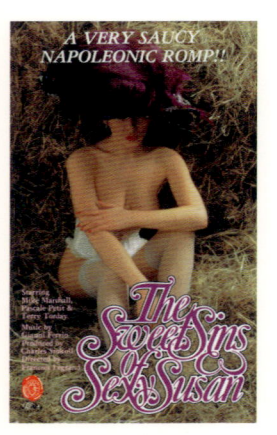

The Sweet Sins of Sexy Susan
Original Title: **Suzanne / I dolci vizi... della casta Susanna**
Country: **Austria / Italy / Hungary**
Director: **Francois Legrand**
Year: **1967** Time: **86m 03s**

SS Girls: More Nazi sleaze and another classic cover shot, which was recently re-issued with 3m 34s of cuts.

Starlet!: The ad-line for this sexploitation film ran "The Lure of Motion-Picture Stardom for Young, Pretty Girls Has Always Been Part of the American Dream!" Stuart Lancaster appears, and is still making appearances in films like '**Batman Returns**' and '**Edward Scissorhands**'.

The Sweet Sins of Sexy Susan: It's hard to believe that this camp sex farce, from the maker of '**The Tower of the Screaming Virgins**', was screened at British cinemas during the late Sixties.

88

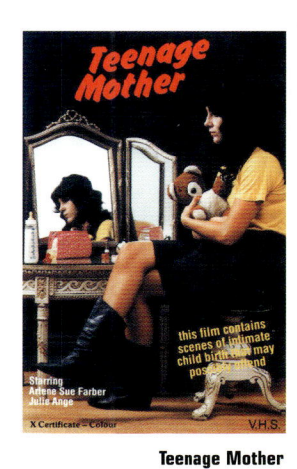

1983 - Seventeen

EMAP, the publisher of Smash Hits, launch fortnightly magazine 'Just Seventeen' – the title is a huge success

Teenage Mother
Country: **USA**
Director: **Jerry Gross**
Year: **1966** Time: **65m 48s**
Video Label: **Portland / MovieMatic**

Too Hot to Handle
Country: **USA**
Director: **Don Schain**
Year: **1976** Time: **82m 10s**
Video Label: **Inter-Ocean**

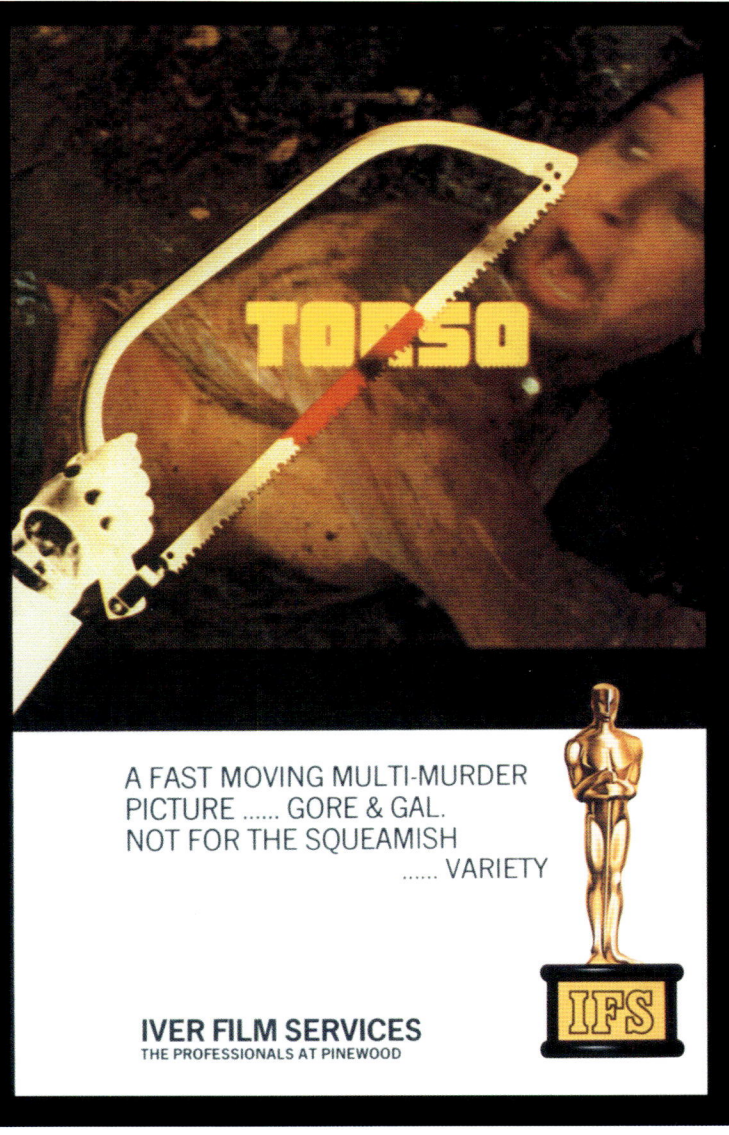

Torso
Original Title: **I corpi presentano tracce di violenza carnale**
Country: **Italy**
Director: **Sergio Martino**
Year: **1972** Time: **85m 13s**
Video Label: **IFS** (Iver Film Services)

Teenage Mother: Following the ups and downs of a teenage girl, the finale featured a graphic child birth sequence, included to attract the inquisitive among us. Not released theatrically in Britain, this film appeared on UK video in both uncut and cut versions.

Too Hot to Handle: A follow-up to the incredibly sleazy '**Ginger**' trilogy, again starring Cheri Caffaro. This one didn't make it to the local flea-pit.

Torso: A classic 'giallo' starring British actress Suzy Kendall. This UK release featured the American 'R' rated version. The Cramps used to run the trailer when playing.

4 · NICE AND SLEAZY DOES IT

89

1984 - 'Divine Retribution'

A thunderbolt strikes 700 year-old York Minster causing fire damage estimated at £1 million

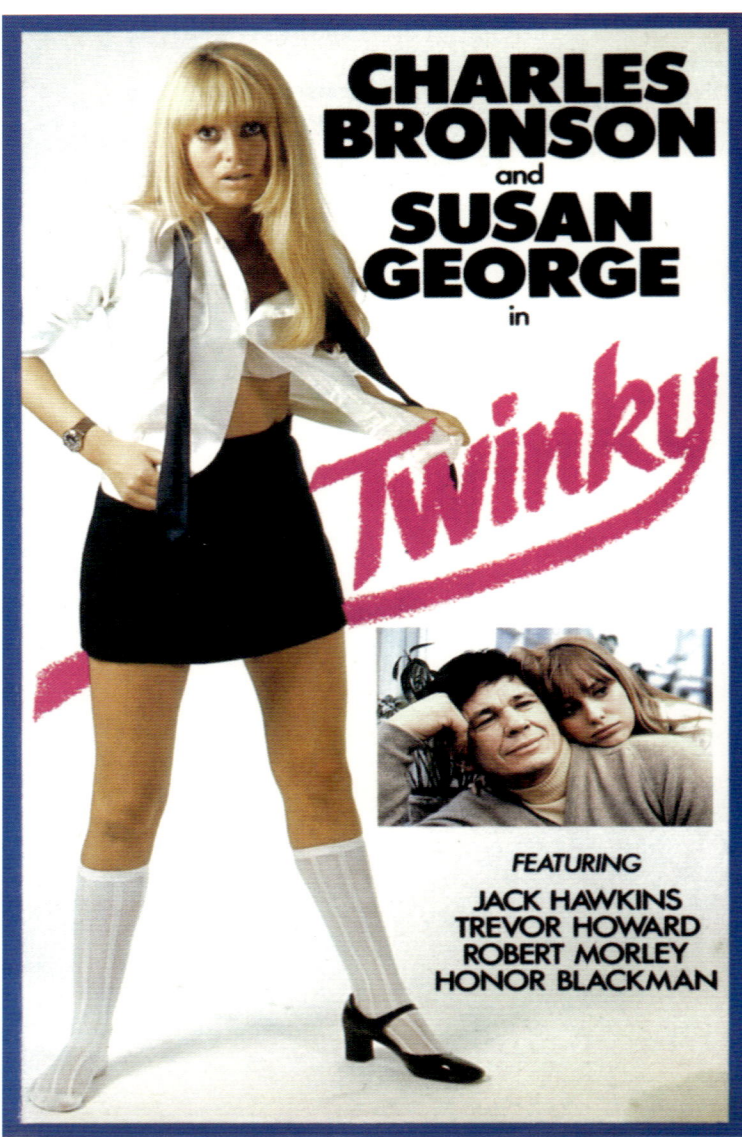

NICE AND SLEAZY DOES IT

Twinky
Country: **Great Britain / Italy**
Director: **Richard Donner**
Year: **1969** Time: **94m 13s**
Video Label: **Rank**

The Vampire Happening
Original Title: **Gebissen wird nur Nachts Happening der Vampire**
Country: **West Germany** Director: **Freddie Francis**
Year: **1970** Time: **95m 58s**
Video Label: **DVS**

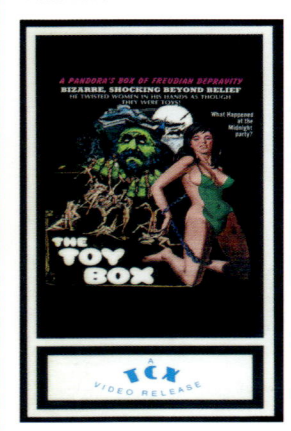

The Toy Box
Country: **USA**
Director: **Ron Garcia**
Year: **1970** Time: **85m 38s**
Video Label: **TCX**

The Toy Box: A very strange piece of sexploitation described by the producers as 'A Pandora's Box of Freudian Depravity'. Garcia is actually an acclaimed cinematographer in his his own right, having recently shot '**Twin Peaks Fire Walk With Me**'.

Twinky: Susan George plays Charles Bronson's teenage lover in this risqué film, which was rather surprisingly passed 'A' by the BBFC in 1969.

The Vampire Happening: Two years after directing Hammer's '**Dracula Has Risen from the Grave**', Francis went to Germany to direct this vampire sex-comedy. Listen out for the groovy soundtrack from easy listening fave Jerry Van Rooyen.

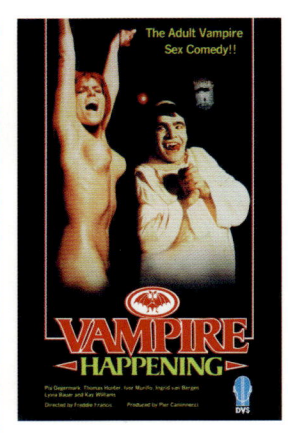

1983 - Lawson elevated

Nigel Lawson becomes Chancellor of the Exchequer

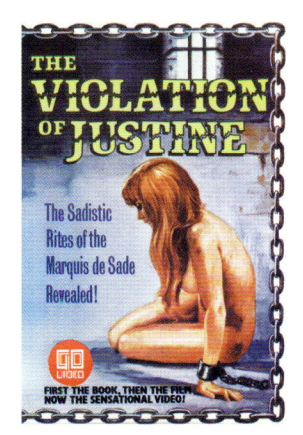

The Violation of Justine
Original Title: **Justine de Sade**
Country: **France / Italy / Canada**
Director: **Claude Pierson**
Year: **1974** Time: **78m 52s**
Video Label: **Go**

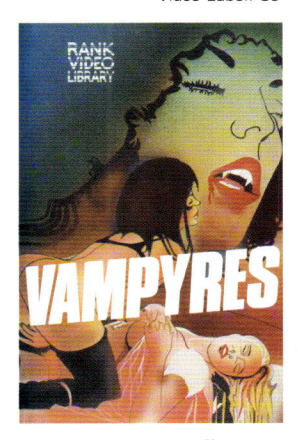

Vampyres
Country: **Great Britain**
Director: **José Ramon Larraz** (as Joseph Larraz)
Year: **1974** Time: **81m 02s**
Video Label: **Rank**

Violation of the Bitch
Original Title: **La Visita del Vicio**
Country: **Spain**
Director: **José Ramon Larraz**
Year: **1978** Time: **67m 17s**
Video Label: **Hokushin**

Vampyres: From the director of '**Violation of the Bitch**' comes this superb tale of supernatural sex and death starring Marianne Morris and Anulka. It was passed 'X' with cuts in January 1975.

The Violation of Justine: Alice Arno plays the title role in another reworking of the Marquis de Sade's '**Justine**'. Passed 'X' by the BBFC in a severely truncated version, Go Video chose to play safe and release the same censored version on video. The overseas version ran 25 minutes longer.

Violation of the Bitch: From the director of '**Vampyres**', this was released theatrically on the UK sex circuit with an 'X' rating. The video art would no doubt have the Video Packaging Review Committee foaming at the mouth!

1983 - CND joins hands

CND organises 14-mile protest of 100,000 people, linking arms between Greenham Common and Aldermaston

Wam Bam Thank You Spaceman
Country: **USA**
Director: **William A. Levey**
Year: **1972** Time: **74m 13s**
Video Label: **TCX**

Werewolf Woman
Original Title: **La lupa mannara**
Country: **Italy**
Director: **Rino Di Silvestro**
Year: **1975** Time: **88m 34s**
Video Label: **Cinehollywood** (Cockney Rebel / Inter-City)

Virgin Witch
Country: **Great Britain**
Director: **Ray Austin**
Year: **1971** Time: **84m 49s**
Video Label: **Intervision**

Virgin Witch: Starring Anne & Vicki Michele, this mixture of sex and witchcraft was originally rejected by the BBFC when submitted in 1971. It was then submitted to London's GLC, who granted it an 'X' certificate. A year later, the BBFC relented and passed it with cuts. It has since been re-released uncut by Redemption Films.

Wam Bam Thank You Spaceman: Featuring Dyanne Thorne, famous for her portrayal in the notorious Ilsa series, this tacky science fiction sex film was made just two years earlier. Levey directed '**Blackenstein**' the same year.

Werewolf Woman: This slice of sleazy Euro-trash was released to UK cinemas in a vain attempt to cash-in on the success of '**The Howling**'. Prior to the Video Recordings Act, it was released by three different video labels. Only the Cinehollywood and Cockney Rebel's versions were intact, as the Inter-City release contained the BBFC 'X' theatrical version. It has since been re-released as '**Naked Werewolf Woman**' with 42s of BBFC cuts.

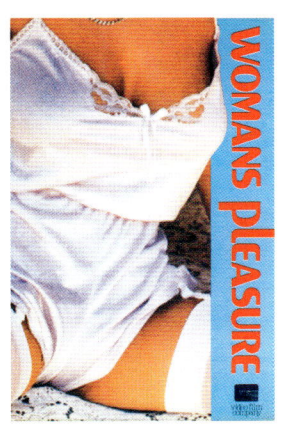

1982 - Laker Falls

Sir Freddie Laker, pioneer of cut-price air travel, is devastated as Laker Airways collapses

Woman's Pleasure
Original Title: **Alle Kätzchen naschen gern**
Country: **West Germany**
Director: **Joseph Zacher**
Year: **1969** Time: **72m 18s**
Video Label: **Vision On**

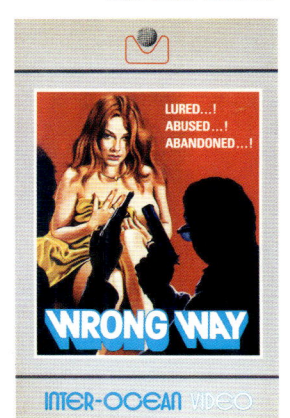

Wrong Way
Country: **USA**
Director: **Ray Williams**
Year: **1972** Time: **77m 36s**
Video Label: **Inter-Ocean**

What Schoolgirls Don't Tell
Original Title: **Was Schulmädchen Verschweigen**
Country: **West Germany**
Director: **Ernst Hofbauer**
Year: **1973** Time: **74m 41s**
Video Label: **World of Video 2000**

What Schoolgirls Don't Tell: Who could resist this entry from the sleazy 'Schoolgirl Report' series, which features an appearance by Christina Lindberg. It had previously been released theatrically as '**Secrets of Sweet Sixteen**'.

Woman's Pleasure: Starring Euro-babe Edwige Fenech who appeared in the best Italian thrillers, this was released to UK cinemas in 1970 as '**The Blonde and the Black Pussycat**'.

Wrong Way: This outrageous sexploitation epic was released theatrically with 20 minutes of cuts. However, the distributors of this video release sneakily tacked a fake 'X' certificate at the beginning of this uncut release.

4 • NICE AND SLEAZY DOES IT

93

5 THE GOOD, THE BAD AND THE VOMIT-INDUCING

1982 - Zepplin Blips

Former Led Zepplin singer Robert Plant's first solo attempt 'Burning Down One Side", scrapes into the charts at Number 73

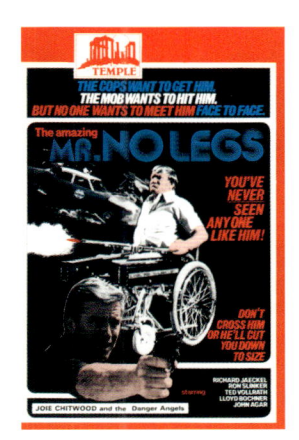

The Amazing Mr. No Legs
Original Title: **Mr. No Legs**
Director: **USA**
Director: **Ricou Browning**
Year: **1975** Time: **85m 15s**
Video Label: **Temple**

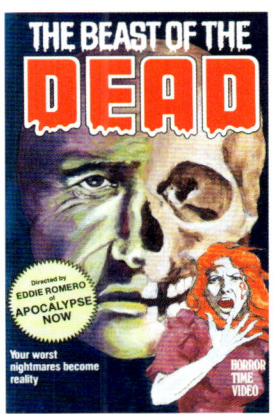

Beast of the Dead
Original Title: **Beast of Blood**
Country: **Phillipines / USA**
Director: **Eddie Romero**
Year: **1970** Time: **86m 23s**
Video Label: **Horror Time**

The Astro-Zombies
Country: **USA**
Director: **Ted V. Mikels**
Year: **1968**
Time: **77m 23s**
Video Label: **Mountain**

The Amazing Mr. No Legs: Unbelievable! A wheelchair-bound mob boss who kung-fu kicks with his stumps is the main villain in this fun, but at times dull, no budgeter. With John Agar from '**Zontar, the Thing from Venus**'.

The Astro-Zombies: '**Faster, Pussycat! Kill! Kill!**'s Tura Satana appears in this bad film from schlockmeister Mikels, about a deranged doctor creating zombies with skeleton masks which look like they're from the local joke shop. Clearly there was no budget for this mess from day one.

Beast of the Dead: The sequel to '**The Mad Doctor of Blood Island**' from the so-called '**Blood Island**' trilogy, Romero was associate producer on '**Apocalypse Now**', hence the rather misleading sleeve quote.

5. THE GOOD, THE BAD AND THE VOMIT-INDUCING.

1982 onwards - Protest and Survive

This CND slogan played on a Government pamphlet 'Protect and Survive', which suggested that by painting the house windows white and hiding under the kitchen table, the population would survive nuclear attack

The Bell of Hell
Original Title: **La Campana del Infierno**
Country: **Spain / France**
Director: **Claudio Guerín Hill**
Year: **1973** Time: **92m 44s**
Video Label: **Duplivision**

The Big Zapper
Country: **Great Britain**
Director: **Lindsay Shonteff**
Year: **1973**
Time: **87m 25s**
Video Label: **Video Network**

Being Different
Country: **USA**
Director: **Harry Rasky**
Year: **1981**
Time: **98m 26s**
Video Label: **Video Network**

The Big Zapper: Linda Marlowe stars in this fun, but at times plain silly, comic strip type spoof which was passed 'X' by the BBFC with cuts for the cinema, although this release was intact.

The Bell of Hell: A superb psycho-thriller, now regarded as something of a minor masterpiece and worthy of a video re-release. The director fell to his death from the bell tower on the last day of shooting. It was screened here theatrically in 1974 with a BBFC 'X' certificate.

Being Different: A bizarre pseudo-documentary featuring real freaks and a modern-day Elephant Man. Narrated by Christopher Plummer, this is pretty disturbing stuff.

1982 onwards - Watch thy Neighbour

A network of crime-prevention schemes called Neighbourhood Watch are introduced, whereby house-holders agree to look out for dodgy geezers in their area

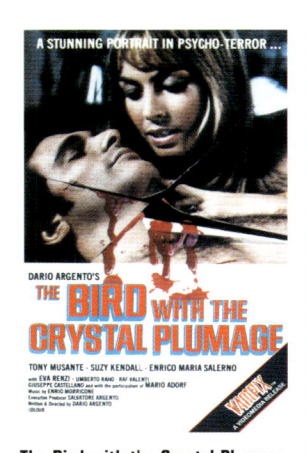

The Bird with the Crystal Plumage
Original Title: **L'uccello dalle piume di cristallo / Das Geheimnis der schwarzen Handschuhe**
Country: **Italy / West Germany**
Director: **Dario Argento** Year: **1969** Time: **92m 10s**
Video Label: **Videomedia / Vampix**

Black Sunday
Original Title: **La maschera del demonio**
Country: **Italy**
Director: **Mario Bava**
Year: **1960** Time: **81m 20s**
Video Label: **Videomedia / Vampix**

The Black Gestapo
Country: **USA**
Director: **Robert Lee Frost**
Year: **1975** Time: **85m 11s**
Video Label: **IFS (Iver Film Services)**

The Bird with the Crystal Plumage: Tony Musante stars as an American writer working in Rome who witnesses what appears to be a murder through the window of an art gallery. He is forced to help the police solve the crime in order to return home.
A collectable video release, although this BBFC 'X' cut version deleted a sequence involving a girl's undies being removed with the aid of a knife. It has since been screened uncut on London's ITV.

Black Sunday: Starring Barbara Steele, this is considered by many to be Bava's best. This release featured the cut-down BBFC 'X' version which had originally been rejected by the BBFC way back in February 1961. It eventually received an uncut TV screening courtesy of the BBC during the late eighties, prompting numerous complaints. It was finally released uncut on UK video with only a '15' certificate by Redemption Films, under the title '**Mask of Satan**'.

The Black Gestapo: A bullied group of blacks unite and set up their own 'Black People's Army' dressed in Nazi-esque uniforms in this incredibly nasty, exploitative but enjoyable (for all the wrong reasons) sleazefest. It was re-released on video as '**Ghetto Warriors**' with 4m 18s cut for an '18' certificate.

99

1982 - Looking good

German techno troupe Kraftwerk get to Number 1 with 'The Model'

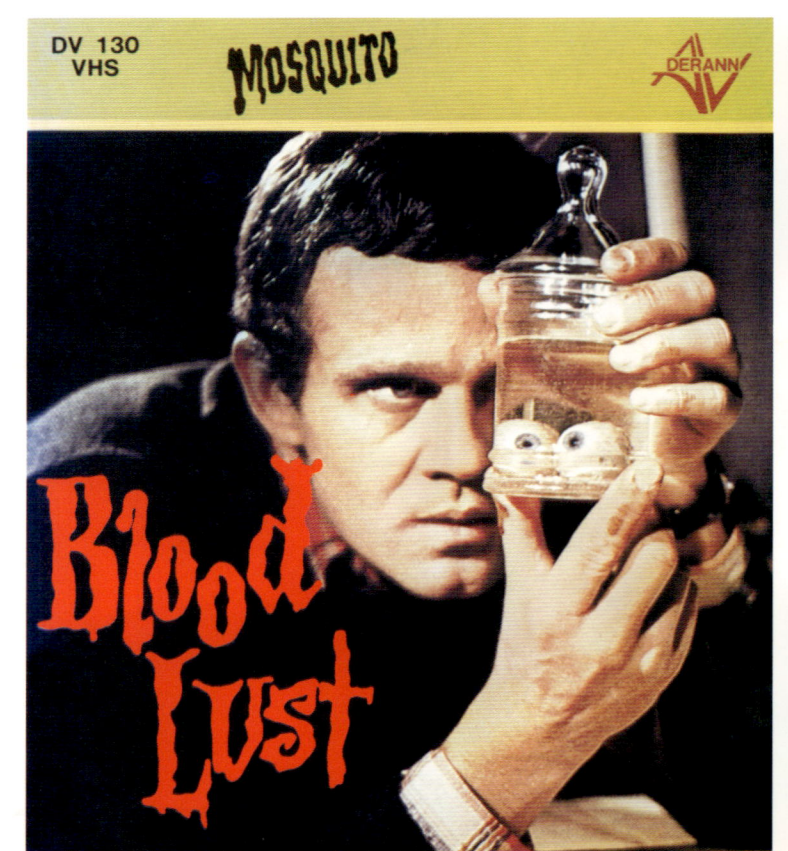

Bloodlust
Original Title: **Mosquito der Schänder**
Country: **Switzerland**
Director: **Marijan Vajda**
Year: **1976** Time: **81m 25s**
Video Label: **Derann**

Blood and Black Lace
Original Title: **Sei donne per l'assassino / 6 Femmes pour L'Assassin / Blutige Seide**
Country: **Italy / France / West Germany**
Director: **Mario Bava** Year: **1963** Time: **79m 48s**
Video Label: **IFS (Iver Film Services)**

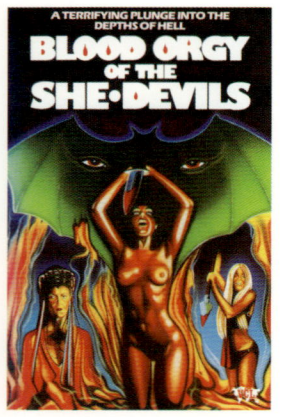

Blood Orgy of the She-Devils
Country: **USA**
Director: **Ted V. Mikels**
Year: **1972** Time: **75m 39s**
Video Label: **VCL (Video Cassette Library)**

Blood and Black Lace: Cameron Mitchell and Eva Bartok star as drug peddlers in this stylish murder mystery set in a fashion house. This release featured the censored BBFC 'X' version, which was re-released on tape with a '15' certificate.

Bloodlust: A deaf and dumb weirdo drinks the blood from corpses and progresses to that of those still living. Another great looking video cover, although the film was cut by 4 mins for an 'X' rating.

Blood Orgy of the She-Devils: More trashy nonsense from Mikels, once interviewed by Jonathan Ross for his 'Incredibly Strange Film Show' back in 1988. Featuring actress Annik Borel, who went on to appear in '**Werewolf Woman**'.

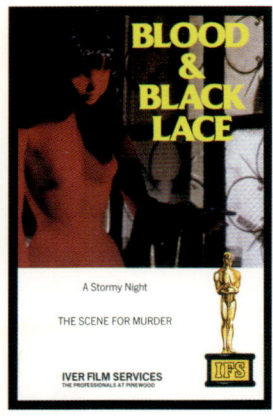

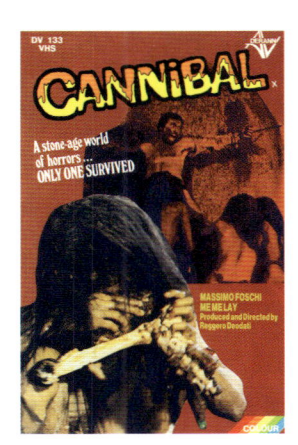

Cannibal
Original Title: **Ultimo mondo cannibale**
Country: **Italy**
Director: **Ruggero Deodato**
Year: **1976** Time: **82m 48s**
Video Label: **Derann**

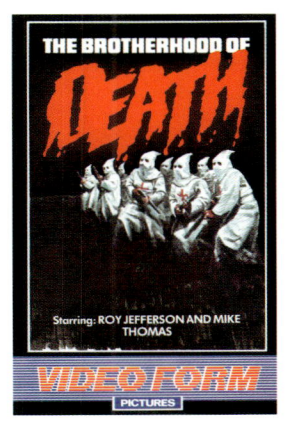

Brotherhood of Death
Country: **USA**
Director: **Bill Berry**
Year: **1976** Time: **70m 09s**
Video Label: **Video Form**

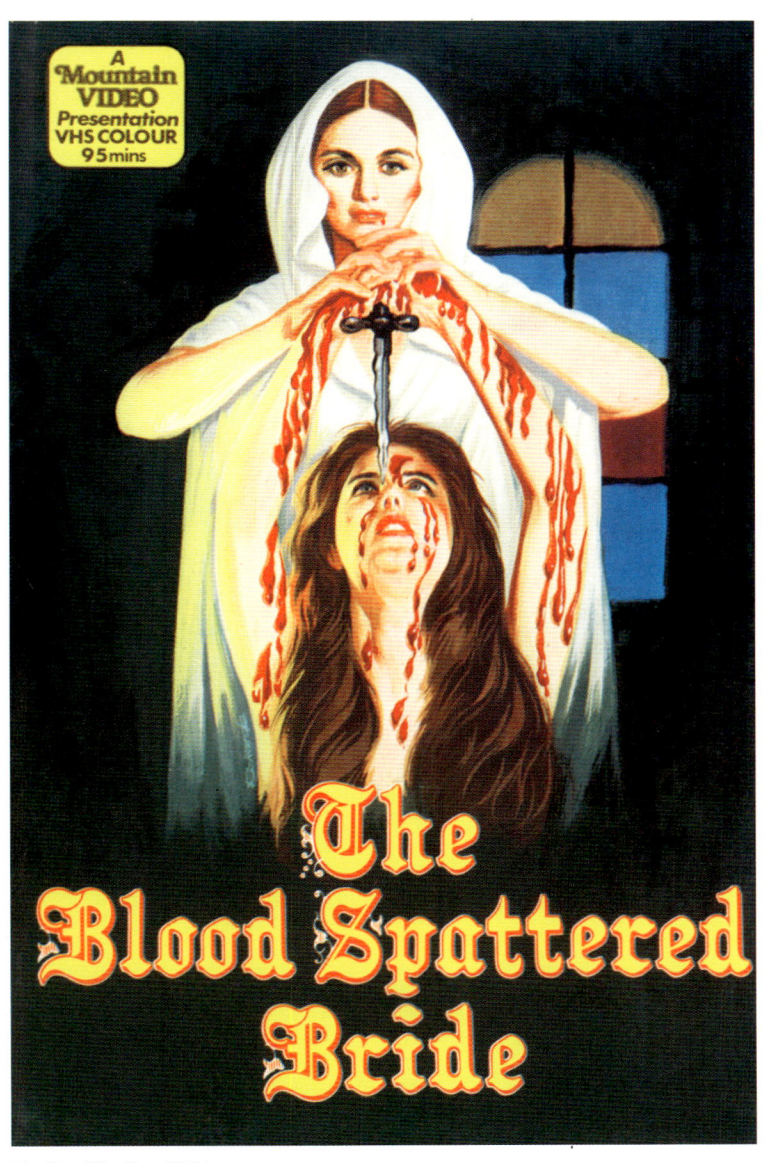

The Blood Spattered Bride
Original Title: **La Novia Ensangrentada**
Country: **Spain**
Director: **Vicente Aranda**
Year: **1972** Time: **96m 14s**
Video Label: **Mountain**

1981 onwards - Nationality

The 1981 Nationality Act redefined British citizenship thus restricting the acquisition of such citizenship.

The Blood Spattered Bride: Based on the famous Carmilla tale, this obscure and highly collectable videotape featured the cut cinema version. Even so, it appears to be more complete than most other video releases around the world.

Brotherhood of Death: This obscurity features more Vietnam vets in a fight against the Ku Klux Klan.

Cannibal: Prior to making '**Cannibal Holocaust**', Deodato made this film about a man whose plane crashes in the Amazon jungle. Taken captive by cannibals, he befriends a young girl (Me Me Lai) and with her aid, escapes. This was the cut-down cinema version, as passed 'X' by the BBFC in November 1977. It almost certainly wouldn't be granted a video certificate today due to its excessive scenes of animal cruelty.

5 THE GOOD, THE BAD AND THE VOMIT-INDUCING.

1983 - Before 'New' Labour there was the 'New' Union

Or rather the 'New Realism', a term coined by the Trades Union Congress to describe attempts to widen the appeal of the Unions following several bitter strikes and an increasingly alienated membership

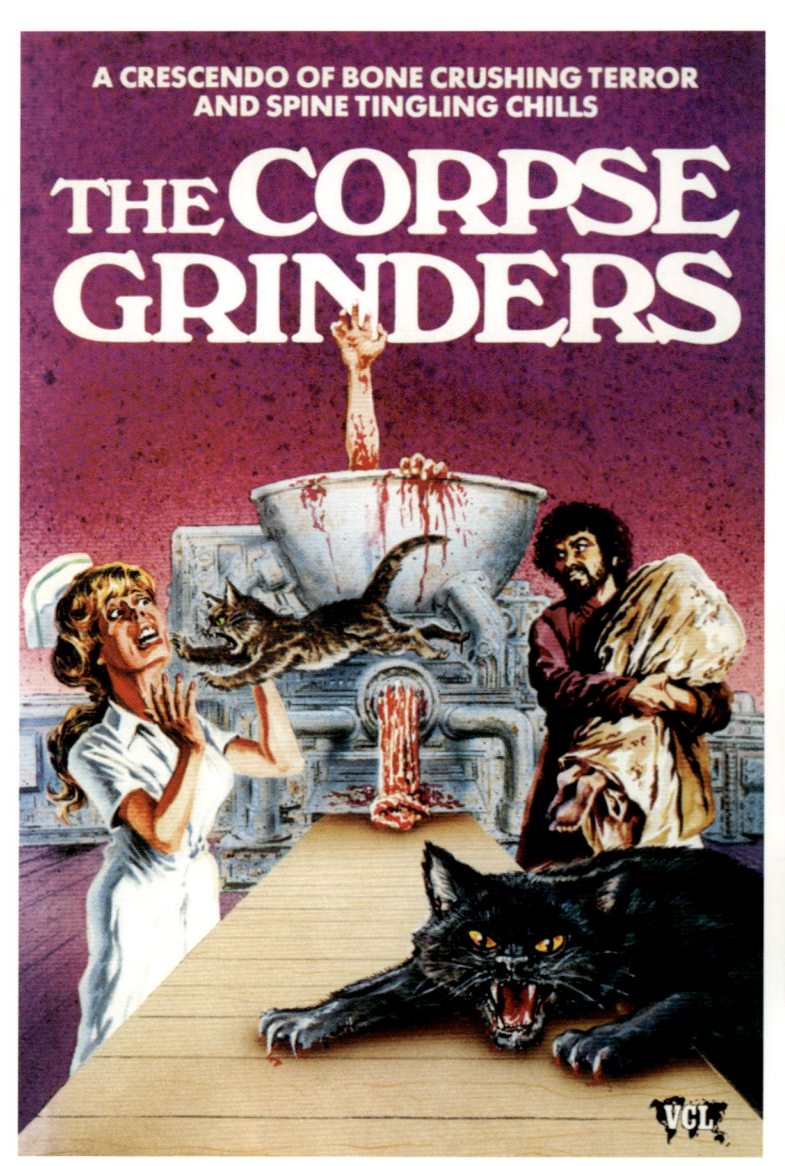

The Corpse Grinders
Country: **USA**
Director: **Ted V. Mikels**
Year: **1971**
Time: **70m 12s**
Video Label: **VCL (Video Cassette Library)**

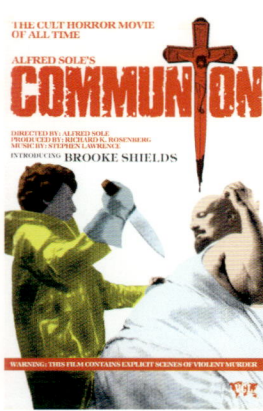

Communion
Original Title: **Alice, Sweet Alice**
Country: **USA**
Director: **Alfred Sole**
Year: **1976** Time: **102m 35s**
Video Label: **VCL (Video Cassette Library)**

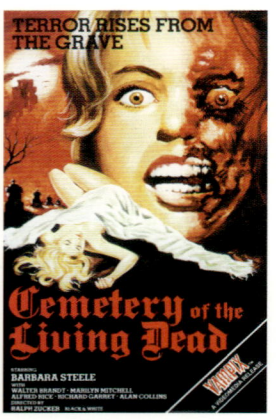

Cemetery of the Living Dead
Original Title: **Cinque tombe per un medium**
Country: **Italy**
Director: **Massimo Pupillo (as Ralph Zucker)**
Year: **1965** Time: **86m 05s**
Video Label: **Videomedia / Vampix**

Cemetery of the Living Dead: Known in the States as '**Terror Creatures from the Grave**', this is another much sought-after classic from the 'golden age of Italian horror', starring horror icon Barbara Steele.

Communion: This must-see, with Brooke Shields' second screen appearance, features a series of brutal murders which appear to be the work of a crazed young girl, in this anti-Catholic film.

The Corpse Grinders: Dodgy cat food factory workers buy human corpses from grave robbers and grind them up using a very obvious cardboard box constructed grinding machine! After developing an unhealthy taste for human flesh, the cats start to attack their owners. You have just got to see this one, which was re-released on video several years back.

102

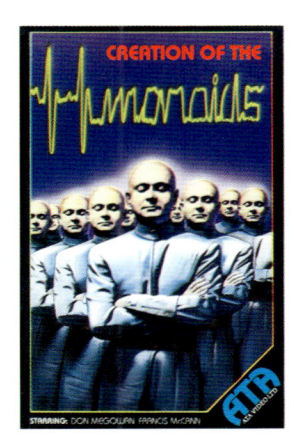

1982 - Lips

US girl group the Go-Gos have their only UK hit with 'Our Lips are Sealed'. Lead singer Belinda Carlisle later enjoys bigger success as a solo artist

The Creation of The Humanoids
Country: **USA**
Director: **Wesley E. Barry**
Year: **1960**
Time: **80m 48s**
Video Label: **ATA**

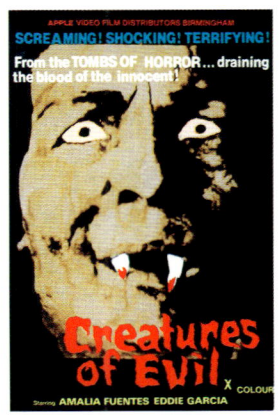

Creatures of Evil
Original Title: **Curse of the Vampires**
Country: **USA / Phillipines**
Director: **Gerardo De Leon**
Year: **1970** Time: **77m 26s**
Video Label: **Apple**

Curse of Death
Original Title: **Death Curse of Tartu**
Country: **USA**
Director: **William Grefé**
Year: **1966** Time: **81m 33s**
Video Label: **Apple**

The Creation of The Humanoids: An interesting slice of science fiction set after the third world war, this was apparently a favourite of Andy Warhol.

Creatures of Evil: Made as a sequel to '**The Blood Drinkers**', this is one of many horror films made in the Phillipines during the Seventies, and played at UK cinemas during the early Seventies.

Curse of Death: Released theatrically in the UK with an 'X' certificate as '**Death Curse of Tartu**', Florida based Grefé went on to direct the sleazy '**Impulse**', with William Shatner and the '**Jaws**' rip-off '**Jaws of Death**' in 1976.

5. THE GOOD, THE BAD AND THE VOMIT-INDUCING.

103

5. THE GOOD, THE BAD AND THE VOMIT-INDUCING.

1981 onwards - 'One of Us'

A tacit description of Conservatives who belonged to the circle in favour with Margaret Thatcher

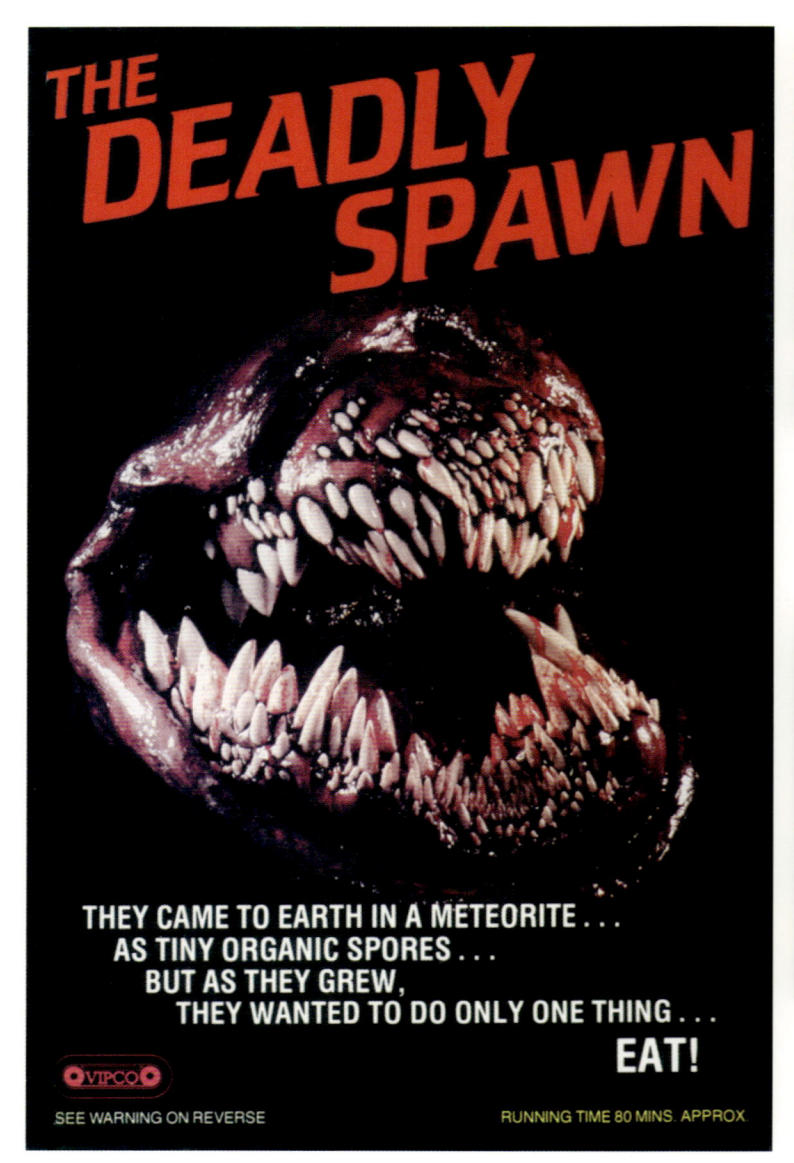

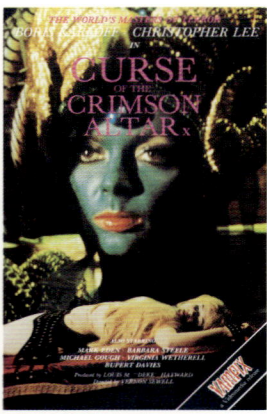

Curse of the Crimson Altar
Country: **Great Britain**
Director: **Vernon Sewell**
Year: **1968**
Time: **83m 32s**
Video Label: **Videomedia / Vampix**

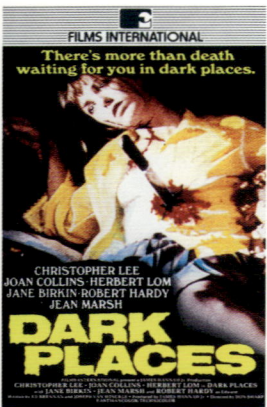

Dark Places
Country: **Great Britain**
Director: **Don Sharp**
Year: **1973**
Time: **86m 55s**
Video Label: **Films International**

The Deadly Spawn
Country: **USA**
Director: **Douglas McKeown**
Year: **1983**
Time: **78m 01s**
Video Label: **Vipco (Video Instant Picture Company Ltd)**

Curse of the Crimson Altar: An expert on the occult helps a couple escape from witches. The star-studded cast features the talents of Boris Karloff, Christopher Lee, Mark Eden and Barbara Steele.

Dark Places: Christopher Lee, Joan Collins, Herbert Lom and Jane Birkin appear in this tale about a heiress possessed by an insane killer's spirit. From a former Hammer director.

The Deadly Spawn: A great little low budgeter about some nasty looking aliens with rows of deadly sharp teeth. Passed uncut by the BBFC for a theatrical '18' certificate. Great packaging, too.

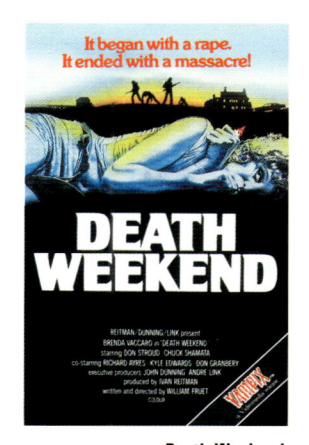

1984 - Virgins

Mega star-to-be, Madonna, has her highest chart placing to date with 'Like a Virgin'

Death Weekend
Original Title: **The House by the Lake**
Country: **Canada**
Director: **William Fruet**
Year: **1976** Time: **84m 54s**
Video Label: **Videomedia / Vampix**

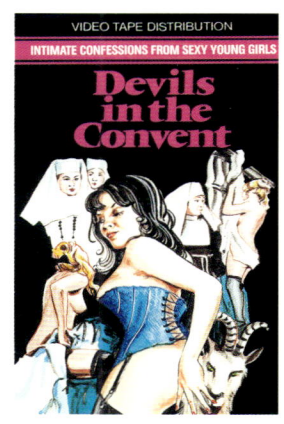

Devils in the Convent
Original Title: **Leva lo diavolo tuo dal... convento / Frau Wirtins tölle Töchterlein**
Country: **West Germany / Italy / Austria**
Director: **Françoise Legrand** Year: **1973** Time: **86m 17s**
Video Label: **Whitmoor International**

Death Row Killer
Original Title: **Enforcer from Death Row**
Country: **Phillipines**
Director: **Efren C. Piñon**
Year: **1977** Time: **80m 00s**
Video Label: **DVS**

Death Row Killer: A man is rescued from Death Row and is sent on a kung-fu mission to save the world from a deadly virus. Unbelievable trash.

Death Weekend: A couple are attacked by four vicious thugs and mayhem ensues. Fruet later made '**Spasms**' with Peter Fonda and Oliver Reed.

Devils in the Convent: Femy Benussi and Gabriele Tinti starred in this sexy nunsploitation film, released to UK cinemas as '**Knickers Ahoy**'.

THE GOOD, THE BAD AND THE VOMIT-INDUCING.

105

5. THE GOOD, THE BAD AND THE VOMIT-INDUCING.

1983 - Hungry Goths

The defining Goth/Vampire movie 'The Hunger' is released, ensuring that Bauhaus track 'Bela Lugosi's Dead' is used in every Gothy film for the next decade

Don't Answer the Phone!
Original Title: **The Hollywood Strangler**
Country: **USA**
Director: **Robert Hammer**
Year: **1979** Time: **89m 32s**
Video Label: **World of Video 2000 / Jaguar**

Die Sister, Die!
Country: **USA**
Director: **Randall Hood**
Year: **1974**
Time: **81m 00s**
Video Label: **Video Form**

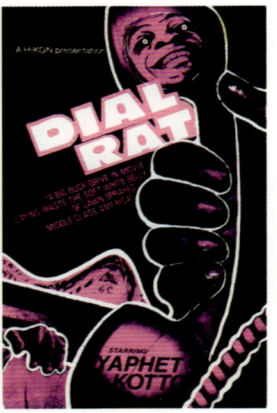

Dial Rat
Original Title: **Housewife**
Country: **USA**
Director: **Larry Cohen**
Year: **1972** Time: **87m 27s**
Video Label: **Hikon**

Dial Rat: Yaphet Kotto (Mr Big from '**Live and Let Die**') holds a married couple hostage in this release from Hikon, whose cover art designer was obviously an acid casualty.

Die Sister, Die!: A very obscure title featuring Edith Atwater, who had previously appeared in William Castle's '**Strait-Jacket**'.

Don't Answer the Phone!: This is one sick movie. A vile, fat Vietnam vet (yep, another one) is on the rampage strangling and raping his way through Hollywood's women. You'll want to take a shower after watching this, even though it's the theatrical BBFC 'X' version, as cut by 1 minute. They don't make them like this anymore...

106

Don't Open the Door
Country: **USA**
Director: **S. F. Brownrigg**
Year: **1979** Time: **81m 51s**
Video Label: **Video Form**

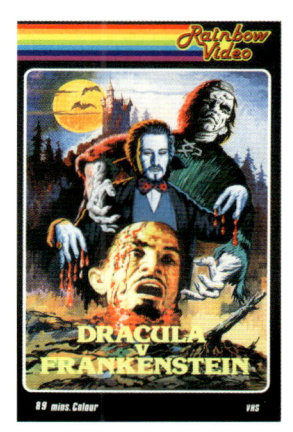

Dracula vs. Frankenstein
Country: **USA**
Director: **Al Adamson**
Year: **1971** Time: **86m 53s**
Video Label: **Rainbow**

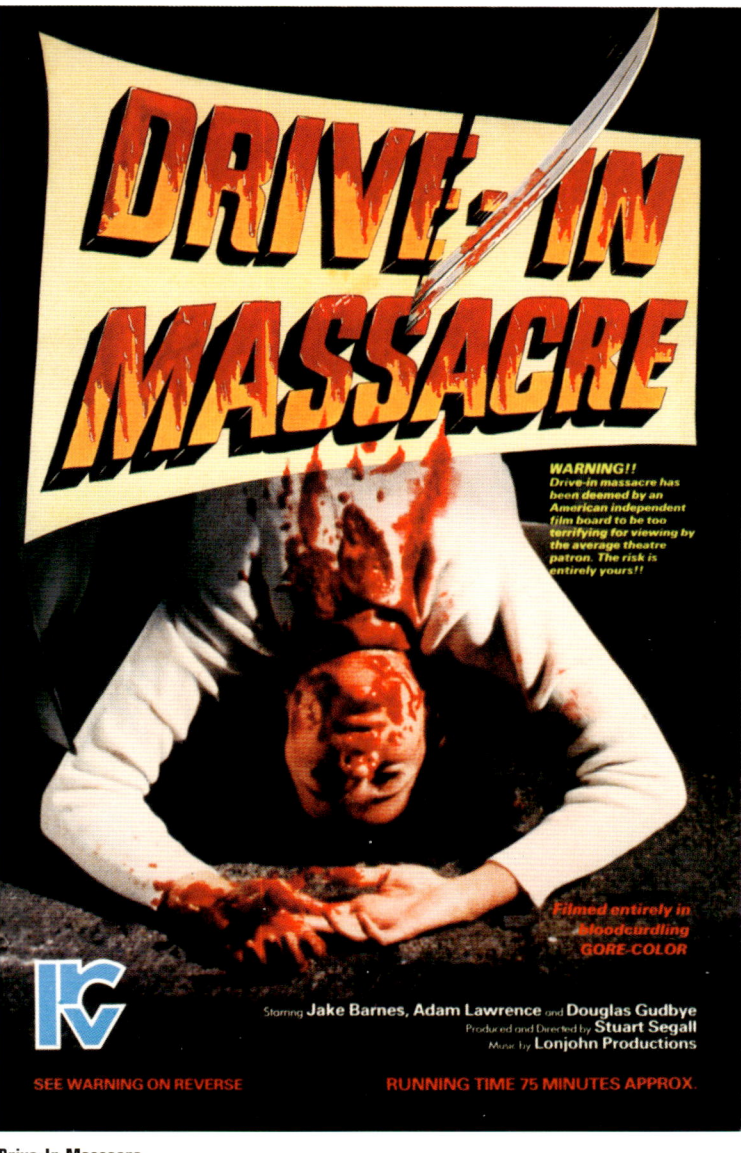

Drive-In Massacre
Country: **USA**
Director: **Stuart Segall**
Year: **1976** Time: **71m 01s**
Video Label: **LRV**

1983 - Gandhi Wins, again

Sir Richard Attenborough's film Gandhi is awarded 8 Oscars

Don't Open the Door: Another entry in the Don't series, this time from the maker of 'nasty' '**Don't Look in the Basement**'. Don't waste your time tracking this down.

Dracula vs. Frankenstein: Lon Chaney Jr stars in this z-grade mess Russ Tamblyn ('**Twin Peaks**' Dr Jacoby) also features. It was released to UK cinemas as '**Blood of Frankenstein**'.

Drive-In Massacre: More low-budget horror about two detectives investigating some gory murders at the local drive-in. It's since been re-released on sell-through, minus the graphic video art.

THE GOOD, THE BAD AND THE VOMIT-INDUCING.

107

1983 - To CD or not CD

The Compact Disc is marketed in Britain and the United States

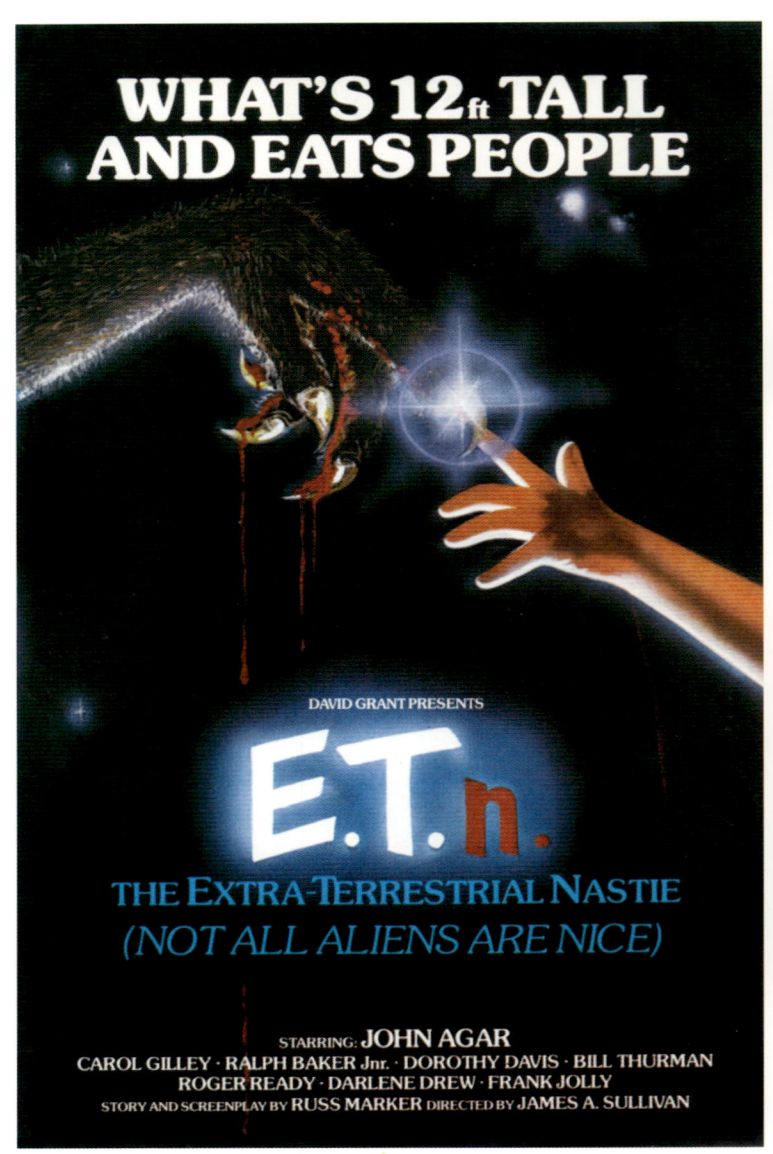

E.T.n. (The Extra Terrestrial Nastie)
Original Title: **Night Fright**
Country: **USA**
Director: **James A. Sullivan**
Year: **1965** Time: **64m 57s**
Video Label: **World of Video 2000**

Drops of Blood
Original Title: **Il mulino delle donne di pietra / Le Moulin des supplices**
Country: **Italy / France**
Director: **Giorgio Ferroni** Year: **1960** Time: **82m 02s**
Video Label: **Market**

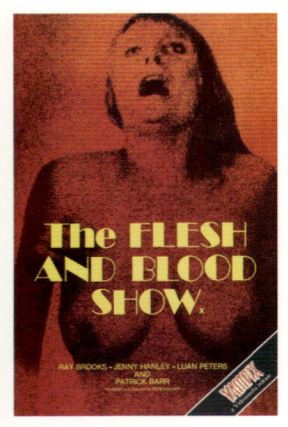

The Flesh and Blood Show
Country: **Great Britain**
Director: **Pete Walker**
Year: **1972**
Time: **91m 38s**
Video Label: **Videomedia/Vampix**

E.T.n. (The Extra Terrestrial Nastie): E.T. wasn't yet available on video (legally, anyway), the nasties scare was in full swing, so what better way to sell an otherwise unknown B-movie? It has since been re-released on tape with its original title.

Drops of Blood: Better known as '**Mill of the Stone Women**'. A scientist keeps his daughter alive with the blood of murdered women, and his statues are actually petrified corpses. From the maker of '**Night of the Devils**'. Also available on tape as '**Tales of Terror 2**'.

The Flesh and Blood Show: Robin Askwith (from the Confessions films) stars in this film about a group of actors being murdered during their rehearsals. With 3D sequences, and from the maker of '**House of Whipcord**'.

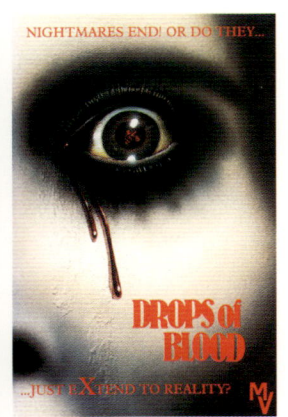

108

G.B.H. Grievous Bodily Harm
Country: **Great Britain**
Director: **David Kent-Watson**
Year: **1983**
Time: **73m 29s**
Video Label: **World of Video 2000**

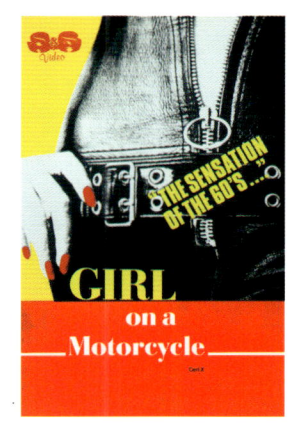

The Girl on a Motorcycle
Country: **Great Britain / France**
Director: **Jack Cardiff**
Year: **1968** Time: **87m 23s**
Video Label: **S&S**

Flesh Feast
Director: **Brad F. Grinter**
Year: **1969**
Time: **67m 31s**
Video Company: **Intercity**

1983 - I Spy

Soviet spy Anthony Blunt, the long sought 'Fourth Man' (in addition to the now infamous trio of spies Burgess, Philby and Maclean), dies.

G.B.H. Grievous Bodily Harm: An early shot-on-video obscurity filmed around Manchester. Three years later the director hired Donald Pleasence for '**Into the Darkness**'.

The Girl on a Motorcycle: Marianne Faithfull stars as a leather-clad biker visiting her lover, recounting previous erotic encounters along the way. It has since been re-released.

Flesh Feast: Veronica Lake came out of retirement to produce and appear in this mess as a mad scientist breeding maggots in order to revive dead skin tissue. Her secret patient turns out to be Hitler. From the maker of the equally inept '**Blood Freak**' and '**Devil Rider**'.

5. THE GOOD, THE BAD AND THE VOMIT-INDUCING.

109

5. THE GOOD, THE BAD AND THE VOMIT-INDUCING.

1982 - Dancing Trotters

Instrumental dance band Pigbag have their only major chart success with 'Papa's got a Brand New Pigbag'

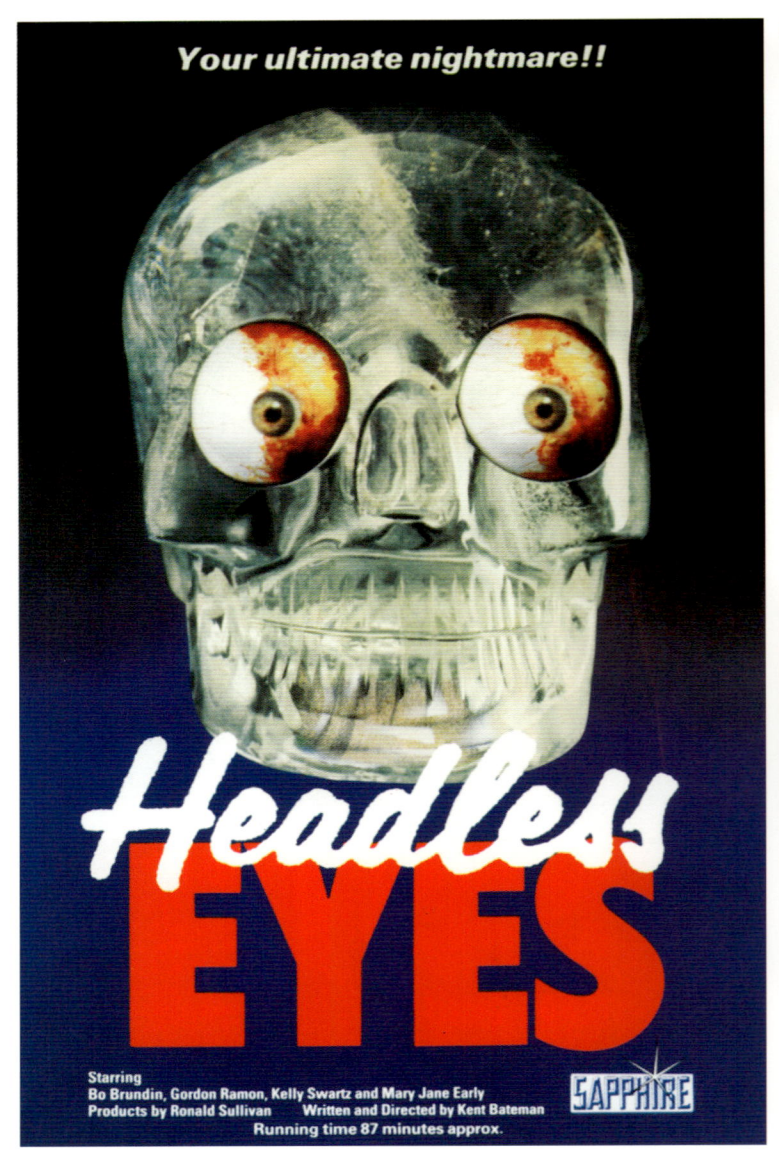

The Headless Eyes
Country: **USA**
Director: **Kent Bateman**
Year: **1971**
Time: **76m 21s**
Video Label: **Sapphire**

The Glass Ceiling
Original Title: **El techo de cristal**
Country: **Spain**
Director: **Eloy de la Iglesia**
Year: **1971** Time: **91m 20s**
Video Label: **EKO**

Grave of the Undead
Original Title: **Tomb of the Undead**
Country: **USA**
Director: **John Hayes**
Year: **1971** Time: **55m 47s**
Video Label: **KM**

The Glass Ceiling: An interesting thriller from the maker of '**The Cannibal Man**', featuring Dean Selmier from '**The Blood Spattered Bride**'.

Grave of the Undead: From the maker of '**Mama's Dirty Girls**' comes this low budget tale of executed prisoners coming back from the dead to wreak vengeance on the sadistic guards that killed them. Filmed in dead colour.

The Headless Eyes: An artist loses an eye in a case of mistaken identity and develops an unhealthy fetish for collecting the eyes of young women. You want bizarre?

1982 - RAB is R.I.P.

'Rab' Butler, the Conservative politician responsible for transforming the UK's post-war education system, dies.

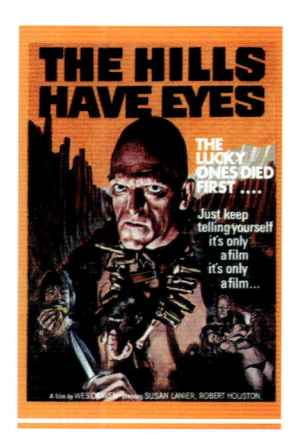

The Hills Have Eyes
Country: **USA**
Director: **Wes Craven**
Year: **1977**
Time: **85m 32s**
Video Label: **World of Video 2000 / Jaguar**

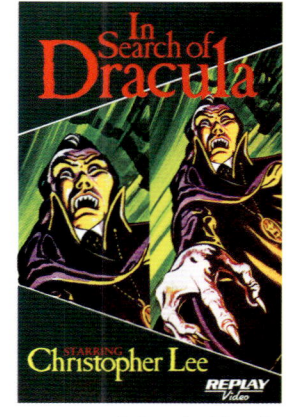

In Search of Dracula
Original Title: **Pa jekt efter Dracula?**
Country: **Sweden / USA**
Director: **Calvin Floyd**
Year: **1972** Time: **78m 12s**
Video Label: **Replay**

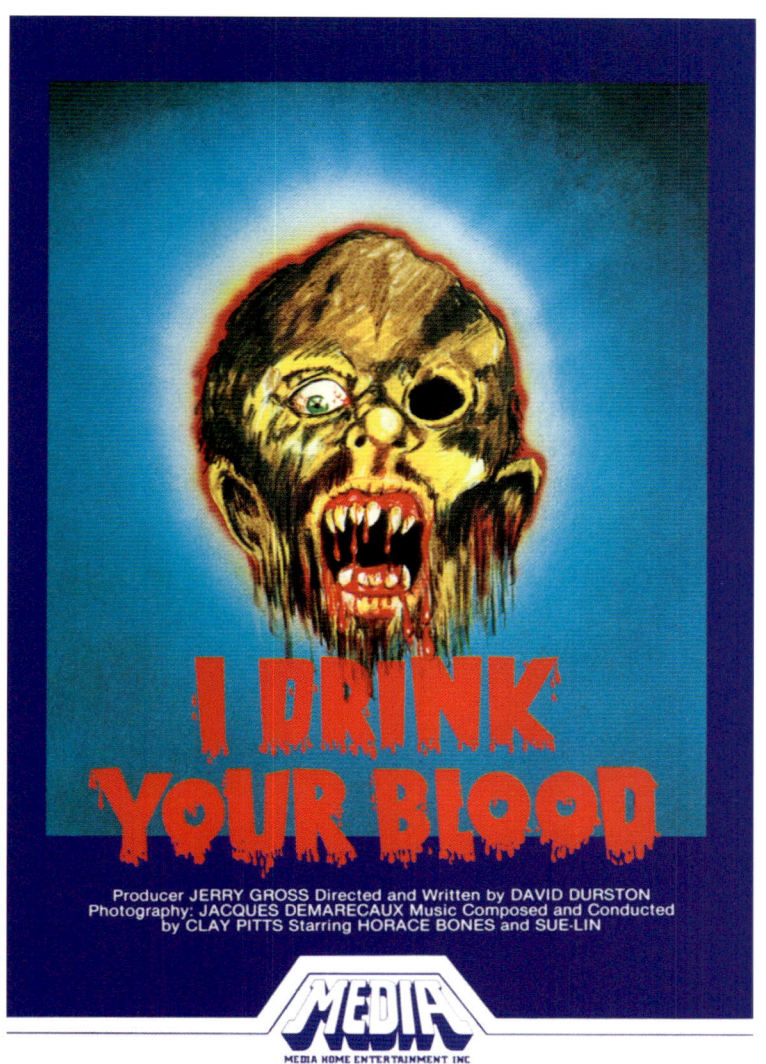

I Drink Your Blood
Country: **USA**
Director: **David Durston**
Year: **1971** Time: **77m 51s**
Video Label: **Media**

The Hills Have Eyes: After making '**Last House on the Left**', Craven directed this tale of a family of deranged inbred hillbillies. This was the trimmed 'X' rated cinema release. It has since been passed at '18' with an additional 2s cut.

I Drink Your Blood: Hippy Satanists become infected with rabies in this grisly outing. The UK release deletes an entire sequence in which a pregnant mother stabs her unborn child for fear of it being born with rabies.

In Search of Dracula: Christopher Lee narrates this rare documentary about the vampire legend, much sought after by goth video collectors.

5 . THE GOOD, THE BAD AND THE VOMIT-INDUCING.

111

1984 - Terrorism

New Legislation allowed arrest without a warrant, and detention for up to seven days, for those suspected of being involved in Terrorism

Invasion of the Blood Farmers
Country: **USA**
Director: **Ed Adlum**
Year: **1972** / Time: **73m 55s**
Video Label: **Rainbow**

Invitation to Hell + The Last Night (double bill)
Country: **Great Britain**
Director: **Michael J. Murphy**
Year: **1982** Time: **41m 28s + 50m 13s**
Video Label: **Scorpio**

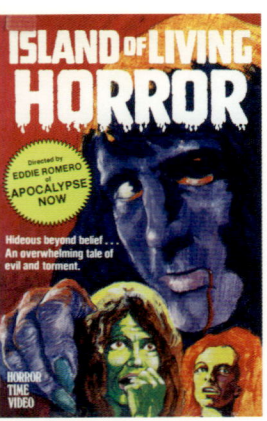

The Island of Living Horror
Original Title: **Brides of Blood**
Country: **Phillipines / USA**
Director: **Gerardo De Leon & Eddie Romero**
Year: **1968** Time: **92m 22s**
Video Label: **Horror Time**

Invasion of the Blood Farmers: People are drained of their blood in this cult low-budget effort from the man who produced '**Shriek of the Mutilated**'.

Invitation to Hell + The Last Night (double bill): Little is known about this double bill of violent, but interesting horror shorts.

The Island of Living Horror: The first in the '**Blood Island**' trilogy, with John Ashley from '**Frankenstein's Daughter**'.

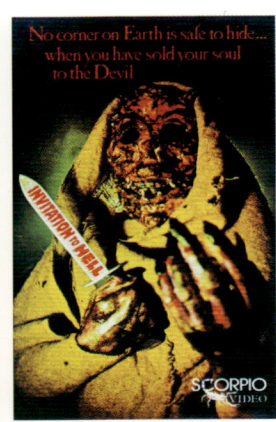

Keep My Grave Open
Country: **USA**
Director: **S. F. Brownrigg**
Year: **1975**
Time: **79m 46s**
Video Label: **Champion**

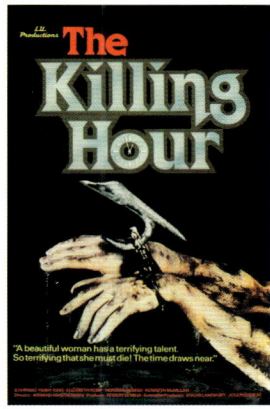

The Killing Hour
Country: **USA**
Director: **Armand Mastroianni**
Year: **1982**
Time: **92m 42s**
Video Label: **World of Video 2000**

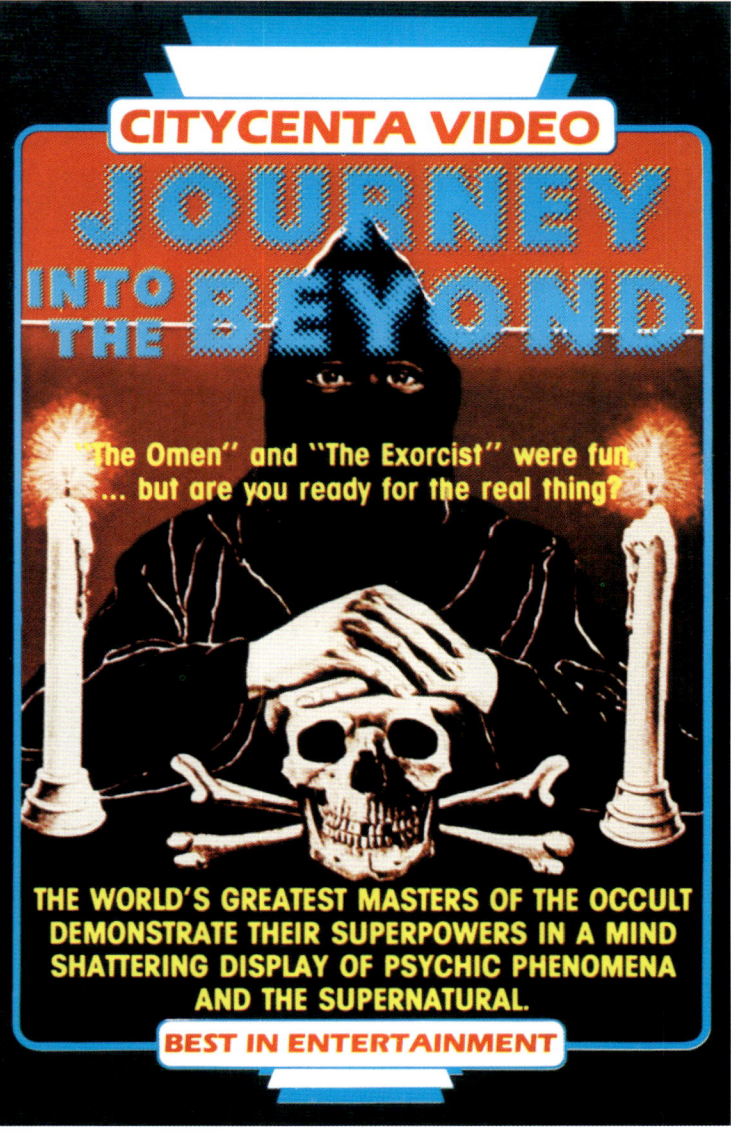

1982 - French Maids

British electro dance band Orchestral Manoeuvres in the Dark get to Number 4 with 'Maid of Orleans'

Journey into the Beyond
Original Title: **Reise ins Jenseits Die Welt des Übernatürlichen**
Country: **West Germany**
Director: **Rolf Olsen** Year: **1975** Time: **103m 52s**
Video Label: **Go / Citycenta**

Journey into the Beyond: An extremely rare 'mondo' movie from the maker of the violent thriller '**Bloody Friday**', this one features psychic surgery, voodoo and… psychic sex!

Keep My Grave Open: A lonely woman thinks that strange murders are the work of her non-existent brother. With Stephen Tobolowsky from '**Thelma and Louise**', this was re-released on video as '**The House Where Hell Froze Over**'.

The Killing Hour: A psychic woman finds that painted visions actually take place in this thriller from Mastroianni, who's now busy directing various TV series. Perry King appears, a year after appearing in the banned-on-video '**Class of 1984**'.

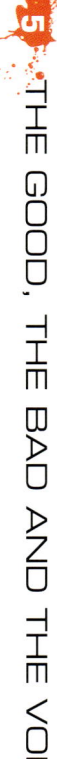

5. THE GOOD, THE BAD AND THE VOMIT-INDUCING.

1984 - Resurrected

Singer Alison Moyet has her first top ten hit since her split from Yazoo, with 'Love Resurrection'

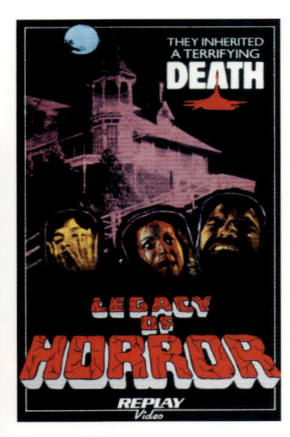

Legacy of Horror
Country: **USA**
Director: **Andy Milligan**
Year: **1978**
Time: **79m 38s**
Video Label: **Replay**

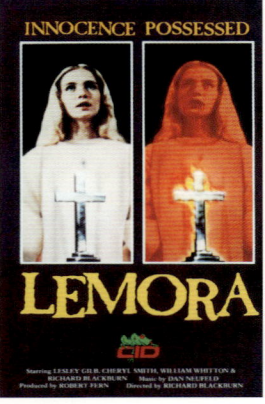

Lemora
Original Title: **Lemora: A Child's Tale of the Supernatural**
Country: **USA** Director: **Richard Blackburn**
Year: **1973** Time: **81m 22s**
Video Label: **CID (Cinema Indoors)**

Macabre
Original Title: **Macabro**
Country: **Italy**
Director: **Lamberto Bava**
Year: **1980** Time: **86m 22s**
Video Label: **Go**

Legacy of Horror: One can only wonder why Milligan chose to remake his '**The Ghastly Ones**'. This one features a gory but dull end sequence.

Lemora: A very effective twist on the vampire legend starring a teenage Cheryl (Rainbeaux) Smith. She went on to appear in the Australian sex film '**Fantasm Comes Again**', as well as Jonathan Demme's 'women in prison' classic '**Caged Heat**'.

Macabre: Bernice Stegers from '**Xtro**' plays a deranged woman who keeps the head of her former lover in the fridge! It was re-released on video as 'Frozen Terror'.

114

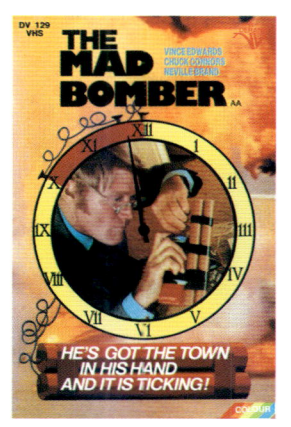

The Mad Bomber
Country: **USA**
Director: **Bert I. Gordon**
Year: **1972**
Time: **83m 51s**
Video Label: **Derann**

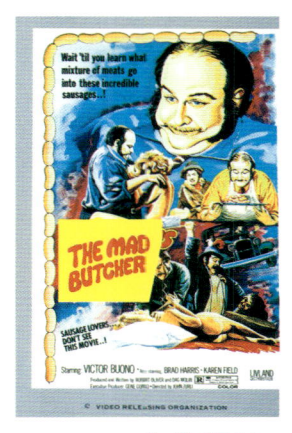

The Mad Butcher
Original Title: **Il strangolatore di Vienna / Der Würger Kommt auf Leisen Socken**
Country: **Italy / West Germany**
Director: **Guido Zurli (as John Zurli)** Year: **1971**
Time: **77m 37s** Video Label: **Video Network / DVS**

Man of Violence
Country: **Great Britain**
Director: **Pete Walker**
Year: **1969**
Time: **97m 39s**
Video Label: **Worldwide**

1984 - Hated Hatton

Deputy leader of Liverpool's Labour Council, Derek Hatton, caused outrage when the hard-left Council set illegal Rates. Labour leadership denounced Hatton as a demagogue

The Mad Bomber: This oddity features a deranged Chuck Connors as the title character, and Neville Brand as a rapist. Gordon also made '**Village of the Giants**'.

The Mad Butcher: Also released on tape here as '**Strangler of Vienna**', this silly horror comedy starred TV regular Victor Buono and Karin Field from Radley Metzger's '**The Alley Cats**'.

Man of Violence: Michael Latimer and Luan Peters star in this gritty film, made the same year as his more successful '**School for Sex**'. It was also released here on tape as '**Moon**', and was passed 'AA' by the BBFC for the cinema.

THE GOOD, THE BAD AND THE VOMIT-INDUCING.

1983 - Brinks Mat Robbery

On 17th November 3.4 tonnes of gold bullion, diamonds and platinum valued at £27,000,000 was stolen from a security depot at Heathrow Airport.

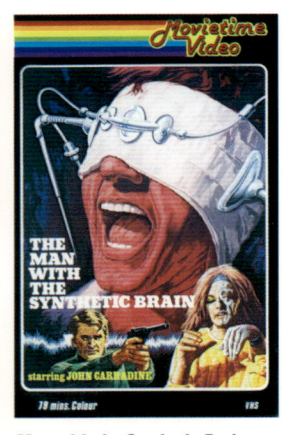

Man with the Synthetic Brain
Original Title: **Blood of Ghastly Horror**
Country: **USA**
Director: **Al Adamson**
Year: **1971** Time: **78m 23s**
Video Label: **Rainbow**

Mark of the Witch
Country: **USA**
Director: **Tom Moore**
Year: **1970**
Time: **74m 29s**
Video Label: **Lone Star**

The Mask
Original Title: **The Eyes of Hell**
Country: **Canada**
Director: **Julian Roffman**
Year: **1961** Time: **73m 10s**
Video Label: **Prestige**

Man with the Synthetic Brain: Better known Stateside as '**Blood of Ghastly Horror**', this one has to be seen to be believed. Regular, John Carradine, appears in this mess about a Vietnam vet sent to rob jewellers with an electronic gadget in his brain.

Mark of the Witch: A very low budget horror obscurity shot in Dallas. Moore's name can now be seen gracing the directorial credits of many recent TV series including '**Cheers**', '**L.A. Law**' and '**ER**'.

The Mask: An entertaining film with some incredible and nightmarish 3D sequences. Roffman went on to produce '**The Pyx**', starring Karen Black. This video release came with some great looking 3D specs.

116

Nightmare in Blood
Original Title: **The Horror Convention**
Country: **USA**
Director: **John Stanley**
Year: **1978** Time: **89m 10s**
Video Label: **Cyclo**

The Night of the Seagulls
Original Title: **La Noche de los Gaviotos**
Country: **Spain**
Director: **Amando De Ossorio**
Year: **1975** Time: **84m 47s**
Video Label: **Archer**

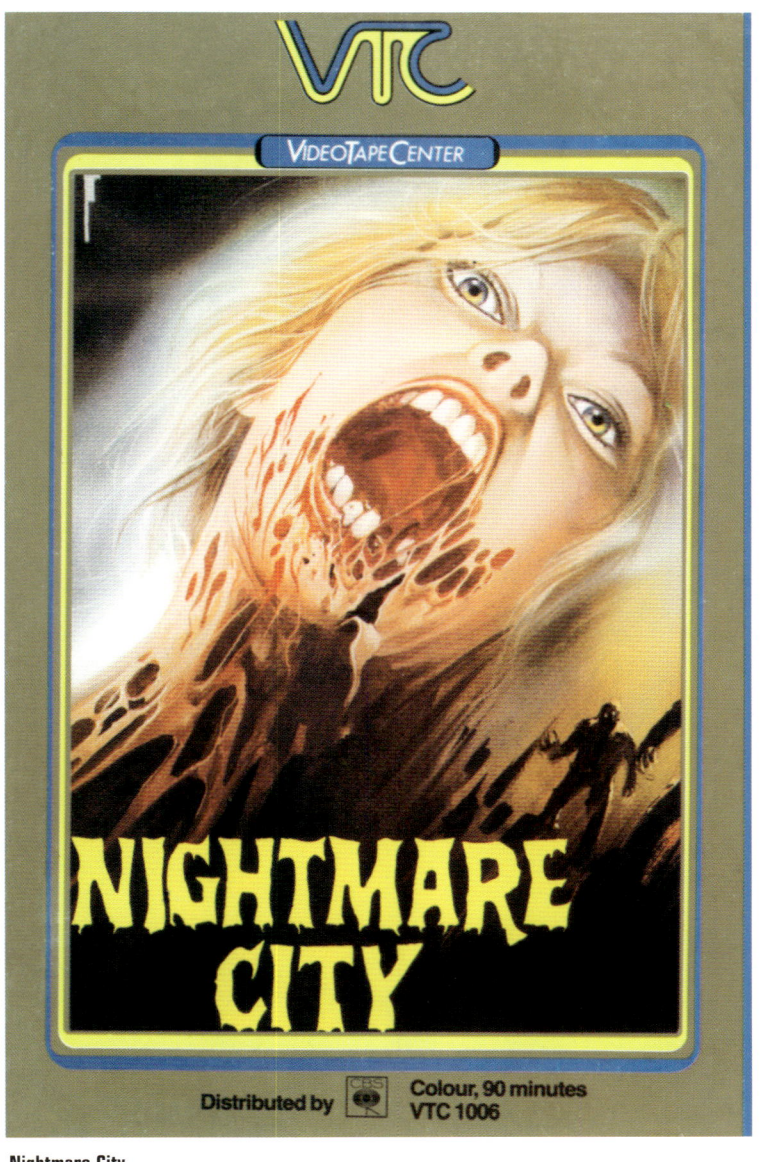

Nightmare City
Original Title: **Incubo sulla città contaminata / La Invasión de los Zombies Atomicos**
Country: **Italy / Spain** Director: **Umberto Lenzi**
Year: **1980** Time: **87m 36s**
Video Label: **VTC (Video Tape Centre)**

1983 - Council Houses up for Grabs

The Conservatives 'home owning democracy', encouraged by the 1980 Housing Act which allowed Council tenants to buy their homes, had by 1983 removed over half a million homes from the public sector.

Nightmare City: A silly but fun film in which actor Hugo Stiglitz dreams that a mysterious plane lands at the airport, with dozens of flesh-eating radiation-infected zombies aboard. A very gory film which was precut by the distributor.

Nightmare in Blood: A low budget feature about an actor who attends a meeting of his fan club, where it is revealed that he is a real vampire. A dull film which had two pre-VRA video releases, this one with gruesome video art.

The Night of the Seagulls: The fourth and final in Ossorio's excellent '**Blind Dead**' series, re-released on video as '**Don't Go Out at Night**' with 1m 6s cut for an '18' certificate.

5. THE GOOD, THE BAD AND THE VOMIT-INDUCING.

1984 - Supermac's SuperSlur

Former Conservative Prime minister, Harold Macmillan, uses his 90th birthday Earldom to pillory the Thatcher Government's privatisation policies saying it was 'selling off the family silver'.

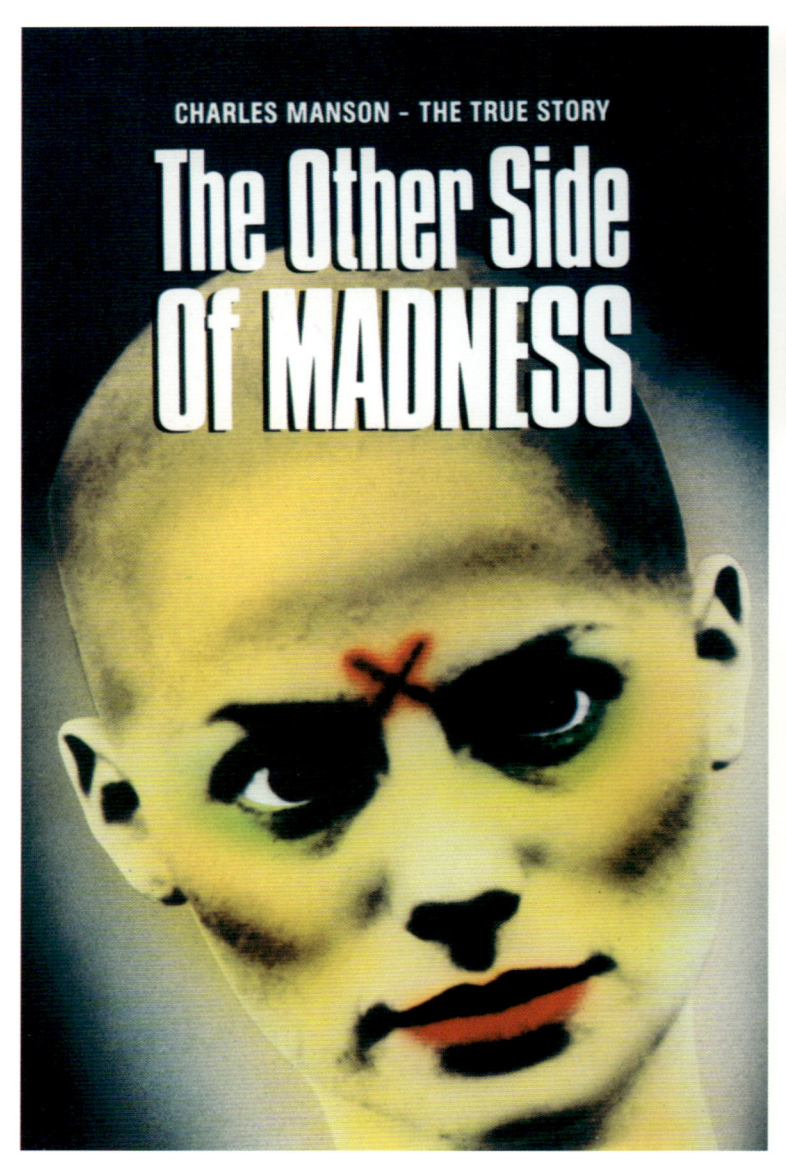

The Other Side of Madness
Country: **USA**
Director: **Frank Howard**
Year: **1970**
Time: **81m 21s**
Video Label: **Palace / Worldwide**

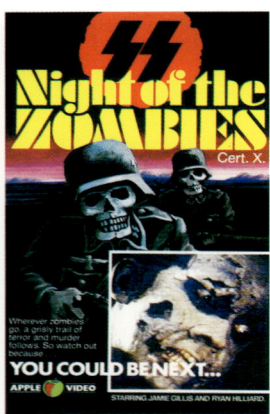

Night of the Zombies
Original Title: **Gamma 693**
Country: **USA**
Director: **Joel M. Reed**
Year: **1979** Time: **75m 08s**
Video Label: **Apple**

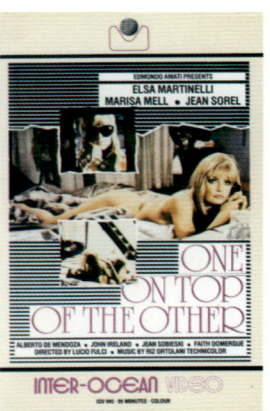

One on Top of the Other
Original Title: **Una sull'altra / Perversion Story / Una Historia Perversa**
Country: **Italy / France / Spain**
Director: **Lucio Fulci** Year: **1969** Time: **98m 47s**
Video Label: **Inter-Ocean**

Night of the Zombies: From the director of cult nasty '**Bloodsucking Freaks**' comes this awful low budget zombie film with porn star Jamie Gillis. It has since been re-released on video as '**The Chilling**'.

One on Top of the Other: After appearing in Bava's superb '**Danger: Diabolik**', actress Marisa Mell starred in this erotic drama with Jean Sorel. It was released theatrically in the UK and was slightly trimmed for an 'X' rating in 1971.

The Other Side of Madness: Based on Charles Manson and his 'family', his song 'Mechanical Man' is used as the theme tune. Shot in black and white, it was released in the States as '**The Helter Skelter Murders**'.

1982 - Fizzes at 1

Euro winners and skirt-lifters, Bucks Fizz, are at Number 1 with 'The Land of Make Believe'

Paranoia
Original Title: **Orgasmo / Une folle envie d'aimer**
Country: **Italy / France**
Director: **Umberto Lenzi**
Year: **1969** Time: **85m 10s**
Video Label: **Video Form**

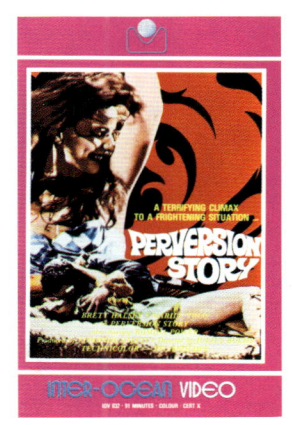

Perversion Story
Original Title: **I caldi amori di una minorenne**
Country: **Italy / Spain**
Director: **Julio Buchs**
Year: **1969** Time: **89m 34s**
Video Label: **Inter-Ocean**

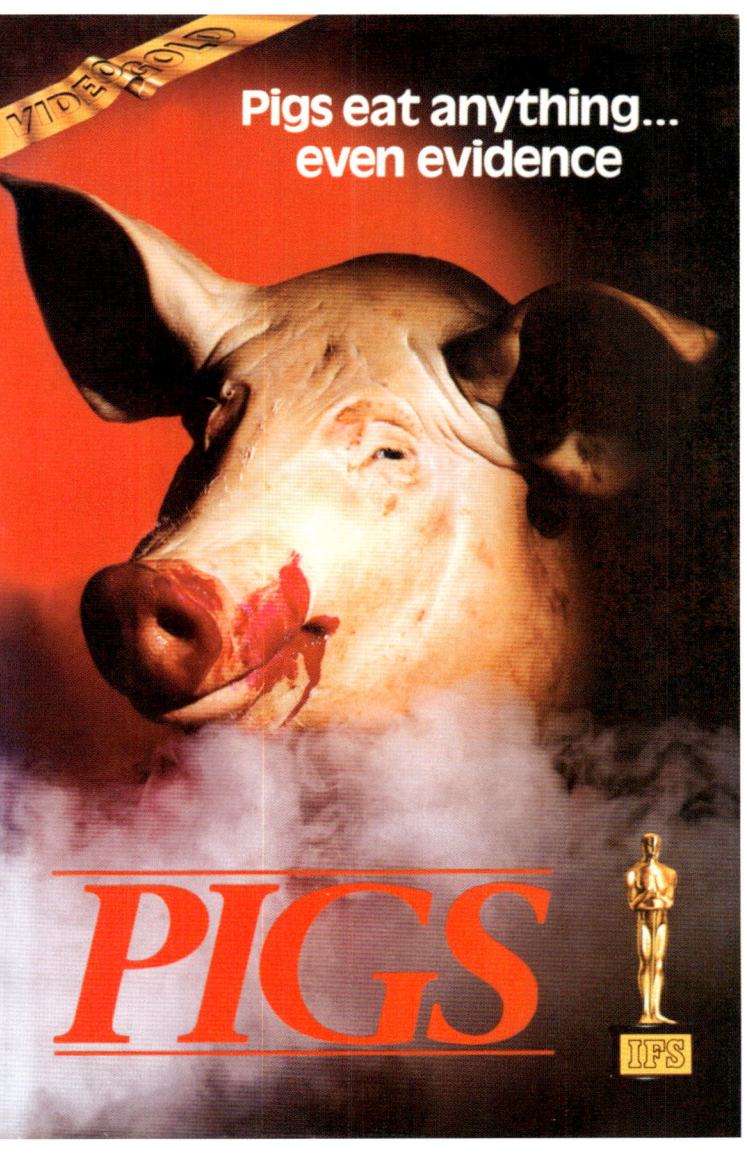

Pigs
Original Title: **Daddy's Deadly Darling**
Country: **USA**
Director: **Marc Lawrence**
Year: **1972** Time: **79m 43s**
Video Label: **IFS (Iver Film Services)**

Paranoia: '**Baby Doll**' star Carroll Baker, is a wealthy woman who is driven to drink by a handsome con-man, who prevents her from leaving her own home. Director Lenzi followed this with another erotic thriller entitled '**So Sweet... So Perverse**'.

Perversion Story: Actor Brett Halsey stars in this stylish Euro-thriller, and appeared in Mario Bava's '**Four Times that Night the same year**'.

Pigs: After appearing in a bit-part in '**Diamonds are Forever**', Lawrence directed this horror quickie about a murderous couple who feed the corpses of their victims to pigs. Four years later Lawrence turned up in '**Marathon Man**', and has gone on to appear in over 120 films to date, including '**From Dusk Till Dawn**' and '**Four-Rooms**'.

THE GOOD, THE BAD AND THE VOMIT-INDUCING.

119

1984 - Ice Dance

Jayne Torvill and Christopher Dean become World, European and Olympic ice-dance champions

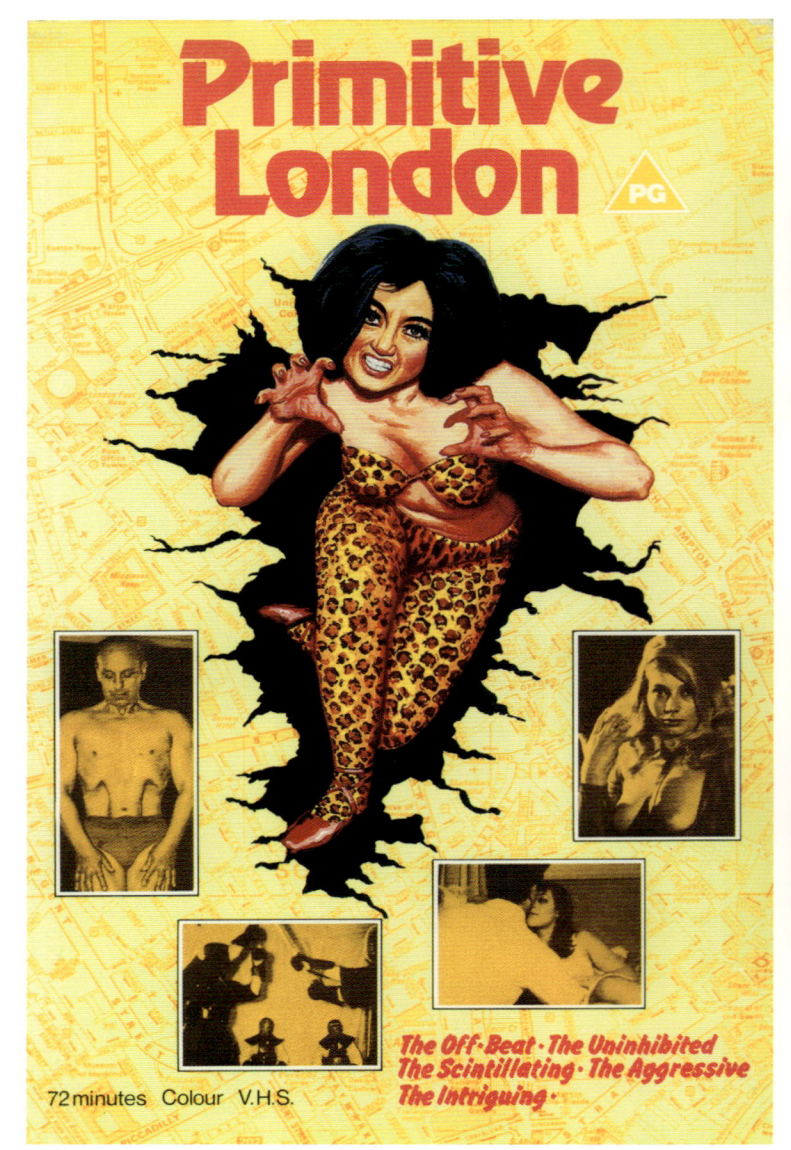

Plan 9 from Outer Space
Country: **USA**
Director: **Edward D. Wood Jr.**
Year: **1958**
Time: **78m 05s**
Video Label: **Palace**

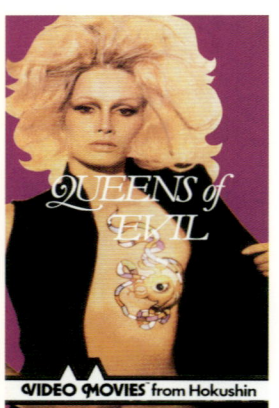

Queens of Evil
Original Title: **Le regine / Il delitto del diavolo / Les Sorcières du Bord du Lac**
Country: **Italy / France** Director: **Tonino Cervi**
Year: **1970** Time: **87m 20s**
Video Label: **Hokushin**

Primitive London
Country: **Great Britain**
Director: **Arnold Louis Miller**
Year: **1965**
Time: **73m 51s**
Video Label: **Portland / Video Revelations**

Plan 9 from Outer Space: This legendary Z-grade epic should need no introduction to those who've sat through Tim Burton's '**Ed Wood**'. Made to capitalise on the few minutes of Bela Lugosi footage shot just days before he died, this collectable release appeared on tape in May 1982.

Primitive London: A Pseudo-documentary on Britain and its youth. Child birth, Mods, Rockers, strippers, tattooed girls and Billy J. Kramer are featured. Released to UK cinemas with an 'X' rating.

Queens of Evil: Ray Lovelock plays a hippy-hedonist, who is taken in by three beautiful girls. After preaching to them about free love, he ends up not being able to live without them.

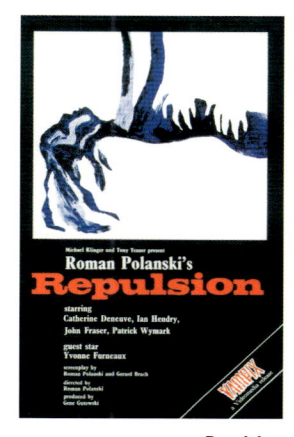

Repulsion
Country: **Great Britain**
Director: **Roman Polanski**
Year: **1965**
Time: **100m 21s**
Video Label: **Videomedia / Vampix**

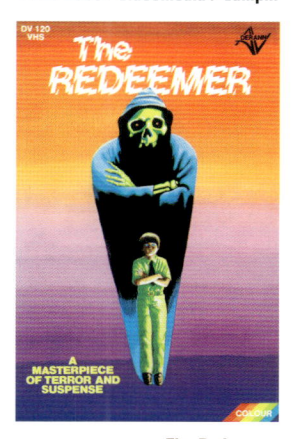

The Redeemer
Country: **USA**
Director: **Constantine S. Gochis**
Year: **1976**
Time: **79m 00s**
Video Label: **Derann**

The Sadist
Country: **USA**
Director: **James Landis**
Year: **1963**
Time: **88m 18s**
Video Label: **Hikon**

1984 - Porritt is Crowned Green

Environmentalist Jonathon Porritt becomes director of 'Friends of the Earth', a post he successfully held until 1990

The Redeemer: Another poor entry in the low budget slasher cycle, this is also known as 'Class Reunion Massacre'. Passed 'X' by the BBFC in April 1978.

Repulsion: Catherine Denueve plays a single girl repelled by men in this classic, set in London's South Kensington. Passed 'X' by the BBFC, it has since been released on sell-through.

The Sadist: Arch Hall Jr and his girlfriend hold a group of schoolteachers at gunpoint throughout this gem, forcing one to kneel down and drink from a bottle before shooting him in the head! Rejected by the BBFC in May 1964, it was later cut by 10 minutes and passed with an 'X'. This video release reproduces the original BBFC cuts list on the back. It's now available on DVD in the States.

5. THE GOOD, THE BAD AND THE VOMIT-INDUCING.

1983 - Get a Haircut

The follically enhanced Kajagoogoo get to Number 1 with the understandable in the circumstances 'Too Shy''

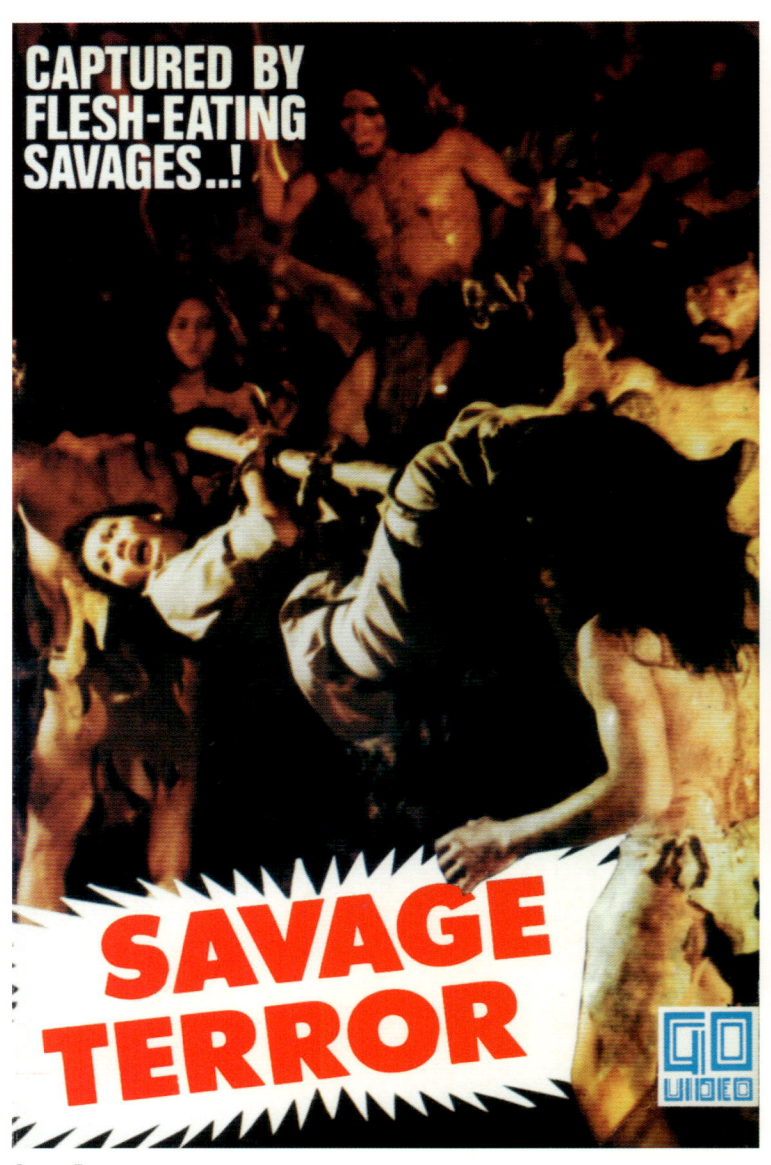

The Search for the Evil One
Country: **USA**
Director: **Joseph Kane**
Year: **1967**
Time: **78m 13s**
Video Label: **MVM (Magical Video Movies)**

The Severed Arm
Country: **USA**
Director: **Thomas S. Alderman**
Year: **1973**
Time: **85m 07s**
Video Label: **IFS (Iver Film Services)**

Savage Terror
Original Title: **Primitif**
Country: **Indonesia**
Director: **Sisworo Gautama Putra**
Year: **1979** Time: **86m 36s**
Video Label: **Go**

Savage Terror: A bizarre Indonesian copy of Cannibal, with Kraftwerk's music used for the soundtrack. Where did Go Video find their films?

The Search for the Evil One: More nonsense with the tag line 'Hitler is still alive - find him'. Forgettable and dull.

The Severed Arm: A group of students are trapped in a cave and draw lots to see who should sacrifice their arm for food. The arm is sliced off, and as luck would have it they are then freed. The rest of the group start to meet nasty deaths..This was passed 'X' by the BBFC in April 1974.

122

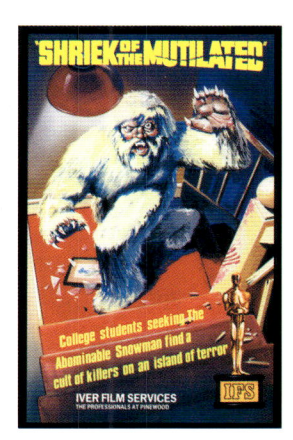

1982 - The Queen Bedded

35 year old Irishman, Michael Fagin, climbs into Buckingham Palace, pinches a bottle of wine and sits down on the Queen's bed for a bedside chat

Shriek of the Mutilated
Country: **USA**
Director: **Michael Findlay**
Year: **1974**
Time: **81m 10s**
Video Label: **IFS (Iver Film Services)**

Smashing the Crime Syndicate
Original Title: **Faker$**
Country: **USA**
Director: **Al Adamson**
Year: **1972** Time: **86m 15s**
Video Label: **KM**

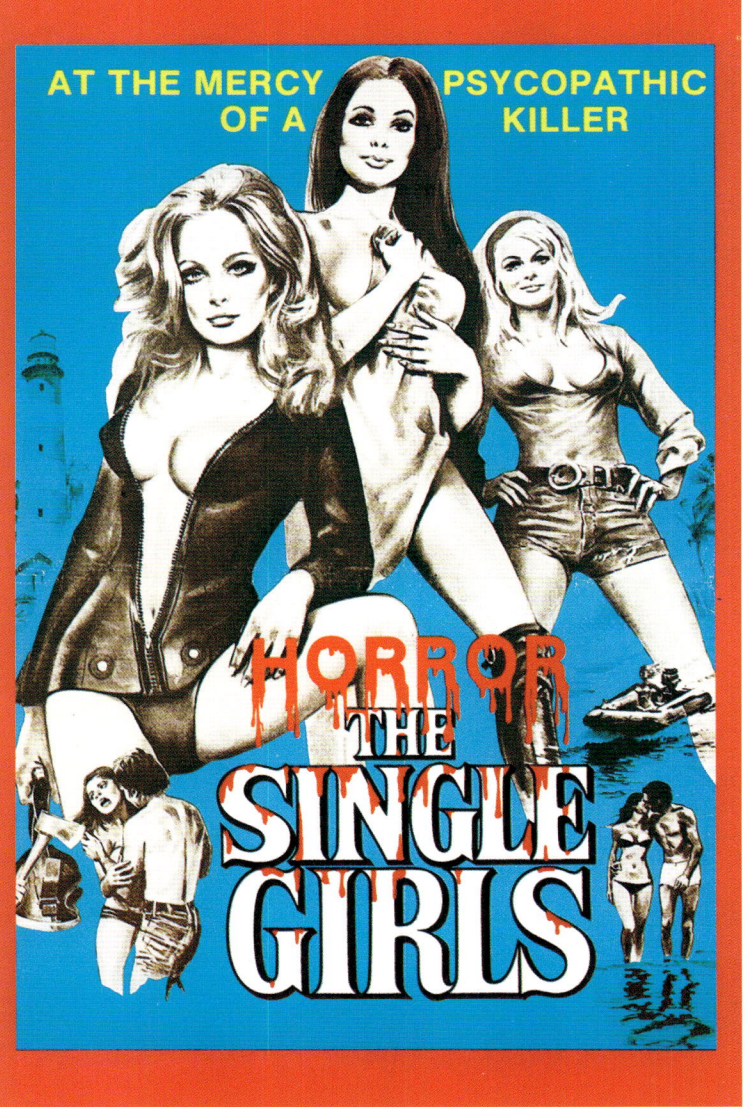

The Single Girls
Country: **USA**
Director: **Ferd & Beverly Sebastian**
Year: **1973**
Time: **73m 19s**
Video Label: **Condor**

Shriek of the Mutilated: Made just two years before Findlay's notorious '**Snuff**' comes this ridiculous film about a student's hunt for the abominable snowman. Truly awful, but what a title!

The Single Girls: After making '**Gator Bait**', the Sebastian's hired Claudia Jennings to appear with other B-movie cuties in this drive-in quickie about a psycho on the loose at a Caribbean resort. Trailered on '**The Best of Sex and Violence**', this is another of those very obscure video releases.

Smashing the Crime Syndicate: Most of Adamson's regulars turn up in this, which was re-released with added biker footage as '**Hell's Bloody Devils**'.

123

5. THE GOOD, THE BAD AND THE VOMIT-INDUCING.

1983 - Religious Riots

Following in the wake of inner city rioting, the Church of England set up an enquiry. When it reported in 1985 the Conservative Government said it was inspired by the 'extreme left' and that it was 'pure Marxist theology'.

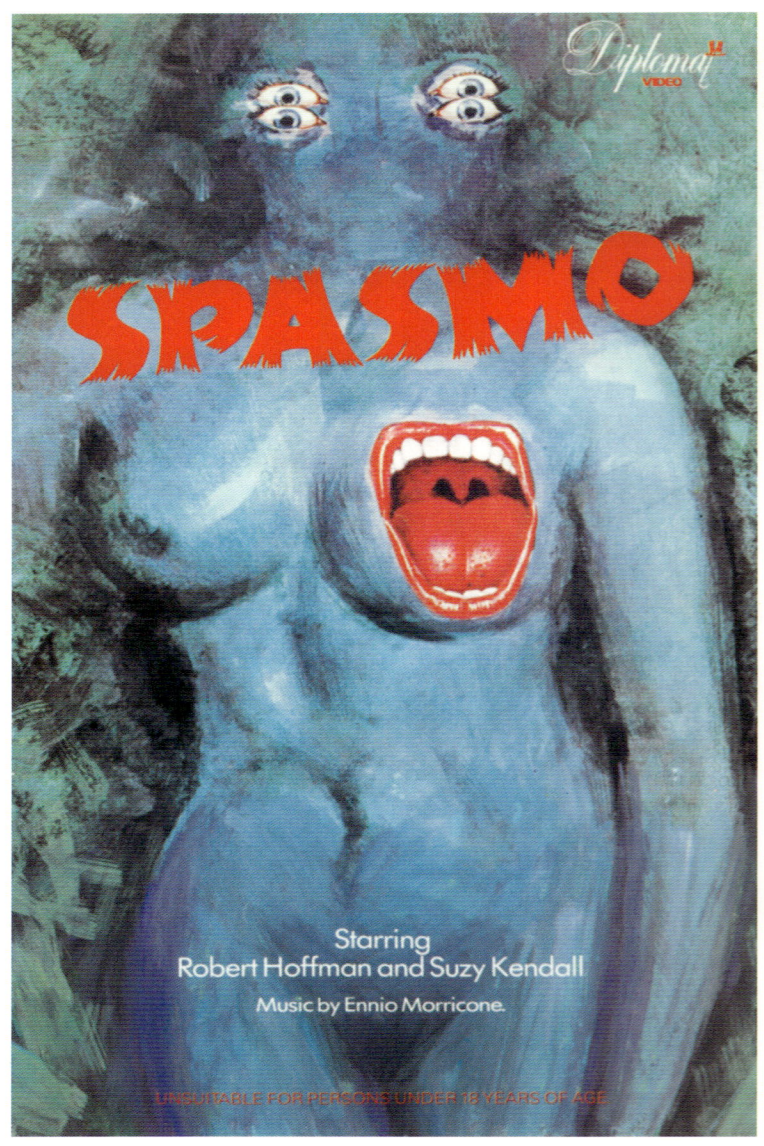

Spider Baby + Reefer Madness (double bill)
Country: **USA**
Director: **Jack Hill / Louis Gasnier**
Year: **1964 / 1936**
Time: **77m 48s + 63m 25s**
Video Label: **Hikon**

The Spook Who Sat by the Door
Country: **USA**
Director: **Ivan Dixon**
Year: **1973**
Time: **98m 21s**
Video Label: **Mountain**

Spasmo
Country: **Italy**
Director: **Umberto Lenzi**
Year: **1973**
Time: **89m 32s**
Video Label: **Diplomat**

Spasmo: From the maker of video nasty '**Cannibal Ferox**' comes this rather subdued thriller starring Suzy Kendall and Ivan Rassimov from '**Cannibal**'.

Spider Baby + Reefer Madness (double bill): Another gem from Hill, '**Spider Baby**' featured a theme tune sung by Lon Chaney. Double billed with '**Reefer Madness**', a camp classic anti-marijuana film that made anybody who saw it want to smoke pot. This release wins hands-down as featuring the UK's most bizarre video cover art.

The Spook Who Sat by the Door: Lead actor Lawrence Cook had previously appeared in Blaxploitation classic '**Cotton Comes to Harlem**'. In these politically correct times it's no surprise to learn that this film's subsequent re-releases have been re-titled '**The Keepers**' and '**Certain Heat**'.

Street Killers
Original Title: **La belva col mitra**
Country: **Italy**
Director: **Sergio Grieco**
Year: **1977** Time: **89m 56s**
Video Label: **Astra**

Sweet Kill
Country: **USA**
Director: **Curtis Hanson**
Year: **1971**
Time: **80m 56s**
Video Label: **Cyclo**

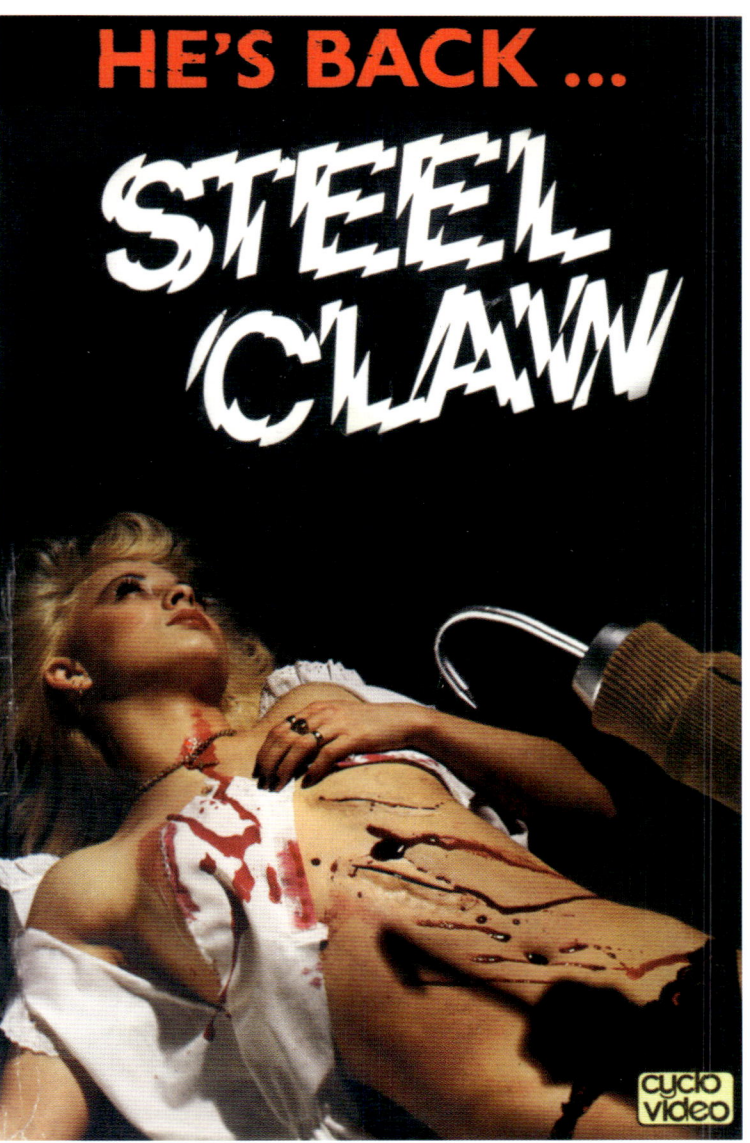

The Steel Claw
Country: **USA**
Director: **George Montgomery**
Year: **1961**
Time: **92m 32s**
Video Label: **Cyclo**

1984 - All Gas, Gaiters and Nylons

The Church of England's General Synod supports the ordination of women as deacons, but not as priests

The Steel Claw: A classic example of how low some of the distribution companies of the early Eighties could go. This dull war movie, granted an 'A' certificate by the BBFC in 1971, was packaged with graphic cover art making it look like a gore film!

Street Killers: This crime movie is better known to most die-hard fans as '**Mad Dog Murderer**'. It was glimpsed in Tarantino's '**Jackie Brown**' when being watched on TV by Bridget Fonda, who remarks that lead actor "Helmut Berger is on TV". Perhaps somebody would consider a re-release?

Sweet Kill: Tab Hunter stars in this cult psycho-sexual nasty, also known as '**The Arousers**', which was rejected outright by the BBFC in March 1973.

5. THE GOOD, THE BAD AND THE VOMIT-INDUCING.

1982 - No Go for Nalgo

In 1982 highly influential trade union, The National Association of Local Government Officers, voted to reject Labour Party affiliation.

Switchblade Sisters
Country: **USA**
Director: **Jack Hill**
Year: **1975**
Time: **86m 17s**
Video Label: **IFS (Iver Film Services)**

Ten Violent Women
Country: **USA**
Director: **Ted V. Mikels**
Year: **1979**
Time: **92m 52s**
Video Label: **Cinehollywood**

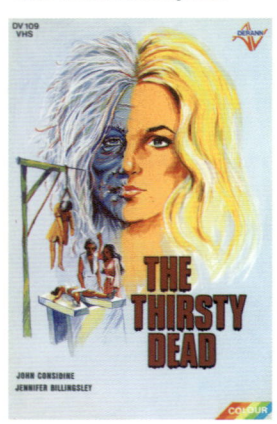

The Thirsty Dead
Country: **USA / Phillipines**
Director: **Terry Becker**
Year: **1973**
Time: **84m 12s**
Video Label: **Derann**

Switchblade Sisters: Also known as '**The Jezebels**', this was recently re-released in the States by Quentin Tarantino's Rolling Thunder Pictures. Hill also directed the Blaxploitation greats '**Coffy**' and '**Foxy Brown**', both with Pam Grier.

Ten Violent Women: After making '**The Doll Squad**', Mikels' made this low-budget not-so-sleazy women in prison film. Mikel's next was '**Angel of Vengeance**', an early addition the BBFC's 'Refused Video Classification' list.

The Thirsty Dead: Jennifer Billingsley had previously worked with Ann Margret in the biker film '**C.C. & Company**' before appearing in this terrible film. It was was re-released on UK video as '**Dream No Evil**'.

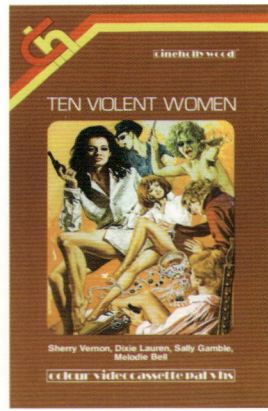

126

1984 - Hong Kong Ditched

The Sino-British agreement is made, by which Hong Kong reverts to Chinese sovereignty on 1 July 1997

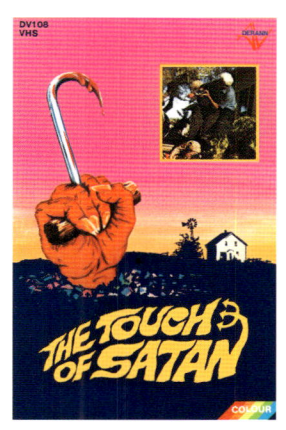

The Touch of Satan
Country: **USA**
Director: **Don Henderson**
Year: **1971**
Time: **84m 54s**
Video Label: **Derann**

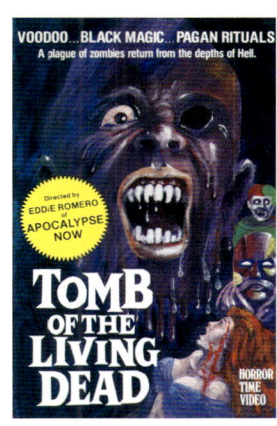

Tomb of the Living Dead
Original Title: **The Mad Doctor of Blood Island**
Country: **Phillipines / USA**
Director: **Gerardo De Leon & Eddie Romero**
Year: **1968** Time: **85m 24s**
Video Label: **Horror Time**

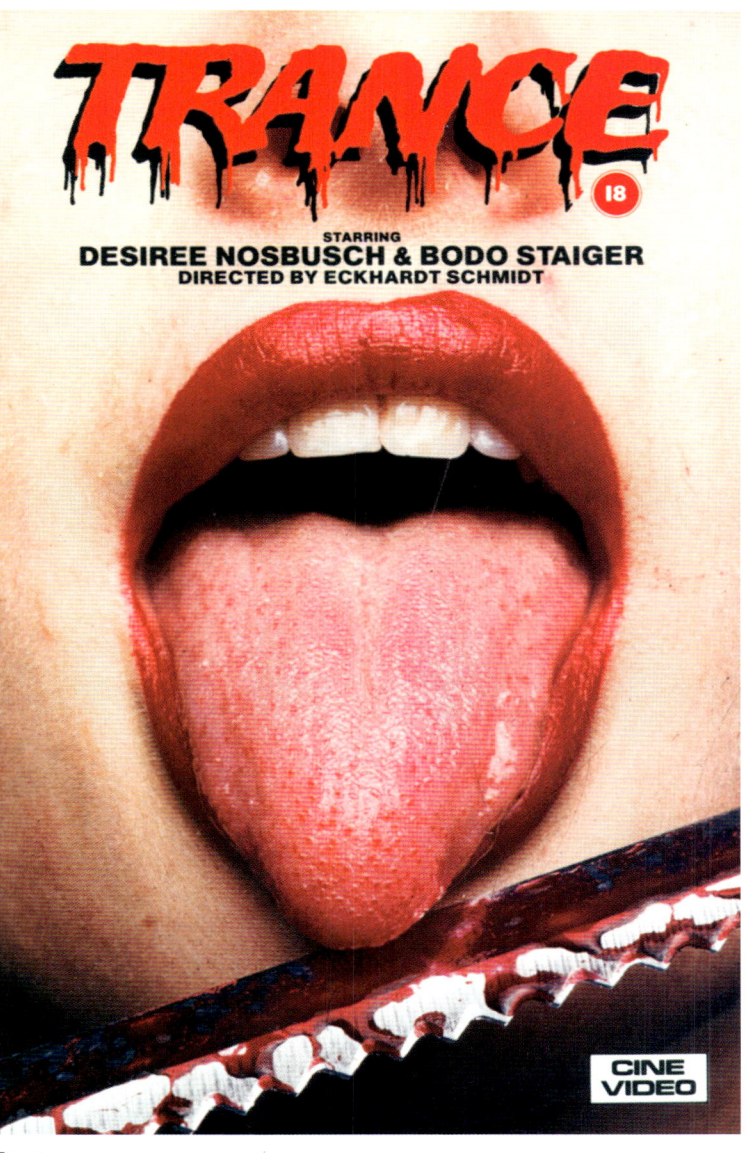

Trance
Country: **West Germany**
Director: **Eckhart Schmidt**
Year: **1981**
Time: **88m 15s**
Video Label: **Palace / Cine**

Tomb of the Living Dead: With Angelique Pettyjohn, this is another title from the Blood Island trilogy, which also included '**Tomb of the Living Dead**' and '**Beast of the Dead**'.

The Touch of Satan: This very obscure low budgeter was released theatrically in America with a 'PG' rating. Also known as '**The Touch of Melissa**', it hasn't been re-released on tape in the UK.

Trance: A Gary Numan type rock star is followed by an obsessed fan (Désirée Nosbusch), who kills him when he loses interest in her. She carves up his body, cooks and eats him!

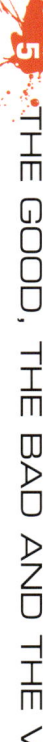

5. THE GOOD, THE BAD AND THE VOMIT-INDUCING.

1983 onwards - Little Englanders

A derogatory term adopted by pro-European Conservatives to describe their more Eurosceptic colleagues

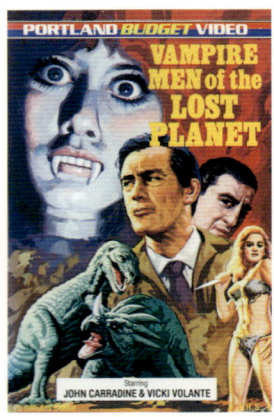

Vampire Men of the Lost Planet
Original Title: **Horror of the Blood Monsters**
Country: **USA**
Director: **Al Adamson**
Year: **1970** Time: **76m 23s**
Video Label: **Portland**

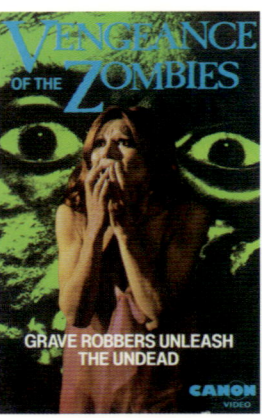

Vengeance of the Zombies
Original Title: **La Rebelión de las Muertas**
Country: **Spain**
Director: **León Klimovsky**
Year: **1972** Time: **83m 28s**
Video Label: **Canon**

Truck Stop Women
Country: **USA**
Director: **Mark L. Lester**
Year: **1973**
Time: **83m 40s**
Video Label: **Inter-Ocean**

Truck Stop Women: Claudia Jennings, later killed in a car crash, appears here as the driver of a mobile whore-house. Lester went on to direct both '**Class of 1984**', now banned on video in the UK, and its sequel, '**Class of 1999**'.

Vampire Men of the Lost Planet: Better known as '**Horror of the Blood Monsters**', this film made use of scenes from other movies, some black and white, which were colour tinted and explained as being filmed in '**Spectrum X**'. With John Carradine, who appeared in no less than half a dozen films this year alone, including as the surgeon in '**Myra Breckinridge**'!

Vengeance of the Zombies: Paul Naschy appears in this tale of a zombie army on a murder mission. Klimovsky is better known for his '**Vampire's Night Orgy**', also shot in 1972.

128

Wanted: Babysitter
Original Title: **Baby sitter un maledetto pasticcio /
La Babysitter / Das ganz größe Ding**
Country: **Italy / France / West Germany**
Director: **Rene Clement**
Year: **1975** Time: **98m 32s** Video Label: **Derann**

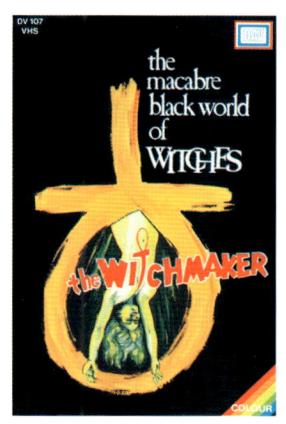

The Witchmaker
Country: **USA**
Director: **William O. Brown**
Year: **1969**
Time: **94m 50s**
Video Label: **Derann**

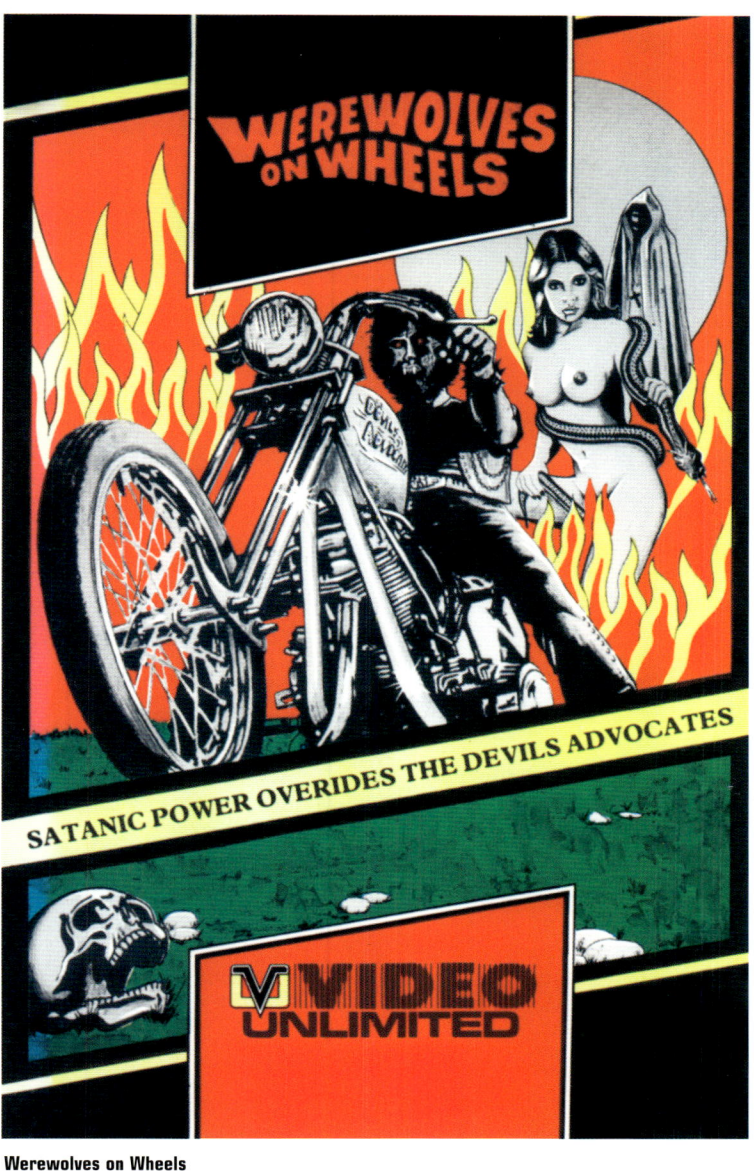

Werewolves on Wheels
Country: **USA**
Director: **Michel Levesque**
Year: **1971**
Time: **81m 51s**
Video Label: **Video Unlimited**

1983 - The Sun Sets on 'Sunny Jim'

Former Prime Minister James Callaghan retires as an MP, having previously stepped down as Party leader in November 1980.

Wanted: Babysitter: '**Last Tango is Paris**' Maria Schneider gets caught up in a plot to kidnap the child she is babysitting. Robert Vaughn also makes an appearance. Dull, but with nice cover art.

Werewolves on Wheels: '**Eve of Destruction**'s Barry McGuire appears in this low budgeter about a group of Satanists who turn two bikers into werewolves. A year later Levesque directed 'women in prison' favourite '**Sweet Sugar**'.

The Witchmaker: Actress Alvy Moore stars in this low-budget thriller where women are being murdered in the swamps. Moore went on to appear in '**A Boy and His Dog**' with Miami Vice's Don Johnson.

LISTINGS

ABACUS:
BLOOD AND GUNS
DANGEROUS HOLIDAY
FRANKENSTEIN'S CASTLE OF FREAKS
HIGH CRIME
LIFE IS BEAUTIFUL
MY NIGHTS WITH SUSAN, SANDRA...
NAUGHTY BLUE KNICKERS
ONE TWO TWO
PASSION ISLAND
PREMONITION
RIDE IN A PINK CAR
SEEDS OF EVIL
SEX SURROGATE
STRIKE BACK
THEY CALL ME HALLELUJAH
VAMPIRE HOOKERS
VICE SQUAD

ABBEY:
LOVE CAMP 7
SADIST
SUMMER SERENADE
WHERE THE BULLETS FLY

ADMIT ONE:
GLEN OR GLENDA
HORROR OF PARTY BEACH, THE
ROBOT MONSTER
TERROR OF TINY TOWN, THE

APPLE:
BLOOD DEVILS
COME MAKE LOVE WITH ME
CREATURES OF EVIL
CURSE OF DEATH
LAST CONCERT, THE
LOVER BOY
NIGHT OF TERROR
NIGHT OF THE ZOMBIES
PRIVATE LESSON, THE
PSYCHO FROM TEXAS
RED LIGHT GIRLS, THE
SWEDISH SEX CLINIC
VICTORY AT SEA

ASTRA:
ABDUCTED
ASTRO ZOMBIES, THE
BEST OF NEW YORK EROTIC FILM FESTIVAL
BEST OF SEX AND VIOLENCE, THE
BLOOD FEAST
CENTRE SPREAD
COUNTRY BLUE
ECHOES
HARRAD EXPERIMENT, THE
HONKY TONK NIGHTS
I SPIT ON YOUR GRAVE
JESUS TRIP, THE
JOAN COLLINS VIDEO SPECIAL
MICROWAVE MASSACRE
REDNECK COUNTY
RIGHT OF PASSAGE, THE
SCHLOCK
SEASON OF THE WITCH
SEIZURE

SHADES OF BLUE 1 & 2
SNUFF
STREET KILLERS
SUNSHINE RUN
THREE WISHES / FLYING HORSE
TIMESLIP
WHEN I AM KING

ASTRA / LYNX:
BOOBY TRAP
DATE WITH A KIDNAPPER
WILBUR AND THE BABY FACTORY

ATLANTIS:
8 MASTERS, THE
ALICE
BARRACUDA
BLUE SUEDE SHOES
DEAD WRONG
DEADLINE
DRAGON'S CLAWS
EAGLE FIST
FACES OF DEATH
FINAL EXECUTIONER, THE
HIDING PLACE, THE
HIT AND RUN
IN SEARCH OF A GOLDEN SKY
INCREDIBLE KUNG FU MISSION, THE
JAWS OF THE DRAGON
JONI
JULIE DARLING
NEXT OF KIN
NIGHTMARE MAKER
ODDBALLS
ONE DARK NIGHT
OPERATION GANYMED
PLATYPUS COVE
SINNER, THE
SORCERESS
TANGLEWOOD'S SECRET
TREASURES OF THE SNOW
TUXEDO WARRIOR

AVATAR:
BIG TIME
BLOOD SABBATH
BRUCE LEE SUPERSTAR
EVA
JAIL BIRDS
JOY
LOST EMPIRE, THE
LOST TRIBE, THE
MOTORHEAD - LIVE IN TORONTO
NIGHTMARE IN WAX
PIECES
PREPPIES
R.S.V.P.
SCARED TO DEATH
SCREWBALLS
STORY OF LINDA
UNHINGED
VALLEY GIRL
WACKO
WHITE TIGER
WITCHING, THE
YOUNG BRUCE LEE, THE

AVI:
ABDUCTORS, THE
ALIEN FACTOR, THE
BEYOND THE DARKNESS
BLOODRAGE
BLOODY FRIDAY
COMMANDO ATTACK
CRY OF THE BLACK WOLVES
DESERT CHASE
ESCAPE FROM CELL BLOCK 3
EVIL COME EVIL GO
GEORGE!
GINGER
GOLD TRAIN
HEADLESS EYES, THE
HELL-HOUNDS OF ALASKA
HONEYMOON HORROR
INVADERS OF THE LOST GOLD
ISLAND OF DEATH
JEKYLL EXPERIMENT, THE
LAST GLORY OF TROY, THE
LION OF THEBES, THE
MAN ON THE RUN
POLICE TRAP
RUN FOR YOUR LIFE
STRANGER FROM SHAOLIN
TIGER GANG
WHEN HEROES DIE

CANON:
BEHIND CONVENT WALLS
BLACK EMMANUELLE GOES EAST
BLUE EYES OF THE BROKEN DOLL, THE
DESERT TIGERS, THE
EXORCISM
LAURA
PRANKS
ROVER, THE
SERPENT, THE
VENGEANCE OF THE ZOMBIES
WE ARE NO ANGELS
WEREWOLF AND THE YETI, THE
WHEN MEN CARRIED CLUBS...

CHAMPION:
BANDITS, THE
CHESTY ANDERSON - U.S. NAVY
DEATH JOURNEY
DEMON LOVER, THE
DIARY OF A SINNER
FLORIDA CONNECTION, THE
KEEP MY GRAVE OPEN
KILLING KIND, THE
MEAN JOHNNY BARROWS
NEW SEEKERS IN CONCERT
NO WAY BACK
ONCE UPON A FABLE
ROAD TO BALI
SEEDS OF EVIL, THE

CINEHOLLYWOOD:
28 MINUTES FOR THREE MILLION DOLLARS
ACQUASANTA JOE
ADOLF HITLER - BENITO MUSSOLINI
BEHIND CONVENT WALLS
BLACK GOLD

BLACK HAND, THE
BORN WINNER
BOSS, THE
CALIBRE NINE
CANNIBALS
CINDY'S LOVE GAMES
COLORADO CHARLIE
COLT CONCERT
CRAZY WORLD OF CARS
CRY BLOOD APACHE
DANGER IS MY BUSINESS
DAY OF VIOLENCE
DEADLY CHASE
DEATHDREAM
DEVIL HUNTER
GANGSTERS
GODMOTHERS, THE
GOLDEN TRIANGLE, THE
GROUND ZERO
HISTORY OF AVIATION, THE
HISTORY OF THE CONQUEST OF SPACE, THE
HOW TO KILL 400 DUPONTS
JOSEPH STALIN - LEON TROTZKIJ
KLEINHOFF HOTEL
LAST GUN, THE
LAST OF THE MOHICANS, THE
LAST STONE AGE TRIBES, THE
LEFT HAND OF THE LAW, THE
LOADED GUNS
LONERS, THE
MAGIC OF THE SEA, THE
MAN HUNT
MESSIAH OF EVIL
MIDNIGHT BLUE
MY NAME IS MALLORY
MY YOUNG MAN
NIGHT TRAIN MURDERS
NORTHEAST OF SEOUL
OCEAN WORLD
ONLY WAY TO SPY, THE
OUR ANIMALS
PERFECT CRIME, THE
PIGMIES OF THE RAIN FOREST, THE
PLACE IN HELL, A
PRICE OF DEATH, THE
PUBLIC ENEMY
RINGO'S WORLD
RITUALS
RULERS OF THE CITY
RUN, MAN RUN
SAFARI RALLY
SAHARA CROSS
SERGEANT KLEMS
SILENCE THE WITNESS
SO SWEET SO DEAD
SPECIAL TRAIN FOR HITLER
TEE TO GREEN
TEN VIOLENT WOMEN
TERROR
TO BE TWENTY
VERY CLOSE ENCOUNTERS OF THE 4TH KIND
VIRGIN OF BALI, THE
WALLS OF SIN
WEREWOLF WOMAN
WINSTON CHURCHILL - CHARLES DE GAULLE
WORLD IN FLAMES, THE : PART 1 - 3

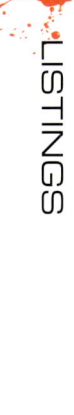

LISTINGS

LISTINGS

ZEBRA FORCE, THE
ZORRO AND THE THREE MUSKETEERS
ZORRO AT THE SPANISH COURT
NO WAY
WILD , HUNGRY, AND FREE

DERANN:
1001 NIGHTS
40 MILLION BUCKS ON A DEAD MAN'S...
ADVENTURES OF CURLEY AND HIS GANG, THE
ADVENTURES OF THE BENGAL LANCERS
ALL MINE TO GIVE
ALLEY CAT, THE
ANDREA, THE NYMPHO
ANTS - PANIC AT LAKEWOOD MANOR
ASSASSIN, THE
BARRACUDA
BATTLE OF OKINAWA
BATTLE OF THE JAPAN SEA
BEDTIME STORIES FOR GROWNUPS
BEIRUT FORMULA
BIG FOOT
BISEXUAL
BLACK EAGLES OF SANTA FE
BLACK EMMANUELLE WHITE EMMANUELLE
BLACK RUBY
BLOODLUST
BLUE BELLE
BOMB AT 10:10
BRUCE LEE - THE MAN, THE MYTH
BRUTES AND SAVAGES
CANNIBAL
CARAVAN TO VACCARES
CAT IN THE CAGE
CAVE OF DIAMONDS
COMEBACK, THE
CON ARTIST, THE
COUNTDOWN TO DOOMSDAY
COVERT ACTION
CRAZED
CYCLONE
DEEP RIVER SAVAGES
DEEP SIX, THE
DEVILS OF DARKNESS
DIE SCREAMING MARIANNE
DJANGO
DOGS, THE
DON'T LOOK IN THE BASEMENT
DRUMMER OF VENGEANCE
EROTIC ADVENTURES OF ZORRO, THE
FIEND, THE
FIND A PLACE TO DIE
FOUR DIMENSIONS OF GRETA
FRANKENSTEIN ISLAND
FRAULEINS IN UNIFORM
FREELANCE
FRIGHTMARE
GAPPA THE TRIPHIBIAN MONSTER
GIRL CALLED JULES, A
GIRL GO-ROUND, THE
GREAT WALL
GROUND ZERO
HANDFULL OF HEROES, A
HAUNTS
HAVE A NICE WEEKEND!
HELL IS EMPTY
HERCULES AGAINST THE SONS OF THE SUN
HOT HONG KONG HARBOR
HOUSE OF SEVEN CORPSES, THE
HOUSE OF THE DAMNED
HOUSE OF WHIPCORD
HOW TO PLAY THE SEDUCTION GAME
ISLAND OF TERROR
ITALIAN STALLION, THE
JOURNEY TO THE CENTRE OF TIME
KILLER PANTHER, THE
LAST TRAIN TO BERLIN
LEOPARD IN THE SNOW
LET ME DIE A WOMAN
LET'S MAKE A DIRTY MOVIE
LICENSED TO KILL
MAD BOMBER, THE
MALIBU HOT SUMMER
MANAOS
MARDI GRAS MASSACRE
MASSACRE AT MARBLE CITY
MONSTERS FROM AN UNKNOWN PLANET
MUTINY IN THE SOUTH SEAS
MY FAVOURITE BRUNETTE
NEW YORK AFTER MIDNIGHT
NIGHT OF THE BIG HEAT
NIGHTMARE COUNTY
NINE AGES OF NAKEDNESS, THE
NORTHEAST OF SEOUL
ONE-EYED SOLDIERS, THE
ORDERS ARE ORDERS
PILOT, THE
PIRATES OF THE MISSISSIPPI
PRICKLY PROBLEMS
PSYCHOPATH
RACKETEER
RAGAN
REDEEMER, THE
RELUCTANT VIRGIN, THE
RICCO
ROCK, ROCK, ROCK
ROGER RAMJET
RUNAWAY GIRLS
SAVAGE ENCOUNTER
SCAVENGERS, THE
SCHOOLGIRL REPORT NO. 11
SEX CONNECTION, THE
SEXY DOZEN, THE
SKIN DEEP
SKY IS FALLING, THE /THE SKY IS FALLING, THE
SPACE CRUISER
STACEY
STACEY
STARBIRDS
STUNTS - THE DEADLY GAME
SUPERMEN
SWEDISH CONFESSIONS
SWINGING CO-EDS
TALES OF MAGIC
TANGERINE MAN, THE
TARANTULAS - THE DEADLY CARGO
TARGET EAGLE
TEN FINGERS OF STEEL
TERROR OUT OF THE SKY
THIRSTY DEAD, THE
THREE WAY SPLIT
TIFFANY JONES
TIGER OF THE SEVEN SEAS
TOUCH OF SATAN, THE
TRADER HORNEE
TREASURE OF JAMAICA REEF, THE
TWO FACES OF FEAR
UNHOLY WIFE, THE
VENGEANCE OF THE BARBARIANS
VERBOTEN!
WANTED: BABYSITTER
WAR OF THE MONSTERS
WHEN GIRLS UNDRESS
WHITE CARGO FROM HONG KONG
WITCHMAKER, THE
WOODEN HORSE OF TROY, THE
WORLD FAMOUS FAIRY TALES

DUPLIVISION:
BELL OF HELL, THE
GIVE ME A RING SOMETIME
GO GIRL
GRAD NIGHT
LONG RETURNING, A
PARTNER, THE
SAY HELLO TO YESTERDAY

EKO:
BOSS, THE
CRY BLOOD, APACHE
DAWN OF THE PIRATES
DEATH IN HAITI
GLASS CEILING, THE
HAWK OF THE CARIBBEAN, THE
KINGS OF FRANCE
LAST OF THE MOHICANS, THE
LOADED GUNS
MIDNIGHT BLUE
PRICE OF DEATH, THE
SERGEANT KLEMS
TICKET TO DIE, A
TREASURE OF BENGAL
WEB OF DECEPTION
ZORRO AND THE THREE MUSKETEERS

EVC:
AFRICA SCREAMS
AT WAR WITH THE ARMY
BAMBOO BROTHERHOOD, THE
BOGUS BANDITS
CANNIBALS, THE
CHILDREN'S CINEMA
CHINESE MECHANIC
CONCORDE AFFAIR
DEATH PROMISE
DRAGON'S EXECUTIONER, THE
ELVIS LIVE FROM HAWAII
FLYING SUPERBOY, THE
GEORGE!
GREAT GUY
HEART OF A FATHER
HEROES OF THE REGIMENT
HOPPITY GOES TO TOWN
HOSTAGES
HOUSE OF THE LOST GIRLS, THE
KEOMA
KINDERBOIS
KISS ME KILLER
LIFE AND TIMES OF GRIZZLY ADAMS, THE
LIFE WITH FATHER
LITTLE LAURA AND BIG JOHN
LITTLE RASCALS
LUCIFER COMPLEX, THE
MAGIC SWORD, THE
MANDARIN MAGICIAN, THE
NIGHT THEY ROBBED BIG BERTHA'S, THE
NORTH COUNTRY
NORTHEAST OF SEOUL
PERILS OF PAULINE, THE
POPEYE AND SUPERMAN
PUMAMAN, THE
REGGAE SUNSPLASH
SICILIAN CROSS
SPECIAL TRAIN FOR HITLER
STAR IS BORN, A
STAR TREK - THE MENAGERIE
SWITCH, THE
TARGET
THAT MAN FROM CHICAGO
UNDER CALIFORNIA SKIES
UTOPIA
VELVET SMOOTH
WATERSHIP DOWN
WOMAN'S PARADISE OR HELL
WOMEN OF THE PREHISTORIC PLANET

FLETCHER:
4 BILLION IN 4 MINUTES
7 WINCHESTERS FOR A MASSACRE
AND GIVE US OUR DAILY SEX
ANONYMOUS AVENGER
ATTILA
BANDIDOS
BELLE STARR STORY, THE
BLACK DECAMERON, THE
BLACK EMANUELLE NO.2
BLUE EYED BANDIT, THE
CANDID CAMERA CLASSICS 1 & 2
CEMETERY WITHOUT CROSSES
CHARLESTON
 BUNYAN
CORBARI
CRAZY CRAZY LOVE
CYNIC, THE RAT AND THE FIST, THE
DAY OF THE COBRA
DAYS OF WRATH
DEADLY INHERITANCE
DEATH OF THE MAFIA
DEEP RED
DENNY LAINE - HELPING HAND (GUITAR)
DESERT COMMANDO
DEVIL WITH SEVEN FACES, THE
DIARY OF PASSION
DIRTY DAM BUSTERS, THE (CHURCHILL'S LEOPARDS)
DIRTY GANG
DJANGO, KILL !
DJANGO'S CUT PRICE CORPSES
EL MACHO
EMERGENCY SQUAD
EXECUTIONER OF THE HIGH SEAS, THE
FACE TO FACE

LISTINGS

FAREWELL AFRICA
FIGHTING FISTS OF SHANGAI JOE, THE
FOUR FOR ALL
GO MAN GO !
GOD FORGIVES - I DON'T
GOODBYE CRUEL WORLD
GREAT ALLIGATOR, THE
GUNMAN'S HANDS
HELL COMMANDOES
HONDO
I'LL DIE FOR VENGEANCE
IDENTIKIT
INSPECTOR GENERAL, THE
KARAMURAT
KILLER NUN, THE
KILLER'S GOLD
LAST CHANCE, THE
LAST REBEL, THE
LAST ROUND, THE
LONG NIGHT OF VERONIQUE, THE
LOVER OF THE GREAT BEAR, THE
LUCKY THE INSCRUTABLE
MASTERS, THE
NEOPOLITAN CAROUSEL
ONE JUST MAN
POLE POSITION
READY FOR ANYTHING
SALOME - WHERE SHE DANCED
SCARLET WOMAN, THE
SHARK HUNTER, THE
SON OF A BITCH
STAR PILOT
SUNSHINE ON THE SKIN
SUPERMAN ADVENTURES NO.1 - 3
SUPERMAN SHOW
SUPPOSE I BREAK YOUR NECK
TE DEUM
TERROR EXPRESS !
THEY BELIEVED HE WAS A SAINT
THREE GUYS STRIKE AGAIN, THE
THREE SUPERGUYS IN THE SNOW, THE
THREE SUPERGUYS, THE
TIGER FROM THE RIVER KWAI
TITBIT
ULYSSES
VENGEANCE WITH A GUN
WILD HORSE HANK
WOMEN PRISONERS OF DEVIL'S ISLAND
YETI
YOUNG, LOVELY AND VICIOUS

GO:
ABDUCTORS, THE
ANGRY DRAGON, THE
APOCALYPSE THE UNTOLD STORY
APPOINTMENT IN BEIRUT
ARMINIUS THE TERRIBLE
BAD BUNCH
BANDITS
BIG CAT, THE
BLOODY PAYROLL
BORN TO KILL
BRAVE BUNCH, THE
CANNIBAL HOLOCAUST
CAPERS
CELESTINE

CURSED VALLEY
DEMONS, THE
DEMONS, THE
DEVIL'S NIGHTMARE
DIRTY DEAL
DOOMED TO DIE
EROTIC RITES OF FRANKENSTEIN, THE
HERO BUNKER
HOUSE OF PERVERSITY
HOUSE OF SECRETS
INSANITY
JOURNEY INTO THE BEYOND
LADY HAMILTON
LADY OF BURLESQUE
MACABRE
MEGAFORCE 7.9
MIRACLE MAN, THE
MOONCHILD
MOUSE AND THE WOMAN, THE
PRELUDE TO HAPPINESS
RAIDERS OF THE TREASURE OF TAYOPA
REACHING FOR THE MOON
SAVAGE TERROR
SCARED TO DEATH
SILENT ACTION
SINNER
SS EXPERIMENT CAMP
STRANGER IN THE HOUSE, A
THEY ALL LOVED HIM
TRIANGLE OF LUST
UNDER THE BIG TOP
VAMPIRE BAT, THE
VIOLATION OF JUSTINE, THE
WOMEN BEHIND BARS

GUILD:
10 TO MIDNIGHT
ADVENTURES OF TOM SAWYER, THE
AFRICA TEXAS STYLE
AGENCY
ALL NEW INCREDIBLE HULK
AMERICAN COMMANDOS
AMERICATHON
AMITYVILLE HORROR, THE
AND BABY MAKES SIX
AND NOW THE SCREAMING STARTS !
APPRENTICESHIP OF DUDDY KRAVITZ, THE
ASYLUM
ATOM ANT 1 - 3
ATTACK FORCE Z
BABY COMES HOME
BABY LOVE - LEMON POPSICLE 5
BANANA SPLITS 1 - 4
BANG THE DRUM SLOWLY
BARON BLOOD
BARRY MANILOW IN CONCERT
BATFINK 1 & 2
BATTLE CREEK BRAWL
BATTLETRUCK
BEAST IN THE CELLAR, THE
BELLS
BEST OF RISING DAMP
BETTER LATE THAN NEVER
BILL
BILL OF DIVORCEMENT, A
BLADE

BLOOD ON SATAN'S CLAW
BLUE SKIES AGAIN
BODY STEALERS, THE
BORN LOSERS, THE
BOUNTY MAN, THE
BREAK THROUGH
BREAKDANCE THE MOVIE
BREAKER MORANT
C.H.O.M.P.S.
CABOBLANCO
CALL OF THE WILD
CAPTAIN AMERICA 1 - 3
CARAVANS
CARBON COPY
CAVERN DEEP
CHILDREN OF THE STONES
CHRISTMAS CAROL, A
CLIFTON HOUSE MYSTERY, THE
CLOUD DANCER
COMMANDOS
CRY OF THE BANSHEE
CUJO
DALLAS VOLS 01 - 18
DANNY
DARK, THE
DASTARDLY AND MUTTLEY 1 - 3
DAY THE EARTH MOVED, THE
DEATH CHEATERS
DEATH CRUISE
DEATH SQUAD, THE
DIRTY TRICKS
DOMINIQUE
DON PASQUALE
DOOMWATCH
DOT AND SANTA CLAUS
DOT AND THE BUNNY
DOT AND THE KANGAROO
DOT AROUND THE WORLD
DRAGON LORD
DRAUGHTSMAN'S CONTRACT, THE
DRESSED TO KILL
DRUM
DUEL IN THE SUN
DUNGEONS AND DRAGONS
DUNWICH HORROR, THE
ENIGMA
ENTERTAINING ELECTRON, THE
ESCAPE TO VICTORY
FALL OF THE HOUSE OF USHER, THE
FANTASTIC FOUR 1 -3
FARMER'S DAUGHTER, THE
FAST WALKING
FEARLESS FLY 1
FIFTH MUSKETEER, THE
FINAL ASSIGNMENT
FISH THAT SAVED PITTSBURGH, THE
FIVE DAYS FROM HOME
FIVE DESPERATE WOMEN
FOR THE LOVE OF IVY
FOR YOUR LOVE ONLY
FOXY BROWN
FROGS
FUTUREWORLD
GALAXINA
GARDEN OF ALLAH, THE
GET KNIGHTED

GETTING OF WISDOM, THE
GOD'S STORY
GODS MUST BE CRAZY, THE
GOLD OF THE AMAZON WOMEN
GRAVE OF THE VAMPIRE
GRAYEAGLE
GREAT HOUDINI, THE
GRISSOM GANG, THE
GUESS WHO'S SLEEPING IN MY BED ?
GUNS AND THE FURY, THE
HANDS OFF
HARRY'S GAME
HEARTACHES
HEATWAVE
HELL IN THE PACIFIC
HENRY'S CAT 1
HIGH RISK
HIGH ROAD TO CHINA
HIGH VELOCITY
HIJACK !
HOLOCAUST 1 - 3
HOME MOVIES
HOUSE OF THE LONG SHADOWS
HOUSE THAT WOULD NOT DIE, THE
HUMAN FACTOR, THE
HURRICANE
I WILL FIGHT NO MORE FOREVER
I'LL BE SEEING YOU
IN BROAD DAYLIGHT
INCREDIBLE HULK 1 & 2
INDISCRETION OF AN AMERICAN WIFE
INTERMEZZO
INVINCIBLE IRON MAN 1 - 3
ISLAND OF ADVENTURE, THE
ISLAND OF DR. MOREAU, THE
ISLAND OF THE LOST
JAYNE MANSFIELD STORY, THE
KELLY MONTEITH - A YANK IN LONDON
KIDNAPPING OF THE PRESIDENT, THE
KILL AND KILL AGAIN
KOTCH
LAST AMERICAN VIRGIN, THE
LEGEND OF VALENTINO, THE
LITTLE NIGHT MUSIC, A
LITTLE SEX, A
LONG WAY HOME, A
LOOKIN' TO GET OUT
LOVE AMONG THE RUINS
LOVE AND MONEY
LOVE AT FIRST BITE
LOVE WAR, THE
LUCKY STAR, THE
MAGNIFICENT 7 DEADLY SINS, THE
MAHLER
MARATHON
MARGIN FOR MURDER
MASSACRE AT FORT HOLMAN
MASTER OF THE WORLD
MATTIE THE GOOSEBOY
MEGAFORCE
MERLIN AND THE SWORD
MIGHTY THOR 1 - 4
MILTON THE MONSTER SHOW
MISS JULIE
MONEY MOVERS
MONTENEGRO

LISTINGS

MOTHER LODE
MURDER ON FLIGHT 502
MY BRILLIANT CAREER
MYSTERIOUS TWO
NANA
NEITHER THE SEA NOR THE SAND
NEVER TO LOVE
NIGHT GOD SCREAMED, THE
NIGHT STALKER, THE
NIGHT STRANGLER, THE
NINTH CONFIGURATION, THE
NOT NOW DARLING
NOTORIOUS
OBLONG BOX, THE
ODD ANGRY SHOT, THE
OLD MAN WHO CRIED WOLF, THE
OUTRAGE
PACKAGE TOUR
PARADINE CASE, THE
PICTURE SHOW MAN, THE
PINOCCHIO IN OUTER SPACE
PIT AND THE PENDULUM
POPE JOAN
PORTRAIT OF JENNIE
POSTMAN ALWAYS RINGS TWICE, THE
PREMATURE BURIAL, THE
PRIME OF MISS JEAN BRODIE, THE
PRIVATE POPSICLE
PROFESSIONALS 1-4
PUPPET ON A CHAIN
RACING GAME, THE
RACQUET
RANSOM
RATS, THE
RAW DEAL
REARDON ON SNOOKER
REBECCA
RELUCTANT HEROES, THE
RETURN OF THE SOLDIER, THE
REVENGE
REVENGE OF THE NINJA
RING OF BRIGHT WATER
ROBBERS OF THE SACRED MOUNTAIN
ROUGHNECKS
RUBY AND OSWALD
RUBY GENTRY
RUNNER STUMBLES, THE
S.O.B.
SAHARA
SAVAGES
SCANDALOUS !
SCANNERS
SCAVENGER HUNT
SECOND-HAND HEARTS
SECRET SQUIRREL 1 - 3
SHOCK WAVES
SIMON SIMON
SINCE YOU WENT AWAY
SLAUGHTER (uncut)
SOGGY BOTTOM, USA
SOMEBODY KILLED HER HUSBAND
SPELLBOUND
SPIRAL STAIRCASE, THE
STORM BOY
STRAW DOGS
STUNT MAN, THE

SUPERTED 1 - 4
SUPPOSE THEY GAVE A WAR...
TALES OF TERROR
TALES OF THE UNEXPECTED 1 & 2
TASTE OF EVIL, A
TERROR EYES (uncut)
THAT CHAMPIONSHIP SEASON
THREE IN THE ATTIC
THRESHOLD
TIME WALKER
TOO LATE THE HERO
TOP CAT 1 - 4
TORN BETWEEN TWO LOVERS
TOUCH, THE
TOWN THAT DREADED SUNDOWN, THE
TRAPPED BENEATH THE SEA
TREASURE ISLAND
TREASURE OF THE FOUR CROWNS
TRIANGLE FACTORY FIRE SCANDAL, THE
TURKEY SHOOT
ULTIMATE THRILL,THE
URGH ! A MUSIC WAR
WARNING, THE
WHEN A STRANGER CALLS
WHITE BUFFALO, THE
WHITE LIONS, THE
WICKED LADY, THE
WILD ANGELS, THE
WILD TIMES
WIND IN THE WILLOWS 1 & 2
WUTHERING HEIGHTS
YOUNG MASTER, THE
YOUNG WARRIORS, THE
YUMA

HIKON:
DIAL RAT
FOXBAT
GIRL ON A MOTORCYCLE
JAZZ ON A SUMMER'S DAY
LIVE WITH LENNY BRUCE
MEAN STREETS
SADIST, THE
SPIDER BABY / REEFER MADNESS

HOKUSHIN:
ANGELS BRIGADE
ANGELS DIE HARD
BIGGEST BATTLE, THE
BLACK BEAUTY
BLOOD BATH
BLUE FANTASIES
BOARDWALK
BRUCE LEE - CHINESE GODS
BUDDY HOLLY STORY, THE
CHOICES
CLONES OF BRUCE LEE, THE
COME PLAY WITH ME
COME PLAY WITH ME 2
CONFESSIONS... DAVID GALAXY AFFAIR
CONFESSIONS OF THE SEX SLAVES
DANCE OF THE DWARFS
DAUGHTER OF EMMANUELLE
DISCO DYNAMITE
EMANUELLE QUEEN OF SADOS
EMMANUELLE 3

EROTIC INFERNO
EVIL IN THE DEEP
FATTY FINN
FEARLESS FUZZ
FOR THE LOVE OF ADA
FREDDY OF THE JUNGLE
GODZILLA VS. THE COSMIC MONSTER
GOING STEADY
GREGORY'S GIRL
HANNIE CAULDER
HUMAN DUPLICATORS, THE
IMPERIAL JAPANESE EMPIRE, THE
INGLORIOUS BASTARDS, THE
ISLAND OF DEATH
JUNGLE BURGER
KISS OF THE TARANTULA
KWAHERI - VANISHING AFRICA
LEMON POPSICLE
LOOSE SHOES
LOVE ME DEADLY
MAGIC CURSE
MARY MILLINGTON'S TRUE BLUE CONF.
MASSAGE GIRLS IN B'KOK
MEAN STREETS
MONDO EROTICO
MORTUARY
NAKED TRUTH, THE
NATURAL ENEMIES
NIGHT FLOWERS
NO PLACE TO HIDE
OH ! CALCUTTA !
ON ANY SUNDAY
PLAYBIRDS, THE
PRISONER OF THE CANNIBAL GOD
PRIVATE NURSE
PRIVILEGED
Q - THE WINGED SERPENT
QUEEN OF THE BLUES
QUEENS OF EVIL
RIVALS
SAVAGE HUNT, THE
SAVAGE WEEKEND
SECRET POLICEMANS BALL, THE
SEX DIARY
SEX WITH THE STARS
SHADOW OF CHIKARA, THE
SHALIMAR
SHARK'S CAVE, THE
SHRUBS, TREES AND HEDGES
SILENCE
SPECIAL COP IN ACTION
SUPER DRAGON
SURVIVAL RUN
SWEET WILLIAM
TEARDROPS
TERROR
THEY CALL ME LUCKY
TITLE SHOT
TOOLBOX MURDERS, THE
TOUCHED BY LOVE
VIOLATION OF THE BITCH
VIOLENT BREED, THE
WHAT'S GOOD FOR THE GOOSE
WHAT'S UP NURSE?
WHAT'S UP SUPER DOC?
WILLA

WITCHFINDER GENERAL
YOUNG AND FREE
ZEBRA FORCE, THE

HVM:
ASH WEDNESDAY
BAD GEORGIA ROAD
BATTLE OF EL ALAMEIN
BEYOND AND BACK
CHARLOTTE'S WEB
DEERSLAYER, THE
DONNER PASS
FALL OF THE HOUSE OF USHER, THE
FIST OF FEAR, TOUCH OF DEATH
HOME BEFORE MIDNIGHT
I WONDER WHO'S KILLING HER NOW ?
INNOCENT BYSTANDERS
KASHMIRI RUN
LAST DAY OF THE WAR, THE
NO WAY BACK
OPTIMISTS OF NINE ELMS, THE
PANIC IN ECHO PARK
PIED PIPER, THE
PRIEST OF LOVE, THE
PROBABILITY ZERO
QUESTION OF LOVE, A
SCORCHY
SHOOT
SNOW TREASURE
SUICIDE COMMANDO
THREE CARD MONTE
TWICE A WOMAN
ZERO POPULATION GROWTH

INTER-OCEAN:
077 FURY IN ISTANBUL
077 MISSION BLOODY MARY
10 MAGNIFICENT KILLERS
ADIOS GRINGO
ADULT FAIRYTALES
ARM OF FIRE
ATTACK OF THE NORMANS
BALLAD OF DEATH VALLEY, THE
BARE KNUCKLES
BELOW THE BELT
BIG RISK, THE
BLACK DRAGON REVENGES... BRUCE LEE
BLACK SABBATH
BRUCE AGAINST IRON HAND
BRUCE LEE AGAINST SUPERMEN
CALIGULA EROTICA
CANDIDO EROTICO
CHALLENGE OF YOUNG BRUCE LEE
CHINESE STUNTMAN
CRYSTAL FIST
CYCLES SOUTH
DEADLY REVENGE
DJANGO
DJANGO SHOOTS FIRST
DRAGON DIES HARD
DYNAMO
ENTER THE DEVIL
EXIT THE DRAGON, ENTER THE TIGER
FALL OF THE GIANTS,THE
FANTASTIC ARGOMAN, THE
FRENCH LOVERS, THE

LISTINGS

GO HOG WILD
GO KILL AND COME BACK !
GREAT DIAMOND ROBBERY, THE
HERCULES CHALLENGE
IMAGE OF BRUCE LEE
INFERNO IN PARADISE
INTIMATE RELATIONS
INVINCIBLE SUPER CHAN, THE
KILLER'S MOON
KUNG FU GANG BUSTERS
KUNG FU GENIUS
KUNG FU MASTER
LADIES' DOCTOR
LAMA AVENGER, THE
LAST OF THE VIKINGS
LITTLE GODFATHER FROM HONG KONG
LITTLE SUPER MAN
LOS ANGELES CONNECTION, THE
LOVE CLINIC
LOVE, LUST AND ECSTASY
LUNCH WAGON
MADIGAN'S MILLIONS
MASTER WITH CRACKED FINGERS, THE
MATCH OF DRAGON AND TIGER
MELODY IN LOVE
MISTRESS, THE
NEEDLES OF DEATH
NEW BLACK EMANUELLE
NIGHTS AND LOVES OF DON JUAN, THE
ONE ON TOP OF THE OTHER
ONE SILVER DOLLAR
PERVERSION STORY
PLEASURE ISLAND
QUEEN FOR CAESAR, A
REFUGE OF FEAR
RETURN OF THE DRAGON
RETURN OF THE TIGER
REVENGE OF THE BARBARIANS
ROME AGAINST ROME
SEASON FOR ASSASSINS
SEVEN GOLDEN MEN
SEVEN GOLDEN MEN STRIKE AGAIN
SNAKE IN THE MONKEY'S SHADOW
SUN DRAGON
SUPER POWER
SUPERSONIC MAN
SWIM TEAM
TASTE OF HELL, A
TENDER LOVING CARE
TEXAS ADIOS
THEY CALLED HIM AMEN
THREE MUSKETEERS OF THE WEST, THE
THUNDERING MANTIS, THE
TIGER STRIKES AGAIN, THE
TOO HOT TO HANDLE
TOYTOWN SERIES NO.1 - 5
TRAP ON COUGAR MOUNTAIN
TROJAN WAR, THE
TRUCK STOP WOMEN
UNDER THE COVER COPS
URSUS
VIKING INVADERS
WAY OF THE BLACK DRAGON
WEAPONS OF DEATH
WHITE WATER SAM
WOMEN GLADIATORS

WRONG WAY
YELLOW EMANUELLE

INTERCITY:
AROUND THE WORLD WITH FANNY HILL
BLONDE VELVET
BLOOD VOYAGE
FISTFUL OF DRAGONS, A
FLESH FEAST
GREEK CONNECTION, THE
HARD STUFF
I FEEL IT RISING
I MISS YOU, HUGS AND KISSES
LOVE AND KISSES
ORIENTAL BLUE
PLEASURE SHOP ON 7TH AVENUE, THE
PROVOCATION
SEXPERT
TANGO OF PERVERSION
TEMPLE OF THE DRAGON
WEREWOLF WOMAN

INTERVISION:
10CC IN CONCERT - LIVE
12 + 1
3 INTO SEX WON'T GO
55 DAYS AT PEKING
67 DAYS - THE LIVING LEGEND...
ABBA MUSIC SHOW 1 & 2
ACCIDENT AT MEMORIAL STADIUM
ADVENTURES OF A PLUMBER'S MATE
ADVENTURES OF A PRIVATE EYE
ADVENTURES OF A TAXI DRIVER
AIB YA LOULOU (SHAME ON YOU LOULOU)
AIDA
AIN'T MISBEHAVIN'
AIR HAWK
ALADDIN'S LAMP
ALADDIN'S LAMP
ALASKA WILDERNESS ADVENTURE, THE
ALICE IN WONDERLAND
ALIENS FROM SPACESHIP EARTH
ALISON'S BIRTHDAY
ALLIGATOR
ALPHA BETA
AMSTERDAM AFFAIR, THE
ANGELS OF THE STREET
ANGELS WITH BOUND HANDS, THE
ANNIE HALL
ARCH OF TRIUMPH
AS THE NAKED WIND FROM THE SEA
ASIAD WA ABEED (MASTERS AND SLAVES)
ASPHYX, THE
ATTIC, THE
BALLAD IN BLUE
BANDITS
BAT PEOPLE, THE
BATTLE OF AUSTERLITZ, THE
BED MANIA
BEDROOM MAZURKA
BEES, THE
BELLE STARR STORY, THE
BEN SIDRAN
BEST OF BOTH WORLDS
BEST OF THE ADVENTURES, THE
BEYOND ATLANTIS

BILITIS
BLACK 6, THE
BLACK DECAMERON
BLACK DEEP THROAT
BLACK PANTHER, THE
BLACK ROOM, THE
BLAZING FLOWERS
BLOOD ON MY HANDS
BLOODSUCKERS
BLOODSUCKERS
BLOW-OUT
BLUE BLOOD
BLUE BLOOD
BODY AND SOUL
BODY AND SOUL
BOLDEST JOB IN THE WEST, THE
BONDITIS
BOOM IN THE MOON
BOOMTOWN RATS
BRIDGE TOO FAR, A
BROOD, THE
BRUCE'S FINGERS
BUCKSTONE COUNTY PRISON
CAN BE DONE AMIGO
CAN YOU KEEP IT UP FOR A WEEK ?
CANADIAN PACIFIC
CANDY CANDY 1 - 3
CANNIBAL MAN, THE
CAPTAIN HARLOCK 1 - 3
CARRIE
CARS THAT ATE PARIS, THE
CASABLANCA
CASABLANCA SPY NEST
CATHY'S CURSE
CAUGHT
CENTREFOLD GIRLS
CERVANTES
CHARLEY ONE-EYE
CHILDREN OF RAVENSBACK, THE
CHILDREN SHOULDN'T PLAY WITH...
CHITTY CHITTY BANG BANG
CIRCUS WORLD
CITY OF THE DEAD
CITY OF THE LIVING DEAD
CLAIRE'S KNEE
CLONES, THE
COME BACK TO THE FIVE AND DIME...
COMING HOME
COMING OUT ALIVE
CONFESSIONS OF A BLUE MOVIE STAR
CONFESSIONS OF A SEX KITTEN
COOL IT CAROL !
COUSINS IN LOVE
CREEPSHOW
CRIES AND WHISPERS
CROCODILE
CRUEL PASSION
CRYPT OF THE LIVING DEAD
CURSE OF EVIL
CURSE OF THE DEVIL
DANISH BED AND BOARD
DANISH DENTIST ON THE JOB
DANISH ESCORT GIRLS
DANISH PILLOW TALK
DARK MIRROR, THE
DARYL HALL AND JOHN OATS

DAY THE EARTH CAUGHT FIRE, THE
DAY TIME ENDED, THE
DEAD OF NIGHT
DEAD OF NIGHT
DEAD OF NIGHT
DEADLY GAMES
DEADLY WEAPONS
DEAREST LOVE
DEATH DIMENSION
DEATH GAME
DEATH OF A HOOKER
DEATH OF A SNOWMAN
DEATHHEAD VIRGIN
DEVIL TIMES FIVE
DICK CLARK SHOW 01 - 20
DOGS TO THE RESCUE
DOLLY PARTON
DON'T GO NEAR THE PARK
DON'T PLAY WITH FIRE
DOUBLE EXPOSURE
DOUBLE LIFE, A
DRACULA VERSUS FRANKENSTEIN
DYNAMITE BROTHERS, THE
EAGLE IN A CAGE
EDDIE KIDD SPECTACULAR, THE
EL CID
ELKIE BROOKS
END OF THE WORLD
EROTIC TALES
ESCORT GIRLS
EUROPA '80
EVERYTHING YOU ALWAYS...
EXPOSE
EXTERMINATOR, THE
EYES BEHIND THE STARS
EYES WITHOUT A FACE
FALL OF THE ROMAN EMPIRE, THE
FAMILY ENFORCER
FELIX THE CAT - NO.1 - 5
FEMALE BUNCH, THE
FIDDLER ON THE ROOF
FIND THE LADY
FLORIDA CONNECTION, THE
FOR A FEW BULLETS MORE
FOR LADIES ONLY
FOXHOLE IN CAIRO
FRIGHTMARE
FROZEN SCREAM
FUNERAL IN BERLIN
FUNNIEST MAN IN THE WORLD, THE
FURY ON WHEELS
GETTING OVER
GHOSTKEEPER
GIRLS FOR PLEASURE
GIRLS FOR RENT
GLOVE, THE
GOD'S STORY
GODFATHER OF HONG KONG
GOOD, THE BAD, AND THE UGLY, THE
GOODBYE, BRUCE LEE
GOODBYE, NORMA JEAN
GORGEOUS BIRD LIKE ME, A
GOT IT MADE
GREAT BALLOON ADVENTURE, THE
GREAT BRITISH STRIP, THE
GREAT MONKEY RIP-OFF, THE

LISTINGS

- GROUP MARRIAGE
- GROUPIES
- GUESS WHAT WE LEARNT IN SCHOOL TODAY?
- HAIR
- HALLELUJAH I'M A TRAMP
- HAPPY HOOKER GOES TO WASHINGTON, THE
- HAPPY HOOKER, THE
- HARDCORE
- HARRY TRACY - DESPERADO
- HE WHO SHOOTS FIRST
- HEIST, THE
- HERCULES
- HERCULES UNCHAINED
- HIGHPOINT
- HOGO AND JOSEFINE
- HOLLYWOOD ON PARADE
- HORROR EXPRESS
- HOUSE OF THE LIVING DEAD
- HOW TO SOLVE THE CUBE
- HOW TO SUCCEED WITH SEX
- HUNTED
- I'M GOING TO BE FAMOUS
- INSIDE MOVES
- INVADERS FROM MARS
- IS THERE SEX AFTER DEATH ?
- JACK AND THE BEANSTALK
- JE T'AIME MOI NON PLUS
- JESSI'S GIRLS
- JOE
- JOE PANTHER
- JOHNNY CASH, THE MAN... HIS MUSIC
- JOURNEY INTO FEAR
- JOYRIDE TO NOWHERE
- KAMPUCHEA EXPRESS
- KHATIAT MALLAK (AN ANGEL'S SIN)
- KILLING KIND, THE
- KING DICK
- KING OF KONG ISLAND
- KING SOLOMON'S TREASURE
- KINGDOM IN THE CLOUDS, THE
- KINGDOM OF THE SPIDERS
- KLONDIKE FEVER
- LA YA OUMI (NO, MOTHER)
- LADY GREY
- LADY IS A WHORE, THE
- LADY, STAY DEAD
- LADY WITH RED BOOTS
- LASERBLAST
- LAST HORROR FILM, THE
- LAST HUNTER, THE
- LAST TANGO IN PARIS
- LAST TRAIN FROM SHANGHAI
- LAST VICTIM, THE
- LEGEND OF ALFRED PACKER, THE
- LENNY
- LET'S GET LAID !
- LETTER FROM AN UNKNOWN WOMAN
- LICENSED TO LOVE AND KILL
- LIFETAKER, THE
- LILI MARLEEN
- LIMBO LINE, THE
- LITTLE GIRL, BIG TEASE
- LITTLE GIRL, BIG TEASE
- LITTLE LULU 1
- LITTLE LULU 2
- LITTLE LULU 3

- LITTLE MERMAID, THE
- LONG ARM OF THE GODFATHER, THE
- LOST MOMENT, THE
- LOVE BUTCHER, THE
- LOVE IN FOUR EASY LESSONS
- LOVE IN THE AFTERNOON
- LOVE IS A SPLENDID ILLUSION
- LUCKY JIM FISHING ADVENTURES 01 - 13
- LUST FOR REVENGE
- LUSTFUL VICAR, THE
- MACBETH
- MAD MISSION
- MAGIC
- MAGIC FLUTE, THE
- MAGNIFICENT MATADOR, THE
- MAID IN SWEDEN
- MALACHI'S COVE
- MALPERTUIS
- MAN FROM BUTTON WILLOW, THE
- MAN OF VIOLENCE
- MAN OUTSIDE, THE
- MAN WHO COULDN'T GET ENOUGH, THE
- MANFRED MANN'S EARTHBAND
- MANIAC
- MARK OF THE DEVIL
- MASTER OF LOVE
- MEAN JOHNNY BARROWS
- MEMORY OF US
- MEN OF SHERWOOD FOREST
- MIDNIGHT
- MIRACLE OF THE BELLS, THE
- MIRRORS
- MISTRESS OF THE APES
- MOHAWK
- MONSTROID
- MOVIES
- MR. KLEIN
- MR. SYCAMORE
- MUSIC MACHINE, THE
- MUSTANG
- MY BOYS ARE GOOD BOYS
- MY FRIENDS NEED KILLING
- MY NAME IS NOBODY
- MYSTERY SUBMARINE
- NAOU MINAI NISAA (A TYPE OF WOMAN)
- NEGATIVES
- NETWORK
- NEVER ON FRIDAY
- NIGHT CREATURE
- NIGHT OF THE LIVING DEAD
- NIGHT PORTER, THE
- NO.1 OF THE SECRET SERVICE
- NO MERCY MAN, THE
- NO MERCY MAN, THE
- NORTHVILLE CEMETERY MASSACRE
- NORTHWEST STAMPEDE
- NORTHWEST STAMPEDE
- OIL - THE BILLION DOLLAR FIRE
- ONE BY ONE
- ONE MAN JURY, THE
- ONE TOUCH OF VENUS
- ONE TWO TWO
- ONIBABA
- OTHER CINDERELLA, THE
- OTHER LOVE, THE
- OTHER WOMAN, THE

- OUTBACK
- OUTLAW RIDERS
- PANIC CITY
- PENTHOUSE PET OF THE YEAR
- PETS
- PINK PANTHER STRIKES AGAIN, THE
- PINK TELEPHONE, THE
- PINOCCHIO'S STORY BOOK
- PINOCCHIO'S STORYBOOK ADVENTURES
- PLAYBACK VIDEO MAGAZINE
- POM-POM GIRLS, THE
- POOR ALBERT AND LITTLE ANNIE
- POOR WHITE TRASH PART 2
- POWER OF FOOTBALL - WORLD CUP 1978
- POWERS OF EVIL
- PRESSURE
- PRINCESS
- PRIVATE RIGHT, THE
- PRIVATE VICES, PUBLIC VIRTUES
- RABID
- RAVINE, THE
- REAL BRUCE LEE, THE
- REDNECK
- RESTLESS BREED, THE
- REVENGE OF THE PINK PANTHER
- RIP VAN WINKLE
- ROAR
- ROBERT GORDON WITH LINK WRAY
- ROCK, SOUL AN' COUNTRY 1 - 8
- ROCKY
- ROCKY 2
- ROLLERBALL
- RUTHLESS
- S.O.S. PACIFIC
- SALAHDIN AL AYOOBI
- SANTA AND THE THREE BEARS
- SANTEE
- SATAN'S SLAVE
- SATURDAY NIGHT AT THE BATHS
- SCRATCH HARRY
- SCREAM BLOODY MURDER
- SCREAM FOR VENGEANCE !
- SECRET BEYOND THE DOOR, THE
- SECRETS
- SEEDS OF EVIL
- SEMI-TOUGH
- SENSUAL ENCOUNTERS OF EVERY KIND
- SEVENTEEN
- SEX CLINIC
- SEX FARM
- SEX SHOP
- SHANGHAI LIL
- SHAPE OF THINGS TO COME, THE
- SHE'LL FOLLOW YOU ANYWHERE
- SHE'LL FOLLOW YOU ANYWHERE
- SHIVERS
- SHOOT FIRST, LAUGH LAST
- SILENT NIGHT, BLOODY NIGHT
- SILENT NIGHT, BLOODY NIGHT
- SILENT SCREAM, THE
- SIN
- SIN
- SISTERS OF DEATH
- SLAVERS
- SLUMBER PARTY '57
- SLUMBER PARTY '57

- SMALL CHANGE (L'ARGENT DE POCHE)
- SMOKEY ROBINSON
- SMURFS AND THE MAGIC FLUTE, THE
- SNAPSHOT
- SOLE SURVIVOR
- SOME MAY LIVE
- SPARROW OF PIGALLE, THE
- SPECIAL DAY, A
- SPECTREMAN 01 - 12
- SPUNKY AND TADPOLE 1 - 3
- SPY STORY
- SQUEEZE A FLOWER
- STAMPING GROUND
- STARSHIP INVASIONS
- STEVE DAVIS' WORLD OF SNOOKER VOL. 1
- STORY OF A LOVE STORY
- STORY OF JOANNA, THE
- STORY OF O, THE
- STUDY IN TERROR, A
- STUNT ROCK
- SUMMERDOG
- SUNBURST
- SUNDAY IN THE COUNTRY
- SUPER SEAL
- SUPERKNIGHTS
- SWORD OF MONTE CRISTO
- TAKE IT TO THE LIMIT
- TAKE TIME TO SMELL THE FLOWERS
- TEMPTER
- TERRIBLE QUICK SWORD OF SIEGFRIED, THE
- THEIR BREAKFAST MEANT LEAD
- THEY PAID WITH BULLETS
- THIS, THAT AND THE OTHER !
- THREE BULLETS FOR A LONG GUN
- TIFFANY JONES
- TIGER AND THE FLAME, THE
- TO BE A ROSE
- TOILET TALK
- TOUCH ME NOT
- TOURIST TRAP
- TREASURE ISLAND
- TRIAL, THE
- TUNNEL VISION
- TWIST, THE
- UNDER THE DOCTOR
- UNFAITHFUL WIFE, THE
- UNION CITY
- UNKNOWN POWERS
- UPS AND DOWNS OF A HANDYMAN, THE
- VELVET HOUSE
- VIGILANTE
- VIOLENT ENEMY, THE
- VIRGIN WITCH
- VIRUS
- VISITOR, THE
- WACKY TAXI
- WEREWOLF'S SHADOW
- WEST SIDE STORY
- WHITE COMANCHE
- WHY WOULD ANYONE WANT TO KILL...
- WINGS OF AN EAGLE
- WINTER COMES EARLY
- WITHOUT A STITCH
- WONDERWALL
- YOU'VE COME A LONG WAY KATIE
- ZOMBIES DAWN OF THE DEAD

ZULU DAWN

IVER FILM SERVICES:
AFRICA EXPRESS
ANDROID
ANGRY JOE BASS
ASSIGNMENT, THE
BEDTIME WITH ROSIE
BETRAYAL
BIRDS OF PREY
BIZARRE
BLACK GESTAPO, THE
BLAZING STEWARDESSES, THE
BLOOD
BLOOD AND BLACK LACE
BLOOD SONG
BLOODY BIRTHDAY
CAGED HEAT
CALL OF THE WILD, THE
CAPTAIN KRONOS - VAMPIRE HUNTER
CHARLES AND DIANA, A ROYAL LOVE STORY
CHERRY PICKER, THE
CHILD BRIDE OF SHORT CREEK, THE
CHINESE HERCULES
CHRISTMAS EVIL
CLARENCE DARROW
CLASS OF '63
CODY
COMPANEROS
CONFESSIONS OF A FRUSTRATED HOUSEWIFE
CONFESSIONS OF A NAKED VIRGIN
CONFESSIONS OF A SEXY PHOTOGRAPHER
CONTRACT
CONVOY BUSTERS
CORRIDORS OF BLOOD
CRYSTAL VOYAGER
CURIOUS FEMALE, THE
DARING GAME
DARK STAR
DEAD KIDS
DEADLY FEMALES, THE
DEEP JAWS
DEVIL'S RAIN, THE
DICK DEADEYE
DISCO FEVER
DON MCLEAN - TILL TOMORROW
DOUBLE POSSESSION
DRACULA'S VIRGIN LOVERS
ELMER
EROTIC EVA
EROTIC YOUNG LOVERS
EXISTANCE
FALLING IN LOVE AGAIN
FALLING MAN, THE
FIGHTING BACK
FIREHOUSE
FIVE BLOODY GRAVES
FOOTSTEPS
FROM CORLEONE TO BROOKLYN
FUNERAL FOR AN ASSASSIN
GAY DECEIVERS, THE
GENTLE GIANT
GENTLEMAN BANDIT, THE
GIRLS ON THE ROAD
GRADUATION DAY
GREAT AMERICAN TRAGEDY, A

HEAD ON
HEARTBREAK MOTEL
HI RIDERS, THE
HOLLYWOOD KNIGHT
HONEYBABY
HONKY
HONOR THY FATHER
HORROR HOSPITAL
HOUSE THAT DRIPPED BLOOD, THE
HUGO THE HIPPO
HUMAN VAPOUR, THE
HURRICANE
IT'S GOOD TO BE ALIVE
KILL THE GOLDEN GOOSE
KILLER'S CURSE
KNIFE FOR THE LADIES
KNOCKING AT HEAVEN'S DOOR
LADY OF THE HOUSE
LAST WAR, THE
LEGACY OF SATAN
LEGEND OF BOGGY CREEK
LEGEND OF THE NORTHWEST
LONG LIVE YOUR DEATH
LONGEST HUNT, THE
LOVE CAMP
LOVE GAMES
LUNATICS AND LOVERS
MAD MAD MOVIE MAKERS
MAN WHO WOULD NOT DIE, THE
MASSACRE IN ROME
MAUI
MESSAGE TO MY DAUGHTER, A
MIDAS RUN, THE
MURDER GANG, THE
MURDER ONCE REMOVED
NAKED EXORCISM
NEW LOOK
NIGHT OF THE ASSASSIN, THE
NIGHT OF THE BLOODY APES
NIGHT OF THE DEMON
NO PLACE TO HIDE
NOT JUST ANOTHER AFFAIR
NOT TONIGHT DARLING
OASIS OF THE ZOMBIES
OCTAMAN
OF MICE AND MEN
ON THE NICKEL
PENELOPE 'PULLS IT OFF'
PEOPLE, THE
PHYSICAL ASSAULT
PIGS
PLANET OF THE DINOSAURS
POCO
PORTRAIT OF A SHOWGIRL
POWDERKEG
PUNCH AND JODY
PURPLE TAXI, THE
RUN, ANGEL, RUN !
RUNNING
S*H*E*
SAMURAI
SATAN'S CHEERLEADERS
SENIORS, THE
SEVERED ARM, THE
SEXY SUPERSTUD
SHARK !

SHRIEK OF THE MUTILATED
SIMON, KING OF THE WITCHES
SLIPPER AND THE ROSE, THE
SOME LIKE IT SEXY
STINGRAY
STRANGER AND THE GUNFIGHTER, THE
STUNT SQUAD
SUMMER OF MY GERMAN SOLDIER
SWINGING CHEERLEADERS, THE
SWITCHBLADE SISTERS
SYMPATHY FOR THE DEVIL
TAKE AN EASY RIDE
TATTERED WEB, A
TEAM-MATES
TEXAS CHAINSAW MASSACRE, THE
THIEF
TORSO
TOWER OF EVIL
TREASURE ISLAND
VENOM
WEREWOLVES ON WHEELS
WHERE HAVE ALL THE PEOPLE GONE ?
WHERE THE RED FERN GROWS
WILLARD
YOUR MONEY OR YOUR WIFE

JVI:
BEAST IN HEAT, THE
CASTLE OF TERROR
FREEDOM TO LOVE
GOKE, BODYSNATCHER FROM HELL
MASTER OF THE FLYING GUILLOTINE
MATANGO, FUNGUS OF TERROR
MORITZ
STRIKE BACK

MVM (MAGICAL VIDEO MOVIES):
BIGFOOT
CAN I COME TOO ?
CHAIN GANG WOMEN
CHANDU ON THE MAGIC ISLAND
DEADWOOD '76
ECSTASY
FIRST CHILD'S BUMPER FUN VIDEO
FROM NASHVILLE WITH MUSIC
GATLING GUN
GRAVE OF THE VAMPIRE
HELL'S CHOSEN FEW
LAUREL AND HARDY DOUBLE BILL
MARS ATTACKS THE WORLD
RISE AND FALL OF IVOR DICKIE , THE
SEARCH FOR THE EVIL ONE, THE
SMOKE IN THE WIND
SON OF BLOB
TILL THE CLOUDS ROLL BY
TOGETHERNESS
VIDEO FUN VOLUME 1

MARKET:
7 DEADLY FEMALES
AFTERMATH
ALTERNATE WAR
ANDREA, THE NYMPHO
ANY GUN CAN PLAY
APACHE WOMAN
BABY BLUE

BEST OF SEX AND VIOLENCE, THE
BIG THUMBS
BLOODY SPA
BOBBY BREWSTER
BUGS BUNNY SHOW
CHOWDOWN
COMIC CARTOONS
DEEP SWAMP
DEVILS IN THE CONVENT
DOLLARS TO DIE FOR
DROPS OF BLOOD
ESCAPE IN THE SUN
FREELANCE
FUN PARADE
FURY AT SUNDOWN
GANG WARS
GOLDEN EXTERMINATOR
GUMDROPS
GUNS OF VICTORY
HECTOR NICHOLS BOODS
HEROINE SYNDICATE
HITCH HIKER, THE
I WANT HIM DEAD
INVINCIBLE FROM HELL
ISLAND OF TERROR
JOHN McENROE STORY, THE
KID AND THE KILLERS
KILLER COP
LEANOR
LIVING FOR SEX
LOONEY TIME
LOVE CAMP 7
MAGIC SWORD, THE
MARDI GRAS MASSACRE
MIKADO KILLERS, THE
MURDER IN PARIS
NEW YORK EROTIC
NIGHT OF THE BIG HEAT
NOON SUNDAY
OPERATION INCHON
PARTY, THE
PEACE FOR A GUNFIGHTER
PRECIOUS JEWELS
PROFESSION GUN
PROFESSIONAL GUN
RAIDING PARTY
RAMRODDER, THE
RELUCTANT VIRGIN, THE
RETURN OF THE DINAS
SATAN WAR
SENSUAL DREAM
SEVEN INTO HELL
SHE FREAK
SILENCE
SOUL SOLDIER
STAR IS BORN, A
STREETS OF L.A., THE
SUPERMAN CARTOON
SUPERWEAPON
SWAMP BAIT
TERMINAL ISLAND
TERROR IN THE JUNGLE
THIS IS AMERICA
THUNDER IN CAROLINA
TREASURE ISLAND
TREASURE OF DEATH

LISTINGS

UPPERCLASS SEX
WHERE THE BULLETS FLY
WOMAN AND THE HUNTER, THE
WOMAN INSIDE, THE

MEDIA:
ACROSS THE GREAT DIVIDE
ADVENTURES OF THE WILDERNESS FAMILY 1 & 2
AMERICAN NIGHTMARE
AMERICAN WILDERNESS
ASSAULT ON PRECINCT 13
ATTACK OF THE KILLER TOMATOES
BLACKENSTEIN
BLOOD BEACH
BOY AND HIS DOG, A
CAN I DO IT...TILL I NEED GLASSES ?
CARTOON CLASSICS OF THE 1930'S
CENTREFOLD GIRLS, THE
CHALLENGE TO BE FREE
CHEERLEADERS, THE
COACH, THE
DEMENTED
DEMONOID
ELECTRIC LIGHT VOYAGE
FADE TO BLACK
FIRST NUDIE MUSICAL
FLESH GORDON
FLOWER OUT OF PLACE, A
FYRE
GO FOR IT
HALLOWEEN
HANSEL AND GRETEL
HAUNTING OF JULIA, THE
HEARSE, THE
HELL NIGHT
HOME SWEET HOME
HOUSE OF SHADOWS
I DRINK YOUR BLOOD
IF YOU DON'T STOP IT YOU'LL GO BLIND
MAN FROM CLOVER GROVE, THE
MOUNTAIN FAMILY ROBINSON
NIGHT BEFORE CHRISTMAS, THE
NINE AGES OF NAKEDNESS, THE
ONCE UPON A GIRL
PRIZE FIGHTER, THE
ROLLER BOOGIE
SEXTETTE
SLITHIS
SS GIRLS
SUDDEN DEATH
SUMMER CAMP
TERROR ON TOUR
TEXAS LIGHTNING
TO ALL A GOODNIGHT
UNSEEN, THE
WACKIEST WAGON TRAIN IN THE WEST, THE

MEDUSA:
ABSURD (uncut)
ATLANTIS INTERCEPTORS, THE
BLASTFIGHTER - THE FORCE OF VENGEANCE
BLAZING MAGNUM (cut)
BLAZING MAGNUM (uncut)
CHARLIE AND THE TALKING BUZZARD
DANGEROUS SUMMER, A
DARKROOM, THE
DOUBLE DEAL
EARLY FROST
EXTERMINATORS OF THE YEAR 3000
FIRST TURN-ON, THE
GOLIATH AND THE BARBARIANS
INN OF THE DAMNED
IRONMASTER
MADHOUSE
MIDNIGHT SPARES
MY NAME IS NOBODY
PINBALL SUMMER
RETURN OF THE DINOSAURS
ROME 2033 - THE FIGHTER CENTURIONS
SCREAMTIME
SEXPLORER
SHERIFF AND THE SATELLITE KID, THE
SPEED FEVER
TORNADO STRIKE FORCE
TOUCH AND GO
WAVELENGTH

MONTE:
36 CHOWRINGHEE LANE
DRAGON FORCE
FOREST OF FEAR
I WANT TO BE A WOMAN

MOUNTAIN:
3 HEADED DRAGON, THE
4D MAN
ADVENTURES OF POPEYE, THE
APHRODISIAC
ASTRO ZOMBIES, THE
AT WAR WITH THE ARMY
BAIT
BIG WHEEL, THE
BLOB, THE
BLOOD ON THE SUN
BLOOD SPATTERED BRIDE, THE
CANNIBAL TERROR
CAR HOPS, THE
CARTOON CAVALCADE
CARTOON SPECTACULAR
CLEOPATRA WONG
COMIC CUTS
CONF OF A YOUNG AMERICAN HOUSEWIFE
COUNTRY CELEBRATION
CRIMSON BAT
CRY UNCLE
DAREDEVIL DRIVERS
DINOSAURUS !
DRACULA
DRACULA VS. FRANKENSTEIN
DRESSED TO KILL
DYING SEA, THE
DYNAMITE JOHNSON
EDDIE CANTOR SHOW, THE
ELSA FRAULEIN SS
ELVIS IN CONCERT
ELVIS IN HAWAII
EMANUELLE AND FRIENDS
EQUINOX
ESKIMO NELL
EVERY DAY'S A HOLIDAY
FABULOUS DORSEYS, THE
FEMALE RESPONSE, THE
FILLMORE ROCK FESTIVAL
FILTHIEST SHOW IN TOWN
FRANK SINATRA SHOW, THE
FRENCH EMMANUELLE
FRENCH NYMPHO
FUN TIME
FURTHER ADVENTURES OF SUPERMAN
G-STRING MURDERS, THE
GHIDRAH THE THREE-HEADED MONSTER
GROUPIE GIRL
GULLIVER'S TRAVELS
GUMS
HOOCH
HORSE CALLED NIJINSKY, A
HOT TIMES
HOW TO SCORE WITH GIRLS
INSPECTOR GENERAL, THE
INVASION OF THE BLOOD FARMERS
JAMES BOND 007 TRAILERS, THE
JAWS OF THE DRAGON
KARATE WARS
KINGS OF THE SQUARE RING
LAUREL AND HARDY IN TOYLAND
LAUREL AND HARDY - BUMPER LAUGHS
LAUREL AND HARDY - THE FLYING DEUCES
LEGEND OF HILLBILLY JOHN, THE
LEGEND OF THE SEA WOLF, THE
LITTLE PRINCESS, THE
LOVE BOX, THE
LOVE SWEDISH STYLE
LOVES OF HERCULES, THE
LUCKY JOHNNY
MADAME ZENOBIA
MAGNIFICENT, THE
MAN WITH THE SYNTHETIC BRAIN
MARTIAL ARTS SPECTACULAR
MOLLY AND LAWLESS JOHN
MONEY, THE
MUSIC UNLIMITED SHOW NO.1 - 13
MY FAVOURITE BRUNETTE
MY SON THE VAMPIRE
MYSTERIES OF THE GODS
NAUGHTY !
NAUGHTY SCHOOLGIRLS
NEW ADVENTURES OF SNOW WHITE, THE
NIGHT OF THE SEAGULLS, THE
NOBODY'S BOY
ON THE GAME
PARTY LAUGHS
PERILS OF PAULINE, THE
RANA - CREATURE FROM SHADOW LAKE
REBEL ROUSERS, THE
RIDING THAT TRAIN
RINGO GOES WEST
RUNNING WILD
SALOME
SANTA FE TRAIL
SCARLET STREET
SECOND CHORUS
SECRETS OF A SUPERSTUD
SEVENTH DWARF, THE
SEX AND THE OTHER WOMAN
SMOKEY AND THE HOTWIRE GANG
SPACE FIREBIRD
SPECTREMAN THE VIDEO SUPERHERO
SPECTREMAN - GIANT ANT INVASION, THE
SPECTREMAN - GIANT SALAMANDER, THE
SPECTREMAN - KILLER SMOG
SPECTREMAN - MAN TURNED MONSTER
SPOOK WHO SAT BY THE DOOR, THE
STAR TREK - AMOK TIME
STAR TREK - DAGGER OF THE MIND
STAR TREK - SHORE LEAVE
STAR TREK - THE TROUBLE WITH TRIBBLES
SUPERMAN CARTOON SPECTACULAR
TECHNO POLICE
TEENAGE HITCH-HIKERS
TEENAGE INNOCENCE
TEENAGE TRAMP
TERROR
TERROR FROM THE SEA
THREE STOOGES CARTOON SHOW
TILL THE CLOUDS ROLL BY
TOGA PARTY
VAMPIRE MEN OF THE LOST PLANET
WAR IN SPACE, THE
WHAT A WAY TO GO
WIFE SWAPPERS, THE
YOUNG STRANGER, THE
ZOMBIES LAKE

PALACE:
AGUIRRE, WRATH OF GOD
ALICE IN THE CITIES
ALPHAVILLE
AMERICAN FRIEND, THE
ANGEL
BASKET CASE
BEAT, THE - GREATEST HITS
BIG MEAT EATER
BITTER TEARS OF PETRA VON KANT, THE
BLOOD OF A POET / TESTAMENT D'ORPHEE
COCAINE FIENDS, THE
COMPLEAT RUTLES
DESPERATE LIVING
DIVA
ENIGMA OF KASPAR HAUSER, THE
ERASERHEAD
EVIL DEAD, THE
FEAR EATS THE SOUL
FEMALE TROUBLE
FITZCARRALDO
FOX AND HIS FRIENDS
GARY NUMAN - MICRO MUSIC
GARY NUMAN - NEWMAN NUMAN
GARY NUMAN - THE TOURING PRINCIPLE '79
HIGH AND LOW
HIT, THE
HONEYMOON KILLERS, THE
JIMI HENDRIX - EXPERIENCE
KURONEKO
KWAIDAN
LAUGHTERHOUSE
LE JOUR SE LEVE
LIVE TODAY, DIE TOMORROW
LIZARDS
LOVELESS, THE
MAN OF FLOWERS
MARLOWE - PRIVATE EYE 1 & 2
MEPHISTO
MERRY CHRISTMAS MR. LAWRENCE
MODERN ROMANCE - LIVE IN TOKYO

MONDO TRASHO
MONSIEUR VINCENT
MOON IN THE GUTTER, THE
MULTIPLE MANIACS
NEW GOOD BIRTH GUIDE, THE
ONIBABA
OTHER SIDE OF MADNESS, THE
PARIS, TEXAS
PINK FLAMINGOS
PIXOTE
PLAN 9 FROM OUTER SPACE
QUERELLE
RETURN OF MARTIN GUERRE, THE
ROBERT PALMER - SOME GUYS...
SALVATORE GIULIANO - THE DREADED MAFIA
SANJURO
SATAN'S BREW
SEX MADNESS
STREETWALKER, THE
STROSZEK
TAXI ZUM KLO
TEMPEST, THE
THAT SINKING FEELING
TRANCE
UK/DK
UNSUITABLE JOB FOR A WOMAN, AN
WHOOPS APOCALYPSE
WOYZECK /HOW MUCH WOOD...
YOJIMBO

RANK:
300 YEAR WEEKEND, THE
80,000 SUSPECTS
ABOVE US THE WAVES
ACT OF VENGEANCE
ADVENTURES OF FRONTIER FREMONT, THE
AGE OF INNOCENCE, THE
ALL COPPERS ARE ...
ALONE IN THE DARK
AMAZING WORLD OF PSYCHIC PHENOMENA
AMERICAN RASPBERRY
AMSTERDAM KILL, THE
ANIMAL FARM
APPLE, THE
ART OF HIGH IMPACT KICKING, THE
ASSAULT
BAD BLOOD
BAD TIMING
BAIT, THE
BALTIMORE BULLET, THE
BANDITS FROM SHANTUNG
BAT, THE
BATTLE OF BILLY'S POND, THE
BATTLE OF THE RIVER PLATE, THE
BEACH OF THE WAR GODS
BELSTONE FOX, THE
BERMUDA TRIANGLE, THE
BIG BOSS, THE
BIRTHDAY PARTY, THE
BLACK GUNN
BLACK NARCISSUS
BLESS THIS HOUSE
BLOOD BATH
BLOOMFIELD
BLOW OUT
BODY AND SOUL

BORN WILD
BOXCAR BERTHA
BOY WHO TURNED YELLOW, THE
BOYS IN BLUE, THE
BOYS IN COMPANY C, THE
BREATHLESS
BRIEF ENCOUNTER
BUGSY MALONE
BULLDOG BREED, THE /SQUARE PEG, THE
CABARET
CAESAR AND CLEOPATRA
CALIFORNIA GOLD RUSH
CAMPBELL'S KINGDOM
CAPTAIN'S TABLE, THE
CARAVAN TO VACCARES
CARD, THE
CARRY ON ABROAD
CARRY ON AGAIN DOCTOR
CARRY ON AT YOUR CONVENIENCE
CARRY ON BEHIND
CARRY ON CAMPING
CARRY ON DICK
CARRY ON DOCTOR
CARRY ON DON'T LOSE YOUR HEAD
CARRY ON ENGLAND
CARRY ON FOLLOW THAT CAMEL
CARRY ON GIRLS
CARRY ON HENRY
CARRY ON LOVING
CARRY ON MATRON
CARRY ON UP THE JUNGLE
CARRY ON UP THE KHYBER
CHARLY
CHEERLEADERS BEACH PARTY
CHERRY HILL HIGH
CITY ON FIRE
CLAIRVOYANT, THE
CLASS
COMEDY OF TERRORS, THE
COPTER KIDS, THE
COUNTESS DRACULA
CRY WOLF
DAUGHTERS, DAUGHTERS
DE SADE
DEAD END STREET
DEATH LINE
DER ROSENKAVALIER
DESPERATE ONES, THE
DEVIL'S ANGELS
DIVORCE HIS, DIVORCE HERS
DOCTOR AT LARGE
DOCTOR AT SEA
DOCTOR IN CLOVER
DOCTOR IN DISTRESS
DOCTOR IN LOVE
DOCTOR IN THE HOUSE
DOCTOR IN TROUBLE
DOLL'S HOUSE, A
DOUBLE CROSSERS, THE
DR. FAUSTUS
DR. HECKYL AND MR. HYPE
DRACULA'S LAST RITES
DREAMER, THE
DRUNKEN MASTER
EAGLE'S WING
EAGLES ATTACK AT DAWN

EARLY BIRD, THE
EARTHLING, THE
EASY MONEY
ELEPHANT PARTS
EMPIRE OF THE ANTS
ENCOUNTER WITH DISASTER
END OF AUGUST, THE
ESCAPE TO THE SUN
FANNY BY GASLIGHT
FAST LADY, THE
FEELING FIT
FERRY TO HONG KONG
FIST OF FURY
FISTS OF THE DOUBLE K
FIVE GUNS WEST
FORGOTTEN MAN, THE
FOUR DEUCES, THE
FRAUD
FRIDAY FOSTER
FRIEND OR FOE
FUTTOCK'S END
GAME OF DEATH
GAS PUMP GIRLS
GENEVIEVE
GENTLE SAVAGE
GEORGIA
GHOST IN THE NOONDAY SUN
GHOST TRAIN, THE
GHOUL, THE
GLITTERBALL, THE
GOD'S GUN
GODSEND, THE
GOLDEN NEEDLES
GOLDEN RENDEZVOUS
GOOD MORNING, BOYS
GOOD TIMES
GORKY PARK
GREAT EXPECTATIONS
GREAT ICE RIP-OFF, THE
GREAT TELEPHONE ROBBERY, THE
GRIFFIN AND PHOENIX
GUNFIGHT, A
GUNSLINGER
H-BOMB
HAMLET
HANDS OF THE RIPPER
HAPPY HOOKER GOES HOLLYWOOD
HAUNTED PALACE, THE
HENRY V
HEROES OF TELEMARK, THE
HIJACK
HITLER - THE LAST 90 DAYS
HOLOCAUST 2000
HOT BUBBLEGUM
HOT T-SHIRTS
HOVERBUG
HOW DO I LOVE THEE ?
HOW TO BEAT THE HIGH COST OF LIVING
HUCKELBERRY FINN
HUMAN FACTOR, THE
IMPORTANCE OF BEING EARNEST, THE
IMPROPER CHANNELS
IN WHICH WE SERVE
INCOMING FRESHMAN
INCREDIBLE ROCKY MOUNTAIN RACE, THE
INTELLIGENCE MEN, THE

IPCRESS FILE, THE
JAGUAR LIVES !
JASPER CARROTT LIVE
JENNY
JUNIOR BONNER
JUST BEFORE DAWN
KID VENGEANCE
KIDNAPPED
KILLING OF SISTER GEORGE, THE
KUNG FU GIRL
LA TRAVIATA
LADY VANISHES, THE
LADY WHIRLWIND
LAST CHILD, THE
LAST OF THE MOHICANS
LAST VALLEY, THE
LEAGUE OF GENTLEMEN, THE
LEGEND OF THE WEREWOLF
LIFE AND DEATH OF COLONEL BLIMP, THE
LIVE A LITTLE, STEAL A LOT
LONE WOLF McQUADE
LONG DUEL, THE
LOVE HATE LOVE
LOVERS AND OTHER STRANGERS
MACKINTOSH AND T.J.
MAGICIAN OF LUBLIN, THE
MAGNIFICENT TWO, THE
MAN FROM HONG KONG, THE
MAROC 7
MASTERMIND
MATILDA
MERRY WIVES OF WINDSOR, THE
MIKADO, THE
MISSILES OF OCTOBER, THE
MONSTER, THE
MOUNTAIN MAN
MUHAMMAD ALI'S GREATEST FIGHTS
MURDERS IN THE RUE MORGUE
MY MOTHER, THE GENERAL
NAKED TRUTH, THE
NATIONAL LAMPOON'S CLASS REUNION
NEVER CRY RAPE
NEW YEAR'S EVIL
NEXT MAN, THE
NIGHT GAMES
NIGHT TO REMEMBER, A
NOBODY RUNS FOREVER
NORSEMAN, THE
NORTHWEST FRONTIER
NOTHING BUT THE NIGHT
NOTHING PERSONAL
NUTCRACKER, THE
ODD MAN OUT
OH ! MR. PORTER
OLIVER TWIST
ON THE RUN
ONE MORE CHANCE
ONE-ARMED BOXER, THE
OPERATION AMSTERDAM
OPERATION THUNDERBOLT
OTHELLO
PAPER TIGER
PEOPLE THAT TIME FORGOT, THE
PERSECUTION
PLEASE SIR !
POPE JOHN PAUL II IN IRELAND

LISTINGS

LISTINGS

POWER PLAY
PURPLE PLAIN, THE
QUARTET
QUEEN'S RANSOM, A
QUEST FOR LOVE
QUILLER MEMORANDUM, THE
RANK TRAILER CASSETTE
RAVEN, THE
REACH FOR THE SKY
RED SHOES, THE
RENTADICK
RETURN TO MACON COUNTY
RIDDLE OF THE SANDS, THE
ROLLING MAN
ROME EXPRESS
ROYAL WEDDING, THE
S.T.A.B.
SABOTAGE
SAPPHIRE
SAVAGE INNOCENTS, THE
SAVAGE SISTERS
SCHIZOID
SCIENCE OF IN-FIGHTING, THE
SEA WOLVES, THE
SEARCH AND DESTROY
SECRET AGENT, THE
SEED OF INNOCENCE
SEVEN
SHAOLIN KUNG FU
SHOUT, THE
SILENT FLUTE, THE
SILKWOOD
SILVER DREAM RACER
SIMBA
SINGER NOT THE SONG, THE
SKY BIKE, THE
SKY PIRATES
SKYWEST AND CROOKED
SLAUGHTER IN SAN FRANCISCO
SNAKE IN THE EAGLE'S SHADOW
SOFT BEDS, HARD BATTLES
SOME GIRLS DO
SOMETHING SHORT OF PARADISE
SONG OF NORWAY
SOUTH OF HELL MOUNTAIN
SPY KILLER, THE
SQUIRM
STARFLIGHT ONE
STONER
STUNTS - THE DEADLY GAME
SUDDENLY SINGLE
SUMMER LOVERS
SURVIVAL RUN
SWAP, THE
SWEET, SWEET RACHEL
SWORD AND THE SORCEROR, THE
TAKE, THE
TAKE THE MONEY AND RUN
TALE OF TWO CITIES, A
TALES THAT WITNESS MADNESS
TARGET : HARRY
TARKA THE OTTER
THAT LUCKY TOUCH
THAT RIVIERA TOUCH
THAT'S CARRY ON
THEY SHOOT HORSES, DON'T THEY ?

THEY'RE A WEIRD MOB
THIRTY NINE STEPS, THE
THIRTY NINE STEPS, THE
THIS SPORTING LIFE
THREE IN THE CELLAR
TIARA TAHITI
TIGER BAY
TIGERS DON'T CRY
TIGHTROPE TO TERROR
TILT
TOWN LIKE ALICE, A
TRACKERS, THE
TRAP, THE
TROUBLE IN STORE / ON THE BEAT
TWINKY
TWINS OF EVIL
ULTIMATE WAY HEALTH AND HARMONY, THE
UNCANNY, THE
UNDER FIRE
VAMPIRA
VAMPIRE CIRCUS
VAMPYRES
VICTIM
WANG YU'S 7 MAGNIFICENT FIGHTS
WAY OF THE DRAGON, THE
WE DIVE AT DAWN
WHAT NEXT ?
WHATEVER HAPPENED TO AUNT ALICE ?
WHEN THE NORTH WIND BLOWS
WHEN YOU COMIN' BACK, RED RYDER ?
WHISTLE DOWN THE WIND
WHO DARES WINS
WHOEVER SLEW AUNTIE ROO ?
WHY SHOOT THE TEACHER ?
WICKED DIE SLOW, THE
WILD GEESE, THE
WILD PARTY, THE
WILD WOMEN
WILDCAT
WOLF LAKE
WOMBLING FREE
X-RAY
YELLOWBEARD
YOUNG AND INNOCENT
YOUNG DOCTORS IN LOVE
YUM-YUM GIRLS, THE
ZACHARIAH

REPLAY:
2 CATCH 2
5 FOR HELL
ALPHA INCIDENT, THE
BARBARIAN, THE
BLOODBEAT
CANNIBAL APOCALYPSE
CANNIBAL FEROX
COMBAT KILLERS
COMING, THE
COMMUTER HUSBANDS
CREATURE FROM BLACK LAKE
DOUBLE AGENT 73
EAST SIDE HUSSLE
FRENCH WAY, THE
GONE IN 60 SECONDS
HERCULES IN NEW YORK
IN SEARCH OF DRACULA

KEEP IT UP JACK !
KENTUCKY FRIED MOVIE, THE
LAST HOUSE ON THE LEFT, THE
LEGACY OF HORROR
LEGEND OF BLOOD CASTLE, THE
NAUGHTY STEWARDESSES, THE
RECOMMENDATION FOR MERCY
ROGUE AND THE GRIZZLY, THE
SCREAM - AND DIE !
SHOCKING ASIA
SUBURBAN WIVES
SWEET SIXTEEN
WEDDING PARTY, THE

REX:
BARBARIAN WOMEN
LION MAN
RETURN OF THE BARBARIAN WOMEN
STARLET !
SWEET SINS OF SEXY SUSAN, THE
TEENAGE INNOCENTS

THORN EMI:
ACCIDENT
ACES HIGH
ADVENTURES OF TIN TIN, THE
ALFIE DARLING
AMAZING HOWARD HUGHES, THE
AMERICA - LIVE IN CENTRAL PARK
AMITYVILLE 2 - THE POSSESSION
AMITYVILLE 3
AND SOON THE DARKNESS
AND THEN THERE WERE NONE
ANGEL
ANTS - PANIC AT LAKEWOOD MANOR
APRIL WINE - LIVE IN LONDON
ARABIAN ADVENTURE
ARE YOU BEING SERVED?
ARENA, THE
ARLENE PHILLIPS' KEEP IN SHAPE SYSTEM
ASHES AND DIAMONDS
ASHFORD AND SIMPSON VIDEO, THE
AT THE EARTH'S CORE
ATOR THE FIGHTING EAGLE
AWAKENING, THE
BAD BOYS
BAL DU MOULIN ROUGE
BALLAD OF JOE HILL, THE
BANANAMAN
BATTLE FOR THE FALKLANDS
BEACH GIRLS, THE
BEASTMASTER, THE
BEGGAR'S OPERA, THE
BEST OF GEORGE AND MILDRED, THE
BEST OF THE BENNY HILL SHOW VOL 1 - 3
BIG BAD MAMA
BILLY LIAR
BILLY SQUIER - LIVE IN THE DARK
BLACK FOX
BLACKMAIL
BLOOD FROM THE MUMMY'S TOMB
BLOODBATH AT THE HOUSE OF DEATH
BLUEBEARD
BOB MARLEY AND THE WAILERS
BODY MUSIC
BODY, THE

BRIGHTON ROCK
BRINGING UP BABY
BRITANNIA HOSPITAL
BUFFALO BILL AND THE INDIANS
BULLSHOT
BURNING, THE (cut)
BURNING, THE (uncut)
BUSHIDO BLADE, THE
BUTTERFLY
CABINET OF DR. CALIGARI, THE
CAN'T STOP THE MUSIC
CANDY STRIPE NURSES
CARRY ON CLEO
CARRY ON COWBOY
CARRY ON NURSE
CAT AND MOUSE
CHAINED HEAT
CHANEL SOLITAIRE
CHERYL LADD - FASCINATED
CHILDREN OF THE CORN
CHRIS RAINBOW - BODY MUSIC
CHRISTMAS CAROLS FROM CAMBRIDGE
CIRCUS OF HORRORS
CITIZEN KANE
CITY UNDER THE SEA
CLASS OF 1984
CLAUDE BOLLING : CONCERTO FOR GUITAR AND JAZZ PIANO
CLIFF AND THE SHADOWS 1984 - TOGETHER
CLIFF RICHARD AND THE SHADOWS "THANK YOU VERY MUCH"
CLIFF RICHARD - THE VIDEO COLLECTION
COLDITZ STORY, THE
CONAN THE BARBARIAN
CONCERT FOR BANGLA DESH, THE
CONDUCT UNBECOMING
CONQUEST OF EVEREST, THE
CONVOY
COOKING AROUND THE WORLD
COUNTRY WAYS
CROSS COUNTRY
CROSS CREEK
CROSS OF IRON
CROSSFIRE
CRUEL SEA, THE
DALEKS INVASION EARTH 2150 A.D.
DAM BUSTERS, THE
DANGER MOUSE VOLUME 1
DANGER MOUSE VOLUME 2
DANGER MOUSE VOLUME 3
DAVID BOWIE (EP)
DAVID BOWIE - JAZZIN' FOR BLUE JEAN
DEAD AND BURIED
DEAD PIGEON ON BEETHOVEN STREET
DEAD ZONE, THE
DEATH OF ADOLF HITLER, THE
DEATH ON THE NILE
DEATH SHIP
DEATH VENGEANCE
DECADE OF BRITISH OPEN
DECADE OF GRAND PRIX / THE FRANK WILLIAMS STORY
DECADE OF WIMBLEDON
DEER HUNTER, THE
DEMONS OF THE MIND
DESPAIR

DEVIL'S ADVOCATE, THE
DIRT BAND, THE - TONITE
DON'T LOOK NOW
DOUBLE EXPOSURE
DOVE, THE
DR. JEKYLL AND SISTER HYDE
DR. MABUSE - THE GAMBLER (DER SPIELER)
DR. WHO AND THE DALEKS
DRIVER, THE
DURAN DURAN - DANCING ON THE...
DURAN DURAN - THE VIDEO ALBUM
ELEPHANT CALLED SLOWLY, AN
ELEPHANT MAN, THE
EMI TRAILER TAPE AUTUMN 1983
EMI TRAILER TAPE MARCH 1982
EMI TRAILER TAPE MARCH 1983
EMI TRAILER TAPE OCTOBER 1982
EMMANUELLE 2 (cut)
EMMANUELLE 2 (uncut)
EMMANUELLE 4
ENJOY BETTER GOLF
ENTERTAINING MR. SLOANE
EUREKA STOKADE
EVENING WITH LIZA MINELLI, AN
EVERY HOME SHOULD HAVE ONE
EVIL UNDER THE SUN
FACE OF FU MANCHU, THE
FAKE OUT
FALLEN IDOL, THE
FALSTAFF
FAR FROM THE MADDING CROWD
FEAR IN THE NIGHT
FEAR IS THE KEY
FEDORA
FINAL PROGRAMME, THE
FINALLY, SUNDAY !
FINEST HOURS, THE
FIRE AND ICE
FIRST BLOOD
FLAME TREES OF THIKA, THE
FLASH GORDON
FORT APACHE
FOUR FEATHERS, THE
FOUR MUSKETEERS, THE
FRANCES
FRIGHT
FRITZ THE CAT
GENERATION, A
GENESIS - THREE SIDES LIVE
GIRL WITH GREEN EYES, THE
GLITTERING CROWNS, THE
GO-BETWEEN, THE
GOLDEN SEAL, THE
GOODIES, THE
GREAT KIDNAPPING, THE
HALLOWEEN 2
HALLOWEEN 3 - SEASON OF THE WITCH
HANDGUN
HARDER THEY COME, THE
HEARTLAND
HEAVENS ABOVE !
HEAVY TRAFFIC
HENRY VIII AND HIS SIX WIVES
HOBSON'S CHOICE
HOFFMAN
HOLIDAY ON THE BUSES

HONKY TONK FREEWAY
HONORARY CONSUL, THE
HOPSCOTCH
HORROR OF FRANKENSTEIN, THE
HOT GOSSIP
HOUSEPLANTS AND PATIO GARDENING
HOW TO BOARDSAIL
HOW TO PASS YOUR DRIVING TEST WITH THE B.S.M.
HUE AND CRY
HUNCHBACK OF NOTRE DAME, THE
HUNDRA
I AM A DANCER
I, MONSTER
I'M ALL RIGHT JACK
ICE COLD IN ALEX
IDOMENEO
IMMORAL TALES
INTERMEZZO
INTERNATIONAL GYMNASTICS
INTIMATE MOMENTS
IRON MAIDEN
IRON MAIDEN - THE BEAST LIVE AT HAMMERSMITH
IRON MAIDEN - VIDEO PIECES (EP)
IT SHOULDN'T HAPPEN TO A VET
IT'LL BE ALRIGHT ON THE NIGHT 3
ITZHAK PERLMAN BEETHOVEN VIOLIN CONCERTO
JAMES BROWN STORY, THE-SOUL CONNECTION
JAZZ SINGER, THE
JUPITER MENACE, THE
KAJAGOOGOO (EP)
KAJAGOOGOO - WHITE FEATHERS TOUR
KANAL
KATE BUSH AT THE HAMMERSMITH ODEON
KATE BUSH - THE SINGLES FILE
KENNETH LO'S TASTE OF CHINA
KENNY EVERETT VIDEO SHOW VOLUME 1- 3
KIM CARNES - VOYEUR
KIND HEARTS AND CORONETS
KIND OF LOVING, A
KING KONG
KING KONG
KING OF COMEDY, THE
KING'S STORY, A
KITTY - RETURN TO AUSCHWITZ
KNIFE IN THE WATER
LA BELLE ET LA BETE
LA BOHEME
LA CENRENTOLA
LA FANCIULLA DEL WEST
LA FILLE MAL GARDEE
LADY CAROLINE LAMB
LADYKILLERS, THE
LANCASTER
LAND THAT TIME FORGOT, THE
LAURA - SHADOWS OF SUMMER
LAVENDER HILL MOB, THE
LE DERNIER MILLIADAIRE
LE SILENCE EST D'OR
LES CONTES D'HOFFMANN
LES ENFANTS DU PARADIS
LES PORTES DE LA NUIT
LET GEORGE DO IT

LET'S SPEND THE NIGHT TOGETHER
LIGHT AT THE EDGE OF THE WORLD, THE
LIKELY LADS, THE
LITTLE LORD FAUNTLEROY
LOCAL HERO
LONELY LADY, THE
LONG GOOD FRIDAY, THE
LONG RIDE, THE
LOOK BACK IN ANGER
LOOT
LORD OF THE RINGS, THE
LUCKY JIM
LUST FOR A VAMPIRE
MAD MISSION 3
MAGGIE, THE
MAKING OF SUPERMAN - THE MOVIE, THE
MAN ABOUT THE HOUSE
MAN AT THE TOP
MAN IN THE WHITE SUIT, THE
MAN WHO FELL TO EARTH, THE
MAN WHO HAUNTED HIMSELF, THE
MANON
MANON LESCAUT
MARCH OF THE WOODEN SOLDIERS, THE
MARILLION - FOREPLAY (EP)
MARILLION - RECITAL OF THE SCRIPT
MARY BERRY'S COUNTRY COOKING
MAYERLING
MAZE - LIVE IN NEW ORLEANS
MEMOIRS OF A SURVIVOR
METROPOLIS
MIRROR CRACK'D, THE
MISSIONARY, THE
MOBY DICK
MONTY PYTHON AT THE HOLLYWOOD BOWL
MONTY PYTHON'S LIFE OF BRIAN
MORECAMBE AND WISE SHOW, THE
MORGAN - A SUITABLE CASE FOR TREATMENT
MOZART IN SALZBURG
MR. MUM
MURDER ON THE ORIENT EXPRESS
MUSIC OF DON MCLEAN, THE
MUTINY ON THE BUSES
MY LEARNED FRIEND
NAKED CIVIL SERVANT, THE
NEVILLE MARINER AND THE ACADEMY OF ST. MARTIN'S
NEW LIFE IN THE GARDEN
NICHOLAS NICKLEBY
NICKELODEON
NIGHT BOMBERS
NIGHTINGALE, THE
NIGHTS OF CABIRIA
NOSFERATU : A SYMPHONY OF HORROR
NOW THAT'S WHAT I CALL MUSIC VOL 1- 4
OLIVIA NEWTON JOHN - PHYSICAL
OLIVIA NEWTON JOHN - TWIST OF FATE (EP)
ON THE BUSES
ONE FLEW OVER THE CUCKOO'S NEST
ONE MILLION YEARS B.C.
ONLY TWO CAN PLAY
OOH ... YOU ARE AWFUL
ORCA ... KILLER WHALE
ORPHEE
OSTERMAN WEEKEND, THE
OUT OF SEASON

OVERLORD
P'TANG, YANG, KIPPERBANG
PAUL McCARTNEY AND WINGS ROCKSHOW
PAYDAY
PELE
PERCY
PERCY'S PROGRESS
PETER COOK AND CO.
PETER GRIMES
PETER TOSH - LIVE
PHOBIA
PICTURE MUSIC
PINK FLOYD (EP)
PLAGUE DOGS, THE
PLAYBOY OF THE WESTERN WORLD, THE
POLICE AROUND THE WORLD
PRINCE CHARLES : A ROYAL PORTRAIT
PRIVATES ON PARADE
PUBERTY BLUES
PUMPING IRON
QUEEN - GREATEST FLIX
QUEEN OF SPADES, THE
QUEEN - THE WORKS (EP)
QUINCY'S QUEST
RACE FOR THE CHAMPIONSHIP, THE
RACE FOR THE YANKEE ZEPHYR
RAGING MOON, THE
RAGTIME
RAID ON ENTEBBE
RAILWAY CHILDREN, THE
RAINBOW
RANSOM
RAQUEL WELCH TOTAL BEAUTY AND FITNESS PROGRAM, THE
RATTLE OF A SIMPLE MAN
READY STEADY GO ! VOLUME 1
READY STEADY GO ! VOLUME 2
READY STEADY GO ! VOLUME 3
RED ARROWS - GNATS AND HAWKS, THE
REILLY, ACE OF SPIES
REWIND : VOLUME 3
RIGOLETTO
ROLAND RAT ROADSHOW, THE
ROSES
ROSTROPOVICH - DVORAK CELLO CONCERTO
ROTTWEILER - THE DOGS OF HELL
ROYAL PHILHARMONIC ORCHESTRA PLAYS QUEEN, THE
ROYAL WEDDING, THE
ROYAL WEDDING, THE + 60 MINS BLANK TAPE
S.O.S. TITANIC
S*P*Y*S
SAMSON ET DALILA
SAVAGE BEES, THE
SCARS OF DRACULA
SCOTT OF THE ANTARCTIC
SCRUBBERS
SECOND THOUGHTS
SERVANT, THE
SEVEN NIGHTS IN JAPAN
SEX THROUGH A WINDOW (not released ?)
SHAKE OUT WITH TV-AM'S MAD LIZZIE
SHALAKO
SHALL WE DANCE ?
SHEENA EASTON LIVE AT THE PALACE

LISTINGS

LISTINGS

SIEGE
SILVER BEARS, THE
SKIING - FOCUS ON FRANCE
SLAYGROUND
SOFT CELL - NON STOP EXOTIC VIDEOSHOW
SOOTY'S ADVENTURES
SOUTHERN COMFORT
SPACE RIDERS
SPITFIRE
STAR FLEET
STARDUST
STEPTOE AND SON
STEVE MILLER BAND - LIVE!
STORIES FROM A FLYING TRUNK
STORY OF JESUS, THE
STRANGE INVADERS
STRANGLERS VIDEO COLLECTION 1977 - 82
STRYKER
SUMMER HOLIDAY
SUMMER IN SAINT-TROPEZ, A
SUPERMAN 3
SURVIVE !
SUSPIRIA
SWALLOWS AND AMAZONS
SWAN LAKE
SWEENEY !
SWEENEY 2
TALES OF BEATRIX POTTER
TARANTULAS - THE DEADLY CARGO
TATTOO
TENDER MERCIES
TERROR OUT OF THE SKY
TESS
THAT'LL BE THE DAY
THAT'S MAGIC
THIRD MAN, THE
THOMAS DOLBY - LIVE WIRELESS
THOMPSON TWINS "SIDE KICKS" - THE MOVIE
THREE MUSKETEERS, THE
THREE SISTERS, THE
THREE WARRIORS
TILL DEATH US DO PART
TIME BANDITS
TIMERIDER
TIMES SQUARE
TINA TURNER NICE 'N ROUGH
TITFIELD THUNDERBOLT, THE
TO THE DEVIL A DAUGHTER
TOM JONES
TOM JONES / THE OSMOND BROTHERS
TOMMY
TOP HAT
TORVILL AND DEAN - PATH TO PERFECTION
TRAIN KILLER, THE
TUBES VIDEO, THE
TWISTED NERVE
TWO-WAY STRETCH
UNDERTONES, THE (EP)
UNKNOWN CHAPLIN
UP POMPEII
UPSTAIRS, DOWNSTAIRS VOLUME 1 - 7
VALACHI PAPERS, THE
VALDEZ THE HALF-BREED
VENOM
VICTORIA THE GREAT
VIDEOHITS

VIDEOSTARS
VIDEOTHEQUE
VILLAIN
WALL, THE - PINK FLOYD
WARLORDS OF ATLANTIS
WATER BABIES, THE
WATERSHIP DOWN
WELCOME TO BLOOD CITY
WHAT A PICTURE! VOLUME 1 - 4
WHISKY GALORE
WHITESNAKE - FOURPLAY (EP)
WHITESNAKE - LIVE !
WICKER MAN, THE
WIDOWS (2 cassettes)
WILLO THE WISP - VOLUME 1 & 2
WIND IN THE WILLOWS, THE
WINSLOW BOY, THE
WONDERFUL LIFE
WOODEN HORSE, THE
YOU TOO CAN DO THE CUBE
YOUNG ONES, THE
ZIGGY STARDUST... SPIDERS FROM MARS
ZOLTAN ... HOUND OF DRACULA

VCL:
10CC LIVE IN CONCERT
67 DAYS
ABBOTT AND COSTELLO
ABDUCTION, THE
ABILENE TOWN
ABRAHAM'S SACRIFICE
ADVENTURE IN VENTANA
ADVENTURES OF SUPERMAN, THE
AGAINST A CROOKED SKY
AGOSTINI - UNTAMED WHEELS
ALAN PRICE
ALEX AND HIS DOG
ALIEN ENCOUNTERS
ALOHA, BOBBY AND ROSE
AMANDA LEAR - LIVE IN CONCERT
AMAZING MR. BLUNDEN, THE
AMERICA SCREAMS
ANGELO BRANDUARDI - CONCERTO
ANIMAL KINGDOM
ANN-MARGRET FROM HOLLYWOOD...
ANOTHER TIME ANOTHER PLACE
ASSASSIN OF YOUTH
ASSASSINATION, THE
AVERAGE WHITE BAND - SHINE
BABY, THE
BARCELONA KILL, THE
BARRY WHITE
BATTLE SQUADRON
BEAST OF THE DEAD
BEAUTY AND THE BEAST
BEHAVE YOURSELF !
BERT KAEMPFERT AND HIS ORCHESTRA
BEST FRIENDS
BEYOND REASON
BLACK ARROW, THE
BLACK JACK
BLACK SABBATH
BLACK SABBATH - NEVER SAY DIE
BLACK TULIP, THE
BLACKOUT
BLOOD ORGY OF THE SHE-DEVILS

BLOOD RELATIVES
BLUE FIRE LADY
BOBBY DARIN
BOBBY DARIN AND LINDA RONSTADT
BOOMTOWN RATS - TONIC FOR THE TROOPS
BORDER U.S.A., THE
BORN TO BUCK
BRAINWASH
BRAINWASHED
BREAKING GLASS
BROTHER O'TOOLE
BROTHERS AND SISTERS LIVE IN CONCERT
BROTHERS O'TOOLE, THE
BULLDOG DRUMMOND ESCAPES
BURY ME AN ANGEL
BUTCHER, THE
BUTTERFLY BALL, THE
CALIFORNIA GIRLS
CALL IT MURDER
CANDIDATE FOR A KILLING
CAPTAIN APACHE
CARMEN
CARQUAKE
CARRY ON EMMANNUELLE
CATCH ME A SPY
CATCHING UP
CLASH BY NIGHT
CLUTCH OF POWER, THE
COBRA
COMMUNION
CONNECTING ROOMS
CONVERSATION PIECE
CORPSE GRINDERS, THE
COUNT BASIE
CRASH !
CRUCIBLE OF TERROR
CRY OF THE INNOCENT
CUBA CROSSING
DANIEL AND NEBUCHADNEZZER
DEADLY ENCOUNTER
DEADLY HUNT, THE
DEATH CHASE
DEATH THREAT
DEATH TRAP
DELINQUENT COLLEGE GIRLS
DELTA FACTOR
DELUGE, THE
DISAPPEARANCE, THE
DOLL SQUAD, THE
DON'T CALL US
DOOMED TO DIE
DOUBLE TROUBLE
DOWN MEMORY LANE
DR. JEKYLL AND MR. HYDE
DRAGON LIVES AGAIN, THE
EDDY GRANT
ELO - LIVE IN CONCERT
ELTON JOHN - CENTRAL PARK
ELVIS - THE MOVIE
EMBASSY
ENGLAND MADE ME
EROTIC ADVENTURES OF PINOCCHIO, THE
ESCAPE FROM GALAXY 3
EVENING WITH CHARLES AZNAVOUR, AN
FAMILY ENFORCER
FANTASTIC PLASTIC MACHINE, THE

FAREWELL TO ARMS, A
FAST COMPANY - JACKIE STEWART
FEMALE MUD WRESTLING
FERRIA DE APRIL
FIFTH DIMENSION WITH DIONNE WARWICK,
THE CARPENTERS
FINAL HOUR, THE
FLASHPOINT AFRICA
FLIGHT TO HOLOCAUST
FOOLIN' AROUND
FRENCH QUARTER
FROM AFRICA WITH LOVE
FROM THE EARTH TO THE MOON
GAMES THAT LOVERS PLAY
GARY GLITTER - LIVE AT THE RAINBOW
GENERAL STONE
GET MEAN
GIANT SPIDER INVASION, THE
GIANTS OF BRAZIL
GIRL STROKE BOY
GIRL WHO COULDN'T SAY NO, THE
GOLD
GOLDEN LADY, THE
GONE WITH THE WEST
GREAT GOLDEN HITS OF THE MONKEES, THE
GREAT GUNDOWN, THE
GUERILLAS IN PINK LACE
GULLIVER'S TRAVELS
GYPSY, THE
HALF A HOUSE
HARLEQUIN
HEADING FOR GLORY
HEIST, THE
HELL ON WHEELS
HER FIRST AFFAIR
HOAX
HOLD-UP
HOUND OF THE BASKERVILLES, THE
HURRICANE EXPRESS
IMAGES
IMPULSION
ISLAND OF LIVING HORROR, THE
IVANHOE
JACKSON 5 IN CONCERT, THE
JAZZ FESTIVAL
JOHN MILES - LIVE IN CONCERT...
JOSEPH AND HIS BROTHERS
JOSHUA AT JERICHO
JOURNEY
JOYRIDE
JUBILEE
JUDGEMENT OF SOLOMON
JUST A GIGOLO
KENNY BALL AND HIS JAZZMEN
KGB CONNECTIONS, THE
KIDNAPPED
KLANSMAN, THE
KUBLAI KHAN
LACEMAKER, THE
LASSIE
LAST FIGHT, THE
LAST PLANE OUT
LAST ROMAN, THE
LAST TRAIN, THE
LEGEND OF FRENCHIE KING, THE
LEGEND OF LOCH NESS

LEROY GOMEZ	RACHEL'S MAN	TENNIS	CRYPT OF HORROR
LIONS FOR BREAKFAST	RANDY EDELMAN	THAT LUCKY TOUCH	CURSE OF THE CRIMSON ALTAR
LIVING FORM	RAPE OF THE THIRD REICH	THEATRE STARS	DEATH WEEKEND
LONDON BRIDGE SPECIAL, THE	RAQUEL WELCH	THEY MADE ME A CRIMINAL	EATEN ALIVE !
LOU RAWLS	REACHING FOR THE MOON	THIN LIZZY - LIVE AND DANGEROUS	FLESH AND BLOOD SHOW, THE
LOVE MACHINE FROM THE U.S.A.	RED NIGHTS OF THE GESTAPO, THE	THIRST	HAUNTED HOUSE OF HORROR, THE
LOVE TO ETERNITY	REGGAE SUNSFLASH PART 1 & 2	THIS YEAR 1980	HOUSE BY THE CEMETERY, THE
LUSTY MEN, THE	RIDING HIGH	THIS YEAR 1981	PREY
MAD FOXES, THE	RIGHT OF WAY	TICKET TO HEAVEN	REPULSION
MADRON	ROBIN HOOD	TINA TURNER	SHOCK
MAFIA WARFARE	ROBINSON CRUSOE	TINA TURNER QUEEN OF ROCK 'N' ROLL	STRANGLER OF VIENNA
MARCO POLO	ROCK AND ROLL REVIVAL	TINTORERA	STUDY IN TERROR, A
MARIHUANA - THE DEVIL'S WEED	ROGER DALTREY - RIDE A ROCK HORSE	TOM JONES WITH THE CARPENTERS	TENEBRAE
MARRIAGE OF MARIA BRAUN, THE	ROGUE LION	TOMB OF THE LIVING DEAD	TERROR OF DR. HICHCOCK, THE
MARY WILSON AND THE SUPREMES	ROLLERMANIA	TOMORROW MAN, THE	TODD KILLINGS, THE
MASSACRE AT CENTRAL HIGH	ROMANTIC ENGLISHWOMAN, THE	TOMORROW NEVER COMES	
MAX	RUNNERS	TOWER OF BABEL	**VFP (VIDEO FILM PROMOTIONS):**
McMASTERS, THE	SAD CAFE	TREASURE ISLAND	ANTHROPOPHAGOUS THE BEAST
MEETING OF THE SPIRITS	SANTANA AND TAJ MAHAL LIVE	TREASURE OF PANCHO VILLA, THE	BLOOD AND BULLETS
MEMORIES IN MY MIND	SCARED TO DEATH	TRESPASSER, THE	BLUE ISLAND
METAL MESSIAH	SCREAM BLOODY MURDER	TRIP TO KILL	GESTAPO'S LAST ORGY, THE
MICHELLE LAUREN	SCUM	TRIPLE CROSS	GIRL FROM TRIESTE, THE
MIDSUMMER NIGHT'S DREAM, A	SEA QUEST	TRIPLE ECHO, THE	GRAND DUEL, THE
MIGHTY MOUSE IN THE GREAT SPACE CHASE	SECOND CHORUS	TWIN GAMES	RINGS OF FEAR
MINA LIVE	SEDUCER, THE	TWO IN BLACK BELT	SACHA THE WONDER DOG
MINX, THE	SEVEN ALONE	UFC JOURNALS	SWORD OF THE BARBARIANS, THE
MIRRORS	SEWERS OF PARADISE, THE	UNIVERSAL SOLDIER, THE	TERMINATORS, THE
MISSILE-X	SHAMWARI	UP A TREE	
MOBY DICK	SHINBONE ALLEY	URANIUM CONSPIRACY, THE	**VIP (VIDEO INDEPENDENT PRODUCTIONS):**
MONTANA TRAP	SHOCK TREATMENT	VAMPIRE BAT, THE	ATTACK FORCE NORMANDY
MOSES	SILENT WILDERNESS	VIRGIN AND THE GYPSY, THE	CONTAMINATION
MR. ROBINSON CRUSOE	SINGLE ROOM FURNISHED	VIRGIN CAMPUS	DIRTY HEROES, THE
MUHAMMED ALI VS. ARCHIE MOORE	SISTER-IN-LAW, THE	VOICES	EAGLES OVER LONDON
MURDER AT MIDNIGHT	SLIGHTLY PREGNANT MAN, THE	WALDORF TRAVERS	GENTLEMAN TO RESPECT, A
MURPHY'S WAR	SMITHEREENS	WANDERERS, THE	LIVING DEAD AT THE MANCHESTER MORGUE, THE
MUTINY AT FORT SHARP	SNAPSHOT	WHALE OF A TALE, A	
MY PLEASURE IS MY BUSINESS	SNAPSHOT - AUSTRALIAN STYLE	WHERE DOES IT HURT ?	LIZARD IN A WOMAN'S SKIN, A
MYSTERIES FROM BEYOND EARTH	SODOM AND GOMORRAH	WINGS OF AN EAGLE	RISKING
MYSTERIOUS HEROES	SOMEONE BEHIND THE DOOR	WONDER WOMEN	THOR THE CONQUEROR
NANCY WILSON	SOMEONE IS BLEEDING	YOU AND ME	
NAZARETH - LIVE	SOMETHING TO HIDE	YOUNG GRADUATES, THE	**VIDEO NETWORK:**
NEW ADVENTURES OF HEIDI, THE	SOMETHING TO SING ABOUT	ZOMBIE CREEPING FLESH	AXE
NIGHT OF THE JUGGLER	SONNY AND CHER		BEING DIFFERENT
NINA VON PALLANDT	SPACE BANDIT	**VIDEOMEDIA:**	BIG ZAPPER, THE
NUCLEAR COUNTDOWN	SPECIALIST, THE	LOVE VARIATIONS	CHILD, THE
OFF ON A COMET	SPEEDTRAP / CARQUAKE	PENITENTIARY	DARK EYES
ONCE UPON A BROTHERS GRIMM	STARBIRD AND SWEET WILLIAM	PENITENTIARY 2	DAYS OF FURY
ONCE UPON A WHEEL	STARFIRE		DEATH FORCE
OPERATION BLACK SEPTEMBER	STATUS QUO - OFF THE ROAD	**VIDEOMEDIA / RAMPIX:**	DEVIL'S EXPRESS
OSIBISA - LIVE AT THE RAINBOW	STEPFORD WIVES, THE	AU PAIR GIRLS	DON'T GO IN THE WOODS... ALONE!
OSMONDS, THE	STICKS OF DEATH	INTIMATE GAMES	DON'T OPEN THE WINDOW
PACO DE LUCIA	STORY OF ESTHER	MCNIGUE	ENFORCER FROM DEATH ROW
PAM'S PARTY	SUGAR COOKIES	PERMISSIVE	EVIL, THE
PANCHO VILLA	SUNBURN	SEX THIEF, THE	FAST KILL, THE
PASSAGE, THE	SUPERMAN	ZETA ONE	HOW SLEEP THE BRAVE
PATRICK	SUPERMAN - THE MUSICAL		MAD BUTCHER, THE
PEKING BLONDE	SUPERSTARS ON STAGE	**VIDEOMEDIA / VAMPIX:**	NAKED FIST
PERFECT FRIDAY	SURABAYA CONSPIRACY, THE	BEYOND, THE	PERFECT KILLER, THE
PHANTASM	SUSAN GEORGE - NATURALLY	BIRD WITH THE CRYSTAL PLUMAGE, THE	SCREAM IN THE STREETS, A
PHILIP GOODHAND-TAIT - SUNSHINE ON ICE	SUSPICION OF MURDER	BLACK SUNDAY	SHOOT THE SUN DOWN
PINOCCHIO	SWING HIGH, SWING LOW	BLACK TORMENT, THE	TAKE SOME GIRLS
PIRANHA, PIRANHA	SWINGIN' SUMMER, A	BLOOD BEAST TERROR, THE	TERROR AT RED WOLF INN
POOR GLASSBLOWER, THE	TALES OF ORDINARY MADNESS	CANDLE FOR THE DEVIL, A	TEXAS BURNS AT NIGHT
PRINCESS AND THE MAGIC FROG, THE	TALES OF WASHINGTON IRVING	CAULDRON OF BLOOD	TRAPPED
PROUD AND DAMNED, THE	TEACHER, THE	CEMETERY OF THE LIVING DEAD	ZAPPERS BLADE OF VENGEANCE
PSYCHOMANIA	TEN COMMANDMENTS, THE	CREEPING FLESH, THE	

LISTINGS

VIDEO UNLIMITED:
20,000 DOLLARS ON NO.7
300 MILES FOR STEPHANIE
5 KUNG-FU DAREDEVIL HEROES
A.W.O.L.
AIRPORT SOS HIJACK
ALCATRAZ - THE FINAL ESCAPE
ALCATRAZ - THE WHOLE SHOCKING STORY
ALL THE KIND STRANGERS
ALL THE LOVING COUPLES
AMAZING DOBERMANS, THE
ANGEL CITY
ANGELS IN HELL
ANTONY AND CLEOPATRA
ASH WEDNESDAY
BETTER LATE THAN NEVER
BIG COMBO, THE
BLOOD QUEEN
BORN TO BE SOLD
BROTHERS OF SHAO-LIN, THE
C.B. HUSTLERS
CAR-NAPPING
CAT AND THE CANARY, THE
CATACLYSM
CHRISTMAS MOUNTAIN
COCAINE COWBOYS
CORRUPTION OF CHRIS MILLER, THE
CRIME STORY
DANNY TRAVIS
DARK NIGHT OF THE SCARECROW
DEAD MAN'S FLOAT
DESPERATE INTRUDER
DESPERATE VOYAGE
DETROIT 9000
DRAGONFLY FOR EACH CORPSE, A
DRIBBLE
FIEND
GOD'S LITTLE ACRE
GODCHILDREN, THE
GOLDRUNNER
GOOD LUCK MISS WYCKOFF
GOYA
GREEN GROW THE RUSHES
HAUNTED
HAWK OF THE CARIBBEAN, THE
HEADIN' FOR BROADWAY
HIDEAWAYS, THE
HOFFNUNG
HOLLYWOOD KNIGHT
INNOCENT BYSTANDERS
JUSTINE
KASHMIRI RUN
KILL THE WICKEDS
KISS DADDY GOODBYE
LAND OF NO RETURN, THE
LAST DAYS OF THE WAR, THE
LINDA LOVELACE FOR PRESIDENT
LONG DAY OF MASSACRE, THE
LOSERS, THE
LOVE IN MONACO
MAGIC ADVENTURE
MAGNIFICENT TONY CARRERA, THE
MEN IN WAR
MESSALINA
MY CHAMPION
NAKED KISS, THE
NOAH'S ANIMALS
ONE AWAY
ONLY ONCE IN A LIFETIME
ONLY WAY, THE
OPTIMISTS OF NINE ELMS, THE
ORDEAL OF BILL CARNEY, THE
PANIC IN ECHO PARK
PIED PIPER, THE
PREACHERMAN
RED LIGHT IN THE WHITEHOUSE
REMEMBRANCE OF LOVE
RETURN, THE
RIBALD DECAMERON, THE
RIDE THE HOT WIND
RIVALS OF THE DRAGON
SENSUOUS NURSE, THE
SHAOLIN IRON FINGER
SHAOLIN MASTER AND THE KID
SHOCK CORRIDOR
SHOOT
SIMON BOLIVAR
SKETCHES OF A STRANGLER
SNOW TREASURE
SURPRISE ATTACK
TRIANGLE OF SUSPENSE
TRICKS OF THE TRADE
TWICE A WOMAN
UNE FEMME EST UNE FEMME
UNKNOWN WORLD
UPPER 7 THE MAN TO KILL
VICTIMS
WALK A CROOKED PATH
WARKILL
WEREWOLVES ON WHEELS
X FROM OUTER SPACE, THE
ZERO POPULATION GROWTH

VIPCO:
BED HOSTESSES
BEYOND EVIL
BIG BOSS 2
BLACK FIST
BLACKJACK
BLOOD BRIDE
BLOOD FOR DRACULA
BOGEYMAN, THE
BREAKER ! BREAKER !
CAGED WOMEN
CIRCLE OF TWO
DARK SANITY
DEADLY SPAWN, THE
DEATH TRAP
DECEPTION
DIAMOND MERCENARIES, THE
DOUBLE JEOPARDY
DRILLER KILLER, THE
EVIL FORCE, THE
EXECUTION
FIGHT FOR FREEDOM
FLESH FOR FRANKENSTEIN
GROOVE TUBE, THE
HEY ABBOTT
HIGH NOON PART 2
HOT SEX IN BANGKOK
HUSSY
IMMORAL
INTRODUCING BADMINTON
INVINCIBLE IRON PALM, THE
ISLAND OF MUTATIONS, THE
JUICY CUTS 1
KID WITH THE BROKEN HALO, THE
KILL SQUAD
KING FRAT
LADY ICE
LAZARUS SYNDROME, THE
LEGACY, THE
LEGEND OF SLEEPY HOLLOW, THE
MASSACRE MANSION
NESTING, THE
NIGHTBEAST
NIGHTKILL
PACIFIC CONNECTION, THE
PORTRAIT OF A HIT MAN
PRIVATE AFTERNOONS OF PAMELA MANN
PSYCHIC KILLER
RISE AND FALL OF IDI AMIN
SAVAGE INTRUDER, THE
SHOGUN ASSASSIN
SLAYER, THE
SMOKEY AND THE JUDGE
STARCRASH
SWEET AND SEXY
TIME TO DIE, A
UNCLE SCAM
WAR DEVILS
WEREWOLF OF WASHINGTON, THE
WHEN A WOMAN IS IN LOVE
YOUNG SEDUCERS, THE
ZOMBIE FLESH-EATERS (cut)
ZOMBIE FLESH-EATERS (uncut)

VIRGIN:
AI NO BOREI (EMPIRE OF PASSION)
AI NO CORRIDA (REALM OF THE SENSES)
ATOMIC CAFE, THE
AUTOBIOGRAPHY OF A PRINCESS
BAUHAUS - SHADOW OF LIGHT
BETRAYAL
CAN SHE BAKE A CHERRY PIE ?
CHRIS DE BURGH - THE VIDEO
CULTURE CLUB - A KISS ACROSS THE OCEAN
DEVO - THE MEN WHO MAKE THE MUSIC
EATING RAOUL
ESSENTIAL MIKE OLDFIELD, THE
EXECUTIONER'S SONG, THE
FLESH
GREAT ROCK 'N' ROLL SWINDLE, THE
HANOI ROCKS - ALL THOSE WASTED YEARS
HEAT
HEAVEN 17 - INDUSTRIAL REVOLUTION
HOUSEHOLDER, THE
JAPAN - INSTANT PICTURES
JIMI HENDRIX - RAINBOW BRIDGE
LENNY BRUCE LIVE PERFORMANCE
LONESOME COWBOYS
LOOSE CONNECTIONS
ORCHESTRAL MANOEUVRES IN THE DARK
ORDER OF DEATH
PLOUGHMAN'S LUNCH, THE
PUBLIC IMAGE LTD - LIVE
RICHARD PRYOR - LIVE IN CONCERT
SEBASTIANE
SEX PISTOLS, THE - LIVE IN SWEDEN
SHAKESPEARE WALLAH
SLAPSTICK
SPACE MOVIE
THIRD WORLD - PRISONER STREET
TOO HOT TO HANDLE
TOO HOT TO HANDLE
TRASH
TWISTED SISTER - STAY HUNGRY
U2 - LIVE AT REDROCK
UB40 - LABOUR OF LOVE
UB40 - LIVE
XTC - LOOK LOOK

VISION ON:
ADULTERY ITALIAN STYLE
AFRICA
BEGINNING OF THE END
BIG BAD WOLF, THE
BILLY THE KID TRAPPED
BURNING PASSIONS
CELEBRATION (BURL IVES SHOW)
DR. MINX
FIGHT FOR YOUR LIFE
GALLERY OF HORROR
HAVE A GOOD FUNERAL MY FRIEND
HEMO THE MAGNIFICENT
LET THE BALLOON GO
MAGIC OF CHRISTMAS
MY FRIENDS NEED KILLING
NIGHT AFTER NIGHT AFTER NIGHT
NIGHTMARES
NO MORE NO LESS
ONCE UPON A TIME
PERILS OF MANDY, THE
PERPETUAL MOTION MACHINE
POINT OF TERROR
PURSUIT
SAGEBRUSH TRAIL
SEXY SISTERS
SHARK RIVER
SOMEONE BEHIND THE DOOR
SPIES-A-GO-GO
STRANGE CASE OF THE COSMIC RAYS
THIS IS YOUR CAPTAIN SPEAKING
UNCHAINED GODDESS
UNEARTHLY, THE
VIRGIN ON THE BEACHES
WEST OF THE DIVIDE
WHAT'S UP FRONT !
WOMAN'S PLEASURE
WORKING GIRLS, THE
YELLOWNECK

VTC:
2019 AFTER THE FALL OF NEW YORK
ACAPULCO GOLD
ADVENTURES OF HAMBONE AND HILLIE, THE
ALIEN TERROR
AMBER WAVES
ANGEL OF H.E.A.T.
ANNA TO THE INFINITE POWER
ARK OF THE SUN GOD, THE
ATOR THE INVINCIBLE
AUSTRALIA NOW
BEAST, THE

LISTINGS

BELL JAR, THE
BLACK CAT, THE
BLINDED BY THE LIGHT
BLOODBATH OF DR. JEKYLL, THE
BODY LANGUAGE
BORSALINO AND CO.
BRAINWAVES
BREAKING UP
BRONSON LEE, CHAMPION
BUDO : ART OF KILLING
CAIN'S CUT-THROATS
CHANGELING, THE
CHATTERBOX !
CHRISTMAS TO FEMEMBER, A
CONTROL FACTOR
CORMACK
CRIME BUSTERS
CRUSADERS, THE - MIDNIGHT TRIANGLE
DARTS - THE JOHN LOWE WAY
DEATH COLLECTOR
DEATH MACHINES
DEATH PROMISE
DEATH WATCH
DELIRIUM
DEMON
DEVIL DOG : HOUND OF HELL
DEVONSVILLE TERROR, THE
DIAL M FOR MURDER
DIFFERENT STORY, A
DOUBLE NEGATIVE
DRINKING MAN'S WAR, THE
DYNAMITE CHICKEN
ENDGAME
ENTER THE STREETFIGHTER
FAMILY MAN, THE
FAST COMPANY
FIRST TIME, THE
FLUSH
FOR COUPLES ONLY
FORCE OF ONE, A
FORT APACHE THE BRONX
FRENCH CONSPIRACY, THE
FUGITIVE FAMILY
GOOD GUYS WEAR BLACK
GREAT SMOKEY ROAD BLOCK, THE
GREATEST ATTACK, THE
HAPPILY EVER AFTER
HITCH-HIKE
HOME TO STAY
HOUSE OF EXORCISM, THE
HOUSE THAT CRIED MURDER, THE
IMAGINATION - VIDEO EP
INCUBUS, THE
IT'S CALLED 'MURDER', BABY
KID FROM LEFT FIELD, THE
KINKS, THE - ONE FOR THE ROAD
KOYAANISQATSI
LAST CHASE, THE
LATE GREAT PLANET EARTH, THE
LIQUID SKY
LOVE AT FIRST SIGHT
LOVE BY APPOINTMENT
LOVING COUPLES
MACHINE GUN McCAIN
MACK, THE
MAD MISSION 2

MAMA'S DIRTY GIRLS
MAN CALLED BLADE, A
MANHANDLERS, THE
MARILYN - THE UNTOLD STORY
MEMED MY HAWK
MID-KNIGHT RIDER
MILLION DOLLAR FACE, THE
MIND MACHINE
MIRROR, MIRROR
MISS NUDE AMERICA CONTEST, THE
MOTHER'S DAY
MURDER BY NATURAL CAUSES
NIGHTMARE CITY
NINJA MISSION, THE
NINJA WARS
OCTAGON, THE
OUTING, THE
POSSESSION
PRESIDENT'S MISTRESS, THE
PRIVATE EYES, THE
REBORN
RECKLESS
REDNECK COUNTY
RETRIEVERS, THE
RETURN ENGAGEMENT
RETURN OF THE STREETFIGHTER
REVENGE OF THE BOGEYMAN
RIDING TALL
ROARING FIRE
RUN FOR THE ROSES
RUST NEVER SLEEPS
SAMURAI REINCARNATION
SARTANA - ANGEL OF DEATH
SCARAB
SCAREMAKER, THE
SECOND SPRING, A
SEE CHINA AND DIE
SINAI COMMANDOS
SINNER'S BLOOD
SISTER STREETFIGHTER
SPASMS
STONE
STRANGENESS, THE
STREETFIGHTER'S LAST REVENGE
STRIPTEASE
SUPERSTITION
SUPERVAN
SUZANNE
TANYA'S ISLAND
THEY ALL LAUGHED
TOPPER
TRANSPLANT
TRIBUTE
TRIUMPHS OF A MAN CALLED HORSE
UTILITIES
WARRIORS THREE
WHEN HELL WAS IN SESSION
WHITE FIRE
WITCH WHO CAME FROM THE SEA, THE
YOUR TICKET IS NO LONGER VALID
ZOMBIE HOLOCAUST

WALTON:

ABOMINABLE SNOWMAN, THE
ADULTERESS, THE
AMOROUS MILKMAN, THE

APACHE WOMAN
BLOOD VENGEANCE
BRITAIN'S ROYAL HERITAGE
CHALLENGE OF THE SKY
CHANT OF JIMMIE BLACKSMITH, THE
CIRCLE OF CHILDREN, A
CLAWS
COME AND PLAY
DESERT BATTLE
DIARY OF A TEENAGE HITCHHIKER
DOLEMITE
EARLY ONE MORNING
EBONY, IVORY AND JADE
EVIDENCE OF POWER
HOMEWARD BOUND
HUMAN TORNADO, THE
HUNTERS OF THE GOLDEN COBRA, THE
JOURNEY TO THE STARS
KILLER
LANGUAGE OF BIRDS
LOVLIER THAN LOVE
MEDUSA
MEN OF SHERWOOD FOREST
MUTHERS, THE
NAPLES CONNECTION, THE
NORMAN LOVES ROSE
OPERATION CROSS EAGLES
OVERBOARD
PARTIZAN
QUATERMASS EXPERIMENT THE
SORCERORS, THE
STORY OF TATTERS, THE
STREETS OF L.A., THE
TERMINAL ISLAND
THIS IS LONDON
THREE IMMORAL WOMEN
THRILL SEEKERS
TOUGH
UP THE CREEK
WILDLIFE USA
X THE UNKNOWN

WORLD OF VIDEO 2000:

16 PARK AVENUE
AFTER SCHOOL GIRLS
AFTERMATH, THE
ALICE GOODBODY
ALL THE NAUGHTY BITS
AMATEUR NUDE WIVES NO.1 & 2
ANGEL AND THE BADMAN
ARM OF FIRE
BARBRA STREISAND IN CONCERT SPECIAL
BASIC DEFENCE
BASIC INTRODUCTION TO YOGA, A
BIG SUSAN
BIM
BLOOD SWEAT AND TEARS
BRA BUSTERS
BRUCE LEE STORY, THE
BRUTAL REVENGE
CARTLOAD OF BRADFORD RUBBISH, A
CHAMPION OF CHAMPIONS
CHARLIE CHAPLIN
CHARLOTTE
CHILDREN'S HOUR
COMEBACK

CONFESSIONS OF A SIXTH FORM VIRGIN
COWBOY BROTHEL
DARK COMMAND
DARK STAR
DAVID SOUL IN CONCERT
DESPERATE JOURNEY INTO FEAR
DIRTY EVENING WITH BERNARD MANNING
DON'T ANSWER THE PHONE !
DRAGON LEE VS. FIVE BROTHERS
DRAGON'S TEETH
DRAWS
DREAMS OF THIRTEEN
E.T.n. (THE EXTRA TERRESTRIAL NASTIE)
ELVIS - THE KING OF ROCK AND ROLL
EXHIBITION
EYE FOR AN EYE, AN
FLAMING BULLETS
FRANK SINATRA - OLE BLUE EYES HIMSELF
G.B.H. (GRIEVOUS BODILY HARM)
GIRLS COME FIRST
HEAD STRONG
HILLS HAVE EYES, THE
HUMAN EXPERIMENTS
HURRICANE EXPRESS
I'M NOT FEELING MYSELF TONIGHT
IMMORAL TALES
JULIA
JUNGLE MAN
KID DYNAMITE
KILLING HOUR, THE
LADY OF PARIS
LATE NIGHT TRAINS
LESBIAN LOVERS
LINDA LOVELACE FOR PRESIDENT
LOVE UNDER 17
MARVIN GAYE
MARY MILLINGTON'S STRIPTEASE...
MEMORIES WITHIN MISS AGGIE
MIDNIGHT CENTREFOLD
MISS NUDE UK 1982 VOL.1
NEW YORK MYSTERY
NIGHTMARES IN A DAMAGED BRAIN
PRIVATE SPY VOLUME 1- 3
PUSSY TALK
SECRETS OF A DOOR-TO-DOOR SALESMAN
SEX AND THE MARRIED WOMAN
SEX AT 7000FT
SEX AT SEA
SEX FEVER
SEX SLAVES
SHORT EYES
SINS WITHIN THE FAMILY
SOFT PLACES
SOMEBODY'S STOLEN OUR RUSSIAN SPY
SWEET EMMANUELLE
TASTE OF DECADENCE
THIEF OF BAGDAD
VANESSA
VIDEO BLUE
WAR IN CONCERT
WET AND WILLING
WHAT A PERFORMER
WHAT SCHOOLGIRLS DON'T TELL
WORLD IS FULL OF MARRIED MEN, THE
YOUNG BEDMATES
YOUNG EMMANUELLE

THE ART OF THE NASTY

Bibliography

ALDGATE, ANTHONY *Censorship and the Permissive Society*, Clarendon Press, 1995.

BARKER, MARTIN *The Video Nasties - Freedom and Censorship in the Media*, Pluto Press, 1984.

BARLOW, GEOFFREY and HILL, ALISON *Video Violence and Children*, Hodder and Stoughton, 1985.

BRAITHWAITE, BRIAN *Women's Magazines*, Peter Owen, 1995.

BOUZEREAU, LAURENT *Ultra Violent Movies*, Citadel Press, 1996.

DUNCAN, ALAN and HOBSON, DOMINIC *Saturn's Children*, Sinclair-Stevenson, 1995.

GAMBACCINI, PAUL, RICE, TIM and RICE, JONATHAN *British Hit Singles* (8th Edition), Guinness, 1991.

GODFREY, JOHN (Editor) with i-D magazine *A decade of i-Deas, the encyclopaedia of the '80s*, Penguin Books, 1990.

HARDY, PHIL (Editor) *The Aurum Horror Film Encyclopedia*, Aurum Press, 1993.

JOSEPH, TANYA and SAGAR, D.J. (Editors) *Cassell Dictionary of Modern Britain*, Cassell, 1995.

MARTIN, JOHN *The Seduction of the Gullible* (Revised edition), Procrustes Press, 1998.

PALMER, TONY *The Trials of Oz*, Blond & Briggs, 1971.

WISTRICH, ENID *I Don't Mind the Sex it's the Violence*, A Marion Boyars Book, 1978

Other valuable sources of information were the BBFC's Video Classification list, and their Theatrical Classification list, as well as the extensive databases of Francis Brewster and Marc Morris

Cover Credits:
Art Direction: Nigel Wingrove, Photography: Garrard Martin, Design: Chris Charlston, Model: Savannah, at Sugar Babes, Make-up: Liberty Shaw, Styling: Dena Costello.